Professional Writing

Study Skills

Academic Success
Academic Writing Skills for International
  Students
The Business Student's Phrase Book
Cite Them Right (11th edn)
Critical Thinking and Persuasive Writing for
  Postgraduates
Critical Thinking Skills (3rd edn)
Dissertations and Project Reports
Doing Projects and Reports in Engineering
The Employability Journal
Essentials of Essay Writing
The Exam Skills Handbook (2nd edn)
Get Sorted
Great Ways to Learn Anatomy and Physiology
  (2nd edn)
How to Begin Studying English Literature (4th edn)
How to Use Your Reading in Your Essays (3rd edn)
How to Write Better Essays (4th edn)
How to Write Your Undergraduate Dissertation
  (3rd edn)
Improve Your Grammar (2nd edn)
The Mature Student's Handbook
Mindfulness for Students
The Macmillan Student Planner
The Personal Tutor's Handbook
Presentation Skills for Students (3rd edn)
The Principles of Writing in Psychology
Professional Writing (4th edn)
Skills for Success (3rd edn)
Stand Out from the Crowd
The Student Phrase Book
The Student's Guide to Writing (3rd edn)
Study Skills Connected
The Study Skills Handbook (5th edn)
Study Skills for International Postgraduates
Studying in English
Studying History (4th edn)
Studying Law (4th edn)
Studying Physics
The Study Success Journal
Success in Academic Writing (2nd edn)
Smart Thinking
Teaching Study Skills and Supporting Learning
The Undergraduate Research Handbook (2nd edn)
The Work-Based Learning Student Handbook
  (2nd edn)
Writing for Engineers (4th edn)
Writing History Essays (2nd edn)
Writing for Law
Writing for Nursing and Midwifery Students
  (3rd edn)
Write it Right (2nd edn)
Writing for Science Students
Writing Skills for Education Students
You2Uni: Decide, Prepare, Apply

Pocket Study Skills

14 Days to Exam Success (2nd edn)
Analyzing a Case Study
Blogs, Wikis, Podcasts and More
Brilliant Writing Tips for Students
Completing Your PhD
Doing Research (2nd edn)
Getting Critical (2nd edn)
How to Analyze Data
Managing Stress
Planning Your Dissertation (2nd edn)
Planning Your Essay (3rd edn)
Planning Your PhD
Posters and Presentations
Reading and Making Notes (2nd edn)
Referencing and Understanding Plagiarism
  (2nd edn)
Reflective Writing
Report Writing (2nd edn)
Science Study Skills
Studying with Dyslexia (2nd edn)
Success in Groupwork
Successful Applications
Time Management
Using Feedback to Boost Your Grades
Where's Your Argument?
Writing for University (2nd edn)

Research Skills

Authoring a PhD
The Foundations of Research
  (3rd edn)
Getting to Grips with Doctoral Research
Getting Published
The Good Supervisor (2nd edn)
The Lean PhD
PhD by Published Work
The PhD Viva
The PhD Writing Handbook
Planning Your Postgraduate Research
The Postgraduate's Guide to Research Ethics
The Postgraduate Research Handbook (2nd edn)
The Professional Doctorate
Structuring Your Research Thesis
Writing a Science PhD

Career Skills

Excel at Graduate Interviews
Graduate CVs and Covering Letters
Graduate Entrepreneurship
How to Succeed at Assessment Centres
Social Media for Your Student and Graduate Job
  Search
The Graduate Career Guidebook (2nd edn)
Work Experience, Placements and Internships

Professional Writing

4th edition

Sky Marsen

BLOOMSBURY ACADEMIC
LONDON • NEW YORK • OXFORD • NEW DELHI • SYDNEY

BLOOMSBURY ACADEMIC
Bloomsbury Publishing Plc
50 Bedford Square, London, WC1B 3DP, UK
1385 Broadway, New York, NY 10018, USA
29 Earlsfort Terrace, Dublin 2, Ireland

BLOOMSBURY, BLOOMSBURY ACADEMIC and the Diana logo
are trademarks of Bloomsbury Publishing Plc

This edition published by RED GLOBE PRESS 2020
Previous editions published by PALGRAVE
Reprinted by Bloomsbury Academic

A catalogue record for this book is available from the British Library.

A catalog record for this book is available from the Library of Congress.

ISBN: PB: 978-1-3520-0799-2
ePDF: 978-1-3520-0804-3
eBook: 978-1-3503-1552-5

Series: Bloomsbury Study Skills

To find out more about our authors and books visit
www.bloomsbury.com and sign up for our newsletters.

Contents

Figures, Tables and Examples

Figures

Tables

Examples

Chapter 1

Chapter 2

Chapter 3

Chapter 5

Chapter 6

Chapter 7

Chapter 8

*To my professional writing students – present,
past and future*

Acknowledgements and Thanks

Various people have supported, in different ways, the writing and re-writing of this book since its first edition. Thank you to all.

For this fourth edition, I would like to thank Derek Wallace for reviewing changes and offering valuable advice, and Ben Stubbs for suggesting improvements and giving me detailed feedback on what works and what doesn't. I would also like to thank Robert Biddle for his valuable suggestions on the writing needs of IT students, and Andrei Sleptchenko for explaining probability and statistical reasoning to me.

Many thanks go to colleagues and students at the California Institute of Technology, who have given me valuable feedback on teaching activities and the framing of communication tasks – especially Steven Youra, for our insightful exchanges on communicating technical concepts to non-specialists, and Ken Pickar's engineering teams for their input on teamwork and project management. Thank you also to my writing students at the University of Southern California, for providing a challenging and rewarding environment where many of the tips, examples and activities were developed. Also, thanks to all those who have used the book in their classes and given me feedback, especially Donna Banicevich Gera for discussing the book with me on many occasions and giving me useful tips.

My gratitude goes to Jill and Rob Bradley, for giving me a lovely writing room in their home in Auckland, where this fourth edition came into being. Finally, many thanks to my editors, Suzannah Burywood and Rosemary Maher, for their helpful guidance.

Preface

Under current trends, the 21st century will be characterized by an increasing diversification of the consumer market, global communications and the collapse of traditional professional boundaries. In this climate, competence in transferring skills, addressing diverse audiences and understanding emerging needs becomes paramount for professional success. To a very large extent this competence is enhanced by the ability to understand, construct and manipulate written information in order to use it effectively in a variety of situations. Good business means good writing!

This book is a brief but comprehensive introduction to major aspects of professional writing for different media. Its content is interdisciplinary, offering a rare opportunity to synthesize methods and ideas developed in text analysis, journalism and management. By combining conceptual aspects of written communication with practical applications, the goal of this book is to assist readers to express ideas effectively in different written formats, in a variety of professional contexts internationally.

Distinctive features

The main features of the book, in its fourth edition, are:

1 An eclectic theoretical foundation, informed by genre theory, rhetoric, discourse analysis and narrative theory. In addition to its theoretical background, the fourth edition is informed by information on business practices collected through communication with professionals in the United States, Australia, New Zealand and Hong Kong, from both corporate and entrepreneurial fields. The aim was to gather and then disseminate information that is relevant for professionals communicating in international business today.

2 As in its previous editions, a direct, concise and student-oriented approach. The book has expressly avoided the density of many other books on writing, opting instead for a more hands-on approach, which student-writers should find very accessible. The aim was to design an easily consultable text that includes clear instructions on selected areas of interest, gives analysed examples that place the instructions into perspective and provides opportunity for practice.

Audience

The book was written primarily as a university text for one-semester undergraduate courses in professional writing or business communication. However, it is by no means limited to this audience. Because it gives useful tips and conceptual resources to overcome the most common troublespots in professional writing, it will serve as a practical guide to anyone who wants to become more confident in choosing an appropriate style and layout to suit the occasion. Those who will benefit most from the guidelines offered here include:

- Students in professional writing and business communication courses
- New professionals, who may be thrust into a professional situation that requires the production of formal written documents (such as consulting reports, newsletter articles, or copy for a website) without prior training
- Entrepreneurs, business people and scientists who want to inform management or the public of a new development, product or invention in their field, but lack the linguistic and/or communicative expertise to produce an effectively constructed written text.

Skills

By working through the book, readers will gain the skills to:

- Understand and use essential terminology and key concepts in describing writing within the context of professional communication
- Understand and employ the skills needed for writing problem-solving reports for clients and management, journalistic articles for the wider public and public relations documents in different media
- Adapt written communication for a specific audience and purpose, and understand the role of different media in communication
- Perceive writing as a process involving planning, drafting, revising and editing, and become aware of their own procedures of writing
- Understand the uses of writing in collaborative projects and in project management
- Develop awareness of critical thinking issues in relation to management and business contexts.

Trajectory

In its fourth edition, the book consists of ten main chapters and an appendix:

Chapter 1: The Writing Process

This chapter looks at the planning and thinking aspects of writing. Using an approach informed by genre, rhetoric and narrative, it discusses ways to analyse a brief, understand audiences and plan a writing project.

Chapter 2: Writing Style

This chapter looks at elements of style and their adaptation for different audiences. It outlines a new typology of style going from specialized to public and discusses such aspects of writing as appropriate length of sentences for different effects, word choice and sentence variety as a technique to maintain reader interest.

Chapter 3: Short Business Documents

This chapter overviews and analyses the major short documents produced in business contexts. These include everyday communication texts, such as agendas and minutes of meetings, letters, memos and email. This chapter also discusses techniques that make successful oral presentations.

Chapter 4: Research Methods

This chapter looks at the role and methods of researching in the preparation of professional documents. It provides guidelines on research skills, preparing questionnaires for interviews and obtaining data in different media. It also discusses copyright and plagiarism issues as they relate to professional contexts.

Chapter 5: Journalism

This chapter discusses genres used to inform the public of recent developments in technology, science and business. It overviews journalistic techniques of writing and magazine layout matters, and focuses on feature articles, which can be written for magazines or newsletters.

Chapter 6: Public Relations Writing

This chapter looks at public relations genres, such as press releases, web content and public speeches. It considers the differences between print, broadcast and digital media in communicating with the public, and explores the increasing importance of social media for business.

Chapter 7: Reports and Proposals

This chapter looks at proposals, business plans and problem-solving reports. It discusses the conceptual concerns involved in writing these documents, such as finding convincing evidence, and explains their conventional structures with examples of complete reports.

Chapter 8: Critical Thinking for Management

This chapter looks at aspects of reasoning and persuasion in professional documents and mass media texts. It explains approaches to argument construction in professional texts and examines issues of faulty or manipulative reasoning. It also overviews the uses and abuses of statistics in the popular media.

Chapter 9: Working in Teams

This chapter describes the role of teamwork and collaboration in projects. It explains the different role allocation models for team projects and explains the stages of project management and the terms used to describe its elements. It discusses the presence of conflict in team projects and some ways to manage conflict constructively.

Chapter 10: Revising and Editing

This chapter focuses on sentence structure and grammatical aspects of writing. It provides guidelines on the revising and editing process and explains some common trouble spots at the sentence level. The chapter is a reference tool for all aspects of writing and can be used at any stage in a particular writing task or be revisited at different times in the duration of a course.

Appendix: Job Applications

This chapter looks at some important considerations in the job-hunting process. These include ideological and personal factors, such as assessing values and professional aspirations, as well as practical techniques, such as writing a CV.

For those of you who have used the book in its previous editions, you will find that the fourth edition is updated, extensively revised and reorganized, in light of feedback from instructors who have adopted the book in their courses, and students who have learned from it.

For those of you who are coming to the book for the first time (and possibly to the world of professional communication for the first time too), I welcome you and hope you find the material given here useful and stimulating.

SKY MARSEN

The Writing Process

Focus:

- The writing process
- Rhetorical and genre analysis
- Writing in business contexts
- Planning a writing project

The skill of writing is acquired through conscious and persistent effort: unlike our ability to speak, it is not an innate skill that we are born with. Writing is more complex than speaking for several reasons. One reason is that it is separate from any form of physical interaction: writing can take place at a totally different time and place from reading. This leaves the written text more open to misunderstanding than the spoken text. Since they are not likely to be present when their readers read their document, writers must try to perceive their text from the readers' point of view and write in a way that is clear and relevant to their audience. Another reason is that writing is thought-active. The simple fact that you want to write about a topic triggers thought processes that give this topic a particular shape out of a range of alternatives. To paraphrase Flannery O'Connor, we don't know what we think until we read what we write. The changes that take place from thinking to writing explain why many novice writers state that their final result is not what they initially wanted to express, or that what is in their mind comes out differently on the written page.

Because of the complexity of written communication, a successful written text does not emerge spontaneously, but requires considerable preparation and revision. As Ben Yagoda (2004) comments, "speaking takes place in real time and is an improvisational performance; writing permits, encourages and to some extent requires reflection and revision. It is an artifact" (p. 26). Even a brief email requires some revision to ensure it is clear and accurate. And although much business and technical writing follows standard conventions of style and organization, each task presents a new problem to solve with its own audience and situation. This chapter looks at some major tested techniques for creating effective written documents, from concept to delivery copy. We focus on the conceptual and idea-generating aspects, as well as the organizational and analytical skills that develop through careful revision and editing.

The techniques discussed here are not the only way to write; there are almost as many variations of the writing process as there are writers. Professional writers of all varieties, business, academic, journalistic and creative, gradually develop their own technique of writing. If it works, then stick with it – if not, consider different techniques.

In fact, writers could be classified into two major categories, *top-down* and *bottom-up* writers. Top-down writers begin by brainstorming an outline of their document, and then filling it in with content. They work better when they see the structure of their text, and like to have a "map" or "big picture" of the whole document before writing the details. Bottom-up writers, on the other hand, prefer to free-write their ideas without attention to structure. They are more data-driven, and end up with many points, facts and examples before they consider how to give form and coherence to their draft.

Regardless of what category of writer you are, effective writing is the result of a process consisting of three interconnected stages: the planning or conceptualizing stage, the drafting stage and the revising/editing stage. In contrast to what is commonly believed, it is the first and third stage that require the most time and attention. You will find that by having a clear vision of what you want to accomplish (stage one), and giving yourself adequate time to re-phrase, delete, rearrange and add information to sections (stage three), you are creating your work. In fact, many professionals who make their living from writing state that planning and revising take about 85% of the time assigned to a task. The drafting stage is just a bridge between careful planning and structuring information. All well-prepared professional documents require this process of writing, although how long each stage takes varies depending on the length and significance of the document, and on whether you are a top-down or bottom-up writer.

Rhetoric and genre

US President Theodore Roosevelt once said that "the most important single ingredient in the formula of success is knowing how to get along with people" (Maxwell, 2007, p. 41). Also, research in business communication has repeatedly shown that successful business professionals are those who actively participate in the culture of their organization, that is, those who fit in the organizational environment – the team players. Understanding that the writing you do as business professionals creates and sustains relationships with managers, peers, stakeholders, clients and the public (or, negatively, breaks these relationships) is the first step in conceptualizing business writing as a social activity. The guidelines proposed here are informed by rhetorical and genre theory, which takes into account audience, purpose and context (Bazerman & Prior, 2004; Bhatia, 2004; Cockcroft & Cockcroft, 2005; Swales, 1990).

Rhetoric proposes that all texts aim to have a particular effect on their readers or listeners, for example to persuade, motivate, inform, warn, etc. If this desired effect is not achieved, it most likely means that the writer or speaker did not accurately assess the readers' dispositions or the situation in which the communication took place. It could also mean that the way the information was presented conflicted with or did not meet reader expectations.

In many cases, written material can be classified as a certain document format or genre. As a simple illustration of this point, think about how a shopping list looks when compared with a car manual, or a letter compared with a film script. Knowing what genre we are reading helps to cue us into what sort of language we might expect the writers to use, how they will organize their material, whether they are likely to include graphs and other visuals, and so on. Genre theory proposes that document formats, such as *report, article, essay, email,* etc., exhibit certain standard features that capture the requirements of particular rhetorical situations, and are therefore appropriate for these situations. For example, a magazine feature article is shorter than a scientific article and therefore cannot contain as much detail as the latter; a report is divided into sections with headings for easy skimming and "chunking" information into categories, etc.

Although genres change over time, and indeed need to be revised to reflect changing circumstances and emerging media, the conventional structure of a type of text is shared knowledge between writers and readers and forms a recognized and accepted way to exchange information. Genre considerations include such elements as degrees of formality, document length and the inclusion or not of visuals.

Keeping these factors in mind, when planning a piece of writing consider the five factors in Table 1.1:

Table 1.1 Planning Factors
1. Who is the *audience?* What do they already know about the topic? What do they not know? What do they *not* want to know? In what areas are they likely to be specialized (so that you may form analogies between your topic and those areas)? How much detail do they need? How much of the big picture do they need?
2. What is the *purpose* of the document? For example, does the document inform? Analyse? Clarify? Persuade? Will it be used as the basis for a decision? How do you want to change or affect the readers through your document?
3. What is the most appropriate *genre*? What is the best format in which to present your information related to the situation? Would an email do the job, or do you need to produce a full investigative report?
4. What is the most appropriate *medium* for the audience, purpose and genre? Would your message be clearer if transmitted electronically, or in print, or maybe orally on the phone or in person? If you're sending a report to a client, would a PDF attachment to an email be the best way, or should you send a printed copy through the post? Or both?
5. What is the most appropriate *style* of writing? Different genres are conventionally written in a particular style or register; for example, a report is expected to be written in more formal style than an email, and a newsletter article is expected to have a lighter tone than a contract. How do you want to appear through your writing? Knowledgeable? Considerate? Strict? Friendly? Your style, formed through sentence structure and word choice, will help you to achieve your desired writing persona.

The professional world abounds with examples where making the wrong decision on the above factors led to costly and serious misunderstandings. For instance, a famous case of this occurred during the Columbia Space Shuttle Incident in 2003 (Columbia Investigation Board Report, 2003; Gurak & Lannon, 2007; Marsen, 2014). Columbia disintegrated upon re-entry into the Earth's atmosphere, which led to an Investigation Board being formed to find out what went wrong. Among other things, such as technical damage done to the shuttle wing during the launch, the Board found several serious communication factors that contributed to the accident.

In one of these, the engineers responsible for evaluating the condition of the shuttle during and after the launch suspected that the wing was damaged by a piece of foam that was dislodged during the launch, and they presented their suspicions to management during a briefing session. However, they made a tactical error by choosing a PowerPoint presentation to convey their findings. In fact, they put the most important information in one crammed slide.

The management, who were expecting serious scientific results to be presented in a technical report, did not place as much significance on the presentation as was needed because, for them, information on PowerPoint slides did not carry enough urgency. In this example, engineers and management did not share the same genre expectations, and so important technical findings were lost in communication fog.

Such considerations make it desirable for organizations to take measures to ensure consistency in the uses of language by all employees. Large organizations have what is known as *house style* to maintain a consistent style among all documents, and to induct employees in the uses of language favoured by the organization. This usually comes in the form of a manual or guide that describes the company's templates and conventions for using such techniques as abbreviations, spelling, numbers and fonts.

> **TIP**
>
> When joining a new company find out about the house style. If starting a new company, make house style a priority in your communication plan to support clarity and uniformity in document design.

More on house style is given in the last chapter. More information on genre, medium and style is given in Chapters 2 and 3. The next section looks at audience considerations.

Audience analysis

Every act of writing takes place in a new context, with a unique time, place or reader. *Audience adaptation* (or *accommodation* as it is sometimes called) refers to the skill of arranging words, organizing thoughts and formatting a document to best achieve your desired effect on the target audience. *Audience dynamics* refers to the relationship that writers form with their readers through their style, and through the amount and structure of information that they provide. The audience dynamics are effective when the readers get a sense of satisfaction that the questions raised in the text were relevant to their interests, and the answers or solutions provided were convincing. In contrast, audience dynamics are ineffective when the readers feel frustrated or offended because the writer's tone is condescending, the answers or solutions provided are simplistic in relation to the complexity of the questions, or the argument is emotive and based on generalization.

In all, for a text to be successful, there must be *writer–reader complicity*. In other words, the readers must feel that the writer is on their side, supporting their interests and respecting their needs. If readers feel that a writer treats them as an example of a general category, rather than as specific individuals, they are more likely to resist accepting the information given.

For an example of bad audience dynamics and lack of writer–reader complicity, consider the following text, which comes from a government information leaflet telling employers about laws governing sexual and racial discrimination. It is tactless because, by grouping all employers into one category, it implies that the readers may be practising discrimination. Also, it fails to bring in the main topic (Equal Opportunity Act) till the very end, when there is actually no space to give any information about it.

Example One: Audience Dynamics

Sexual and racial discrimination is practised by various employers, in retail, small business, industry and corporate environments in a number of parts of the country; it is an important community problem and a direct cause of considerable personal distress.

As an employer, as a Human Resources Officer, or as a business owner, it is important for you to know about the Equal Opportunity Act.

Here is a revised version, which creates more complicity between the issuing authority and the readers, by addressing the readers directly and showing them that the information given is for their benefit. Also, this version has improved presentation and appearance by including a title and bullet points, and by introducing the main topic earlier.

Example Two: Improved Audience Dynamics

Employers and the Equal Opportunity Act

You can play an important part in preventing discrimination if you are responsible for employing staff in

- Retail
- Small business

- Industry
- Corporations.

The Equal Opportunity Act has been legally enforced since it was passed by Parliament in 1995. This Act makes it illegal for anyone to discriminate – to treat people unfairly because of their gender, race, colour, descent, or ethnic origin.

If you know of anyone in your business environment that rejects a suitable candidate for a position because of their gender, or ethnic group tell them about the Equal Opportunity Act. You can also ask the Commissioner for Community Relations for more information.

Marketing executives and consumer researchers, who have a strong interest in understanding market responses, and who, therefore, conduct extensive research in mass perceptions, take into account five factors of audience analysis: (a) Education, (b) Status, (c) Attitude, (d) Demographics and (e) Psychographics (Table 1.2).

Table 1.2 Audience Analysis

Education refers to the readers' knowledge (or lack of knowledge) in the topic that you are writing about. What would be the likely interest of the readers in your topic, and what aspects of your topic are most likely to interest them? Should you begin with the big picture to put the readers into perspective, or go straight to the details that you want to focus on? Are you writing to people of the same educational background as yours (that is, peers), or to those of different training?

Status refers to the writer's degree of authority and/or power relative to the readers. Are you writing to your boss, to a group of peers or to someone who is junior to you? Is your reader a client with whom you intend to continue doing business, or the general public that you can only see from a bird's eye view? Are you an expert presenting information to a non-specialist audience, or a novice showing to an authority how much you know about a subject?

Attitude refers to the state of mind you expect the readers to be in when they read your document. Will your message find them hostile, neutral or positive? How motivated are they to read your document? Are you proposing revolutionary changes to a situation you think your readers will resist changing? Are you informing them of a breakthrough that will undoubtedly improve the quality of their lifestyle, and that they will be happy to know about? Are you giving them good or bad news?

Demographic analysis works on the principle that the population can be grouped, and that each group shows a tendency to think or behave in broadly similar ways. Demographic characteristics include gender, occupation, social class (that is, income level), age and location/nationality (that is, international or local audience).

From a person's demographic profile, certain inferences can be made about their degree of knowledge, expectations and aspirations, though they are not always foolproof. For example, in most Western societies a middle-class white woman is probably educated to upper secondary school or tertiary level – but not necessarily. Also, teenagers are not likely to be classical music fans, but, again, this may not be so. Demographic research is based on the lowest common denominator of prevailing social trends, and, therefore, operates mostly on stereotype.

Psychographics refers to the lifestyle, values, leisure activities and social self-image that the readers are likely to have. Marketing research shows that people react favourably towards products and services that they see as representative of themselves. Similarly, readers will respond differently to your message according to their values. What are their interests, opinions and hobbies? In the rapidly changing and diversifying contemporary world, interests and values are less and less tied to demographic issues. For example, when computer games first started to develop, they were associated with a target market of young males in the 15 to 25 age group. As this form of entertainment evolved, the target market changed, and there are now computer games that attract females, older males and other demographic groups. An analysis of the computer game market, therefore, is more likely to benefit from a psychographic examination that would see the computer game market as a special interest group, rather than a demographic.

Demographic and psychographic analyses are especially relevant in journalistic, marketing and public relations writing where you address a wider public.

In addition to these categories, consider whether you have only *primary* readers or also *secondary* and *immediate* readers. In many cases, the person who will first read the document is not the primary audience. It could be a manager or editor, an intermediary between the writer and the primary audience – *the immediate audience*. The immediate audience often acts as a form of filter or quality control agent of the information before it reaches the primary audience. Additionally, you could have a secondary audience who are likely to read the document even if they are not the target group.

Consider an example. If you submit an article for publication to a specialist magazine, you are writing for a public that is interested in the topic of your article; they are your primary audience. However, before the article reaches this audience, it will be read by the magazine's editor, who will make the final decision about whether to publish the article or not. The editor is, then, the immediate audience (and maybe the only audience, if they reject the article!). If published, the article may also be read by readers who are not primarily interested in the topic: they could be journalism students, for example, studying the article as an example of writing. They would be the secondary audience.

Matters get complicated when a document has different levels of audience, primary, immediate and secondary, who have different interests and/or subject-knowledge. Such cases make it difficult to imagine who you are writing to. A solution to this problem is to include a section that gives background and definitions of terminology for novices, or, in reports, to include an appendix with more technical details for experts. This way you would be distributing information in a clearly marked and accessible way to the different groups of readers. Returning to the example of the article to the editor, you could include a letter with your article explaining to the editor your goals in writing the article and justifying your content and stylistic choices (indeed article submissions are generally accompanied by a proposal). This way you address the editor's concerns and cater for your primary audience's anticipated questions.

As a final note to audience analysis, remember to include yourself in the analysis, since you are an interlocutor in the communicative exchange. Analyse your role: as a professional you are always performing a role that is more or less detached from your personal concerns. Also, as part of your professional position, you will be asked to play different roles for different situations. For example, if you are the CEO of a company you would have top management responsibilities, such as making executive decisions on major financial initiatives and making long-term plans on new product development. However, when addressing shareholders in situations such as public relations speeches, conferences and product exhibitions, you assume the sub-role of equal, sharing the same values and working towards the same interests. The language you use should reflect this equality, or your audience will be alienated and discouraged.

Writing in professional contexts

Writing in professional contexts is pervasive. In fact, most tasks in the workplace are accompanied by some form of writing. Even face-to-face interactions, such as meetings, are preceded and followed by such documents as agendas and minutes. Business documents can be *internal*, *external* or both. Internal documents are circulated within the organization, and include such genres as memoranda (memos), in-house templates and style guides. External documents are directed at clients, other companies (business to business or B2B communication), the media and the public, and include such genres as sales letters and disclosure statements. Many genres, such as certain kinds of reports and email, can be both internal and external. Also, some genres are associated with specific professions while others are general. For instance, most business people, no matter what their actual job, write proposals to request funding or approval for a project, while Public Relations officers write annual reports and press releases, and Human Resources officers write employment contracts and job descriptions.

Two terms are important when considering business writing: *Project* and *Brief*. Tasks in management most often take the form of projects. A project at management level brings together specialists from different fields in order to accomplish an aim, which could include developing a new product, creating an advertising campaign, solving a problem or evaluating the company's strategic plan. Most of the work of managers takes place within the scope of defined projects. In all cases, a project takes place within specified time parameters (deadlines are important in business) and a budget. It also addresses particular questions or issues and has specific goals and objectives to achieve. All this information goes to project members through a *brief*.

Basically, a brief (also known as *terms of reference* in longer projects) is an instruction to perform a task. If it is internal, it may be a short and direct command: "Investigate the ways in which the company could recruit more talented professionals." This task would then become your project, and you would need to decide how best to approach it. A brief could also involve detailed specifications spread over several pages. The latter is often the case in briefs requesting lengthy investigations after a crisis. Problem-solving reports are based on a brief provided by the client or manager, which indicates what is required and how the commissioned specialists should structure their report. Similarly, advertising companies that organize competitions on campaign skills issue a brief which candidates must address to win funding and/or a position in the company.

However, a brief is not only a formal document that presents issues to be addressed in a project. It also sets the stage on which project members will perform. This is because writing itself is not, as is often assumed, a purely mental activity. Rather, it involves the whole sensory framework: think of the physical arousal produced by an action novel or a sexy story; words can cause perspiration, a racing heartbeat, laughter and tears. In fact, it could be said that understanding a text means having the sensation of being where the action takes place. This line of reasoning is informed by the narrative approach to business communication, which sees companies as being organized as stories. The narrative approach recognizes that narrative, or storytelling, is a fundamental part of our cognitive framework and manifests in many human endeavours and creations. Narrative exists, not only in the stories we tell or write, but also in our perception of the world (Cooren, 2015; Taylor, 1993; Taylor & Van Every, 2000).

Adapting this approach for professional writing, we can see the brief as giving the information for the story of the project. It contains, explicitly or implicitly, information on stakeholders, issues, problems, strengths and limitations of a business situation. Therefore, a useful way to analyse a brief and establish a plan of action for a project is to read it in terms of three categories: *scene, content and treatment* (Table 1.3).

Table 1.3   Analysis of Brief

Scene: This includes big picture matters, such as the scope and framework of the project, the audience(s) and their relation to you as project member, the stakeholders who may not be the audience of your writing but are involved in some way in the project, and the event or context that triggered the project. Generally, the scene involves the level of power and perspective your project involves. If your project is part of a top management strategy, it will have a larger scope and a more long-term planning orientation, involving more issues and anticipating changes and developments. If it is part of a middle management strategy, it will involve more immediate concerns and specific issues. A top management perspective requires more research and analysis and tends to produce more complicated and lengthier documents than a middle management perspective, which looks at issues concerned with a specific product or service.

Content: This includes the issues that you need to cover, or questions that you must answer. The content is determined to a significant extent by the raw materials, sources and limitations that you are given to handle the project, such as funding, deadlines, access to resources, and equipment. For example, if you have one day to produce a one-page report, obviously what you write will not be as detailed or analytical as when you have two years and unlimited resources to investigate and solve a problem. Historical aspects are also part of the content. For example, if you are investigating the advantages of networking systems for your company, in addition to analysing computer systems, you would need to look at the use of networking in your company and in your industry as a whole.

Treatment: This includes the tasks into which the project should be divided in order to be completed successfully. It is the plan of action and the steps to be taken. The treatment includes physical and interactive actions, such as organizing meetings and conducting interviews and focus groups, and the type of documents that you decide to produce for a situation. For example, a simple email message may be sufficient in some situations. In other cases, you may need to follow-up your email message with a formal letter or maybe a memo, while a more serious situation would require the submission of a proposal leading to a full report. The treatment also includes the ways in which to present information according to audience needs. For example, if you decide that a PowerPoint presentation is enough to inform an audience of your progress on a project, what kinds of data will you use in the presentation? Would a verbal description suffice? Should you use tables, charts and graphs? Should you provide a full financial analysis of the situation?

The problems that can arise when the scene, content and treatment of a project are not properly interpreted can clearly be seen in disaster situations. The NASA space program provides another example of this, in the famous and well-documented example of the Challenger space shuttle disaster in

January 1986. It is now widely recognized that the explosion of the shuttle was largely due to misunderstandings that occurred in the exchange of written information between NASA officials before the launch. Although some officials had detected a functioning error in the shuttle and knew what had to be done to fix it, they did not communicate their finding in an appropriate way to the responsible parties (Herndl et al., 1991).

TIP

A brief can also be productively improvised to assist in the writing process even in cases when it is not handed out by others. For instance, if you find your progress in a project is hindered by some uncertain factor, or if you want to achieve an aim but have no idea how to go about it, you should find that conceptualizing and writing down your situation in the form of a brief (that is, a set of instructions or issue statement to yourself) may prove very productive.

A final point about professional projects: recording and detailing your projects is vital in corporate contexts, where mobility is high and staff are transferred or change position often. The person replacing you should be able to continue your work without interruption. This is known, in some IT contexts, as working in "drop dead" mode, which means that if a team member or manager were to drop dead, s/he should leave adequate documentation and specifications on their work so that projects are not disrupted because they were wholly dependent on their initiator's habits and methods. Keeping notes on a project is, therefore, essential. Below is a template, based on the tripartite model described above, that you can use or adapt to help you document writing tasks in a project.

Document Planning Template

Scene

1 Scenario (situation that triggered the task)

2 Purpose(s) of document

3 Target date for delivery

4 Audience analysis

Content

1 Main message to convey

2 Key Issues
   (a) ——————
   (b) ——————
   (c) ——————
   (d) ——————

Treatment

1 Genre

2 Supplementary Documents
   (a) ——————
   (b) ——————
   (c) ——————

As an opportunity to reflect on the above guidelines, consider what can go wrong in communication. One area that is notorious for miscommunication is the writing of technical instructions or user manuals. In many cases, these instructions are at best obscure, at worst dangerously misleading. Look at Table 1.4 for some real-life instructions from hell and think about how each reflects unsolved problems at the planning stage. What should the writers do to improve these?

Table 1.4 Nightmare Instructions

From a technical manual:
Since the user interface for analyser calibration refers to calibration as "calibration", this chapter will refer to the process of calibration as calibration.

From a manual for a database package:
An action is to be taken on the third non-consecutive day that an event occurs.

From a technical manual for the British military concerning the storage of nuclear weapons:
It is necessary for technical reasons that these warheads should be stored with the top at the bottom and the bottom at the top. In order that there may be no doubt as to which is the top and which is the bottom, for storage purposes it will be seen that the bottom of each warhead has been labelled with the word "TOP." (Cited in a book on computer science published by the Computer Science Department of the University of Virginia – www.cs.virginia.edu/cs/50/book/ch-programming.pdf.)

From a software user manual:
When you first start the application, the options bar appears on the top left of your screen, and is where option settings are set for the options used with the currently selected tool.

WARNING: The options bar may not be located on the top left of your screen.

Generating content

Generating content is an analytical practice. This is where researching and thinking come in. Depending on the audience and purpose, different types of research would be relevant. For example, you may decide that interviewing would supply you with essential facts; or you may decide that doing a historical research on a topic would be more suitable; or perhaps a combination of methods would help. Collecting facts, however, is not sufficient. You need to think about the significance of these facts and to interpret them. This is where your skills of *analysing* ideas (tracing their constituent elements), and *synthesizing* them (evaluating their significance in a given context) come in.

The process of generating ideas tests your capacity for critical and creative thinking: your ability to imagine all possible aspects or factors of a problem. Analytical thinkers do not simply arrive at the most obvious solution to a question; they test out a range of possible answers and keep an open mind. As happens with chaos theory, sometimes information that initially seemed irrelevant proves to be the key. To be able to trace analogies between seemingly disparate topics and to suggest innovative solutions are skills highly sought in professional and corporate environments. In fact, at the cutting edge of many industries and business endeavours are individuals who are not only highly motivated and organized, but also creative and versatile in their thinking.

The following are some ways to generate ideas. Try them and see which combination suits you.

Brainstorming

Brainstorming is a creative technique pioneered by Alex Osborn in the 1950s (Osborn, 1963) and has since been very productive in generating new concepts in business contexts. Brainstorming lets you list all the ideas that come to your mind randomly about a particular topic. Brainstorm by writing single words, phrases or full sentences – whatever comes to mind. Many writers find that brainstorming in groups is particularly productive. In fact, brainstorming sessions are now routine practice in many corporations, used to solve problems and to design new products. For example, IBM holds such sessions regularly both within one department and across departments and sections. Also, many popular products were initially conceived during brainstorming sessions. For instance, *Twitter* was conceived as a Short Message Service (SMS)-based social networking site by Jack Dorsey, during a day-long brainstorming session.

Mind mapping

Mind mapping was devised by Tony Buzan and is similar to brainstorming but more visual and less linear. Create mind maps by:

- Starting with a word or image central to your topic.
- Placing it in the middle of a big sheet of paper and drawing a line radiating out from it to a major subdivision of the topic.
- Circling that subdivision, and drawing a line radiating out from it to a more specific subdivision.
- Continuing the process until you run out of ideas.

Mind mapping is especially useful to those who find it easier to assimilate and understand schematic information than linear or sentence-based reasoning. See Figure 1.1 for an example of a mind map on the subject of digital piracy.

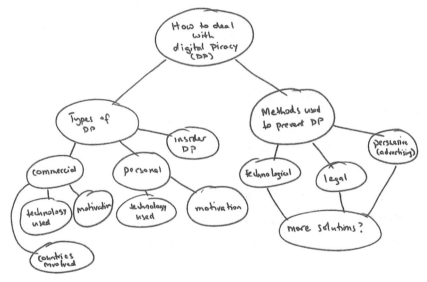

Figure 1.1   Mind map

Asking journalists' questions

Journalists' questions begin with what is known as the 5Ws and 1H interrogatives:

- Who?
- What?
- Where?
- Why?
- When?
- How?

You can approach your task by listing as many journalists' questions about your topic as you can. Questioning encourages you to look at a topic from many different perspectives and may help you to narrow the issue that you are investigating. Journalists' questions are especially useful when your task involves much factual information, because they actually force you to answer them by providing specifics rather than open-ended or ambiguous statements. News reporters, who need to convey facts as quickly and objectively as possible, use these questions to craft their news stories.

Bouncing ideas

Bouncing ideas means talking about your project to someone. The aim here is to listen to yourself talk about your task, so it is not important if your interlocutor is versed in your topic or not. In fact, some writers find that talking about their topic to someone who is a total outsider helps them to clarify issues.

If you are having trouble solving a particular problem, talk about why you are having trouble. Variations on this method include recording yourself, which has the advantage of capturing your thoughts exactly. Some people are most productive in generating and developing ideas when they can move around and create kinetic energy.

Writing scientific categories

If your topic involves interpreting a scientific development or process to a non-specialist audience, simplify and analyse the topic in your own mind by brainstorming as many statements as possible under these categories:

Existence: How can the existence of X be shown?

Quantity: How large/small is X/How fast?

Comparison: Is X greater/less than Y? In what ways is X different from Y?

Correlation: Does the speed of X vary with its weight?

Causality: If X occurs, will Y also occur? How do we know?

Outlining

With outlining you first come up with section topics, then a summary of the document, and then gradually expand your ideas to create the final document. After some brainstorming, extract the key themes that you identified and give them headings. Under each heading, brainstorm some more points that are related to the heading's theme. Having "filled" the headings, you will have chunks of information on each theme, which make up a summary of your final document. You can then decide what sequence would be most appropriate, and re-order your section headings in that sequence. Outlining is effective for top-down writers, those who begin with a big picture plan of the whole document, and then build up the details as they go. When writing a report, the outline acts as a first draft that can be submitted to a manager or client to show the progress of a project.

Storyboarding

This is a spatial type of outlining used in film and multimedia projects. Small screens are drawn on a page depicting the main visual elements of major scenes in a project. Under each screen is some script describing the main action and indicating any areas that need to be developed for the particular scene. In the case of writing, the screen can be replaced with a descriptive heading. Spatial experimentation can help you find a logical order in which to present your ideas; in other words, you can re-shuffle the screens till you find the most appropriate sequence. For both outlining and storyboarding, do not delete documents or files until the project is finished, because you may find that information you thought was redundant becomes relevant again at a later stage.

Figure 1.2 is a storyboard outline of the sections of a report on the causes and consequences of digital piracy. The outline distributes section headings without, at this stage, considering the final sequence.

Figure 1.2   Storyboard

Drafting

When you brainstorm and use the other techniques for generating content described above, you are basically drafting. The drafting stage proper comes when you feel you have gathered enough information and have a clear idea where you are heading, so it is now time to expand confidently. Drafting is when you put into practice the ideas you generated in the previous stage and see how they work in expanded form. When drafting, it helps to be receptive to influences that can provide direction and inspiration. Keep your topic in the back of your mind in your everyday activities, and critically listen to, read and watch all that is productive for your purposes. Also, be open to serendipity – inspiration through sudden, previously unrecognized connections. Many great scientific and technical discoveries were made accidentally, by sudden awareness of previously unseen analogies.

If you get stuck when drafting, do not attempt to complete the draft in one go. Instead, let it incubate by putting it on the "back burner" of your mind and coming back to it later. The time lapse between giving up on a draft and coming back to it could be a few minutes, hours, overnight or more – depending on project deadlines, of course! In the meantime, you can do something that, even though it may seem irrelevant, allows your thoughts to gestate. In fact, in professional contexts more often than not you work on many projects simultaneously, so time management, and letting go of one project to move to another, become significant skills.

Table 1.5 gives a definition of major conceptual actions that you perform when drafting a document. These are common to both academic and professional situations.

Table 1.5 Writing Actions	
Account for	Give reasons; explain why something happened.
Analyse	Take apart an idea, concept or statement inorder to evaluate it. This type of answer should be methodical and logically organized.
Argue	Systematically support or reject a viewpoint by offering justification and evidence for your position while acknowledging the opposite point of view.
Assess	Judge the worth or value of something critically.
Comment on	Discuss, explain and give your opinion on the ideas presented.

Compare	Set items side by side, show their similarities and differences, and provide a balanced description.
Criticize (or Critique)	Point out strengths and weaknesses of the subject; support your judgment with evidence.
Define	Explain the precise meaning of a concept. A definition answer often follows the DEMF model: Definition, Examples, Main Theorist(s) and Further information.
Discuss	Explain an item or concept, and then give details about it with supportive material, examples, points for and against, and explanations for the points you put forward.
Evaluate	Discuss the material, and reach a conclusion either for or against the concept being discussed and evaluated.
Examine	Analyse the topic, give pros (points for) and cons (points against), or offer a critical judgement about it.
Explain	Offer a detailed and exact explanation of an idea, principle or set of reasons for a situation or an attitude.
Generate	Propose new ideas or new interpretations of available subjects.
Hypothesize	Propose a statement or set of statements that can be used as the basis for testing conclusions.
Illustrate	Provide examples to demonstrate, explain, clarify or prove the subject of the question.
Integrate	In a logically related way, draw together two or more subjects not previously connected.
Interpret	Explain the meaning of something, make it clear and explicit, and evaluate it in terms of your own knowledge.
Justify	Give reasons supporting a particular position on the subject. This could be a positive or a negative position.
List	Present issues or subjects in an itemized series. In many cases, listing can be done in point form.
Outline	Give an organized ordering of information stating the main points or idea and omitting details.
Review	Examine, analyse and comment briefly on the main points of an issue.

Overcoming writer's block

If you find that it is difficult to generate ideas about a specific topic, leading to annoying and costly delay, try one or a combination of these "unblocking" techniques.

Freewriting offers one method of clearing and opening your mind. You can freewrite by writing non-stop, on any topic, for a specific length of time. Do not stop to edit or evaluate what you are writing, and, if you cannot think of anything, keep repeating your last word or phrase until you get going again. The point of freewriting is to unblock your thought processes and put you in the mood to express ideas in writing. The topic or relevance of what you are writing is, at this stage, put aside. Many writers find that freewriting allows them to approach their task in an uninhibited way.

Writing to the resistance means writing about why you are having trouble tackling a task, or why you are being frustrated in your investigations. This process may help you break through a puzzle or identify more clearly what it is about the forms of evidence you are dealing with that makes them difficult. Writing to the resistance works especially in cases when you feel so perplexed or overwhelmed by a topic that you find it difficult to write about it in a systematically logical way. It may help you to trace a rational pattern in chaotic thinking.

Responding and mirroring should help you get in the mood for writing, by engaging with other texts. Read a text in the genre in which you are writing (for example, if you are writing a report, choose a report, if a magazine article, choose a magazine article), and write an informal critique of it: if you could ask the writer questions about it, what would you ask? What do you think could have been done better in the document? Rewrite a section to improve it. What is particularly effective in the document, and why? If the document asks a question, answer it. By responding this way to the text, you are building motivation and direction to work on yours.

This technique is also called "mirroring", a term from the world of acting. Trainee actors learn to perform by reflecting in their behaviour what they observe in a partner – responding to a smile with a smile, to a frown with a frown, etc. This is based on the idea that any form of action is also, by extension, a form of communication, that is, it is meaningful in relation to a context and a set of participants – action is reaction. Clearly, then, this is relevant to writing too, and can fruitfully be exploited as a "warm-up" or "unblocking" technique.

"Blind" writing is a solution for compulsive editors. If you feel critical about every word you produce and constantly delete and re-write the same sentence, it may be better not to see what you write. Try typing with a dark screen to help you achieve momentum and mass before crafting your output.

Tips for successful writers

As a conclusion to this chapter, here are some inspirational guidelines for effective writing. These are based on discussions with people from different countries, who make their living from writing of all kinds, professional, creative and academic. Therefore these tips are international and based on practical, life experience.

1 **Be observant.** All kinds of writing emerge from experience, so the more experience you get in your chosen field the better a writer you will become. Also, being a good writer means being good at dealing with people. Writing always has readers and the more you understand people's behaviour and reactions the better a writer you will be. Remember that the writing process begins before you start writing, so keep an eye out for anything that you could use in your writing later.

2 **Record and organize different types of material.** Professional writers keep a record of ideas, objects or events that catch their eye, even if these may not seem relevant to what they are writing at the moment. Writers carry a notebook and pen, or their digital equivalents, everywhere, and many also carry recording devices to record their thoughts and observations immediately as they come. This way you are building a pool of resources that some day will find their way into your writing.

3 **Do not wait for inspiration.** Writing creates itself – rather like eating is said to arouse the appetite. Most professional writers write on a schedule to meet publishing deadlines, whether they initially feel like it or not. So start writing before you have thought out completely what you want to say. It doesn't matter if you start by writing nonsense, repetitions, fragments or mind maps. You will discover what you want to write by writing and not just by thinking. Your document will eventually write itself.

4 **Revise as you write.** Most professional writers do at least two, and sometimes many more, drafts of anything they write. The first version should never be the last version. To be a successful writer, you should see yourself both as innovator (coming up with new ideas and new connections between ideas) and editor (rearranging and cutting out parts of your text). Regarding professional writing, keep in mind that many documents are collaborative and those editing a document may not be the same as those who wrote it.

5 **Learn grammatical rules and genre conventions.** Successful writers know standard English very well. Although writing is based to a large extent on skill, imagination and knowledge, it is still a technical medium dependent on grammatical rules. Even if you want to break those rules, like many writers in fact do, you first need to know what they are. Similarly, find out what the standard conventions are for different genres in your field of writing. If working in a business context, find out about your company's house style. These rules and conventions are the tools of the trade.

6 **Get feedback.** In contrast to what some people wrongly believe, writing is not a solitary activity. A written text is meant to be read, so discuss your projects with friends and colleagues, and distribute your drafts for comments when possible and appropriate. Other people may be able to give you valuable insights on your work that you would have missed if you worked in isolation.

ACTIVITIES

1 Analyse a media text (for example an advertisement, a magazine feature article, etc.) in terms of its target audience.

2 Interpret these briefs using the scene-content-treatment model outlined in this chapter. Plan your course of action and decide what kind of information you would need to gather to write each report.

(a) You are a travel industry expert.

A major airline, LibAir, has commissioned you to assess its competitive position in the travel industry. The airline executives want you to investigate recent developments in aircraft construction, security measures and client services, and to evaluate their airline's advantages and disadvantages in relation to those of competitors. Write a report that identifies pertinent issues and recommends a practical course of action for the airline to follow in order to remain competitive in the current travel market.

(b) You are a security expert.

The Privacy Commissioner has asked you to investigate and write a report on contemporary issues concerning privacy. With developments in surveillance technology, the spread of Internet published information and digitally stored personal information, there is serious concern that individual rights to privacy are being eroded. The increasing presence of computer hackers and state-owned satellite systems mean that individual privacy is being attacked from both private and public sectors. The Commissioner wants you to investigate the extent to which this fear is justified, to evaluate possible consequences and to suggest possible solutions. Write a report that identifies and analyses pertinent issues and puts forward a clear set of recommendations for action.

(c) You are the Human Resources Manager at Law Limited, a leading national law firm.

Law Limited has been having difficulties retaining its junior and intermediate-level lawyers. This is an industry-wide problem with law firms generally losing more than half of their junior lawyers before they reach an intermediate level (3–4 years' experience). The Chief Executive of Law Limited has asked you to prepare a report investigating the problem both within the company and inter-company. Write a report that identifies pertinent issues while taking into account the interests of the company as well as the views of the junior lawyers. Outline a couple of alternative solutions, evaluate them and propose the best solution justifying your recommendation.

References and further reading

Bazerman, C., & Prior, P. A. (eds.) (2004) *What writing does and how it does it: An introduction to analyzing texts and textual practices.* New Jersey: Lawrence Erlbaum.

Bhatia, V. (1993) *Analyzing genre: Language use in professional settings.* London: Longman.

Bhatia, V. (2004) *Worlds of written discourse: A genre based view.* London: Continuum.

Candlin, C. N., & Hyland, K. (1999) *Writing: Texts, processes and practices.* London: Longman.

Cockcroft, R., & Cockcroft, S. (2005) *Persuading people: An introduction to rhetoric,* 2nd edition. Red Globe Press.

Columbia Space Shuttle Accident Investigation Board Report (2003). Retrieved from http://caib.nasa.gov/

Cooren, F. (2015) *Organizational discourse.* New York: Wiley.

Cottrell, S. (2015) *Skills for success: The personal development planning handbook,* 3rd edition. London: Red Globe Press.

Elbow, P. (1998) *Writing with power: Techniques for mastering the writing process,* 2nd edition. New York: Oxford University Press.

Gurak, L. J., & Lannon, J. M. (2007) *A concise guide to technical communication.* New York: Longman.

Herndl, C. G., Fennell, B. A., & Miller, C. R. (1991) Understanding failures in organizational discourse. In C. Bazerman and J. Paradis (eds.) *Textual dynamics of the professions.* Maddison: University of Wisconsin Press, 336–357.

Hyland, K. (2002) *Teaching and researching writing.* London: Longman.

Marsen, S. (2011) Writing the "professional": A model for teaching project management in a writing course. In Martha Pennington and Pauline Burton (eds.) *The college writing toolkit: Tried and tested ideas for teaching college writing.* London: Equinox, 239–254.

Marsen, S. (2014) Lock the doors: Towards a narrative-semiotic approach to organizational crisis. *Journal of Business and Technical Communication,* 28(3), 301–326.

Maxwell, C. (2007) *Ultimate leadership.* New York: Thomas Nelson.

Osborn, A. F. (1963) *Applied imagination: Principles and procedures of creative problem solving,* 3rd edition. New York, NY: Charles Scribner's Sons.

Peeples, T. (2003) *Professional writing and rhetoric: Readings from the field.* New York: Longman.

Swales, R. (1990) *Genre analysis.* Cambridge: Cambridge University Press.

Taylor, J. R. (1993) *Rethinking the theory of organizational communication: How to read an organization.* Norwood, NJ: Ablex Publishing.

Taylor, J. R., & Van Every, J. E. (2000) *The emergent organization: Communication as site and surface.* Mahwah, NJ: Lawrence Erlbaum Associates.

Yagoda, B. (2004) *The sound on the page: Great writers talk about style and voice in writing.* New York: HarperCollins.

Writing Style

Focus:

- Style, format and genre
- Types of style
- Writing clearly, accurately and concisely
- Cohesion

Even if you have all the conceptual aspects of a written project thought out and made a plan of the information that you want to communicate, you may find that you get stuck in some other areas. For example, you may find that you have difficulty in putting ideas into words, cannot think how to begin, or how to end, a sentence or find that your sentences are invariably too short, too long, unclear or monotonous. All these are matters of style. Furthermore, since style differs quite drastically from spoken to written form, attempting to write as you speak can only lead to ineffective communication (unless, of course, you are writing dialogue). As the poet T. S. Eliot famously once said, if we spoke as we write, we would find nobody to listen, and if we wrote as we speak, we would find nobody to read. This chapter gives insights into recognizing and choosing appropriate style and expression for particular genres and in constructing sentences in an effective and clear manner.

As style has been examined since ancient times, definitions and approaches abound. Many definitions focus on style in relation to purpose. For example, the Roman orator Cicero (Wisse, 2007) distinguished three levels of style: high, middle and low. The first is grandiose and elaborate, aiming to move, the second is clear and methodical, aiming to please, and the third is unadorned and simple, aiming to teach. These distinctions have influenced much of contemporary rhetoric, and they also underlie the concept of genre.

More recently, writers have experimented with style, often blurring genre distinctions. An example is Tom Wolfe, who challenged journalistic writing conventions in the 1970s in his "New Journalism", a style which favoured subjective phrases and literary devices, such as incomplete sentences (fragments) and the coinage of new terms – for instance, the phrases "radical chic", "the right stuff" and "good old boy" are attributed to Wolfe (Kaplan, 1987).

Other approaches are more evaluative, and distinguish strengths and weaknesses of style, regardless of genre or purpose. A common element in these approaches is applauding precision and transparency in all prose writing and criticizing opaqueness and verbosity. For instance, the well-respected book *Elements of Style* by William Strunk and E. B. White (2000, original 1918) emphasizes the importance of a tight and concise style that focuses on information rather than author presence. The book even has a section entitled "Place Yourself in the Background". Interestingly, the tenet of transparency is often espoused by creative writers too. For example, novelist George Orwell (1953) ends his essay *Why I Write* by stating that "one can write nothing readable unless one constantly struggles to efface one's personality. Good prose is like a window pane" (p. 46).

Using an eclectic and practical approach, this chapter defines style as the result produced by different combinations of sentence structures, sentence lengths and word choices. It explains how particular arrangements of words emphasize different elements and produce varying degrees of objectivity and subjectivity, making them suited for specific genres and purposes. This approach agrees with journalist Ben Yagoda's (2004) statement that "every time we write a word, a phrase, a sentence, we have to choose from what seems like an infinite number of acceptable candidates. Then just as significantly, we choose how to link the sentences together into paragraphs. Together, these decisions constitute a style" (p. 36). The choice of what style to adopt should take into account context, genre and purpose.

The components of style are *balance, emphasis, register* and *tone*. Balance indicates the amount of information given to a topic in a sentence or paragraph and how information is prioritized and sequenced. Emphasis indicates if information is foregrounded by repetition or emphatic linkers, such as "importantly". Register indicates the degree of formality used. Tone indicates the degree of flow or abruptness (achieved through sentence structure) and the use of jargon or creative devices such as metaphor. Like the clothes we wear, our hairstyle and body language give away much about our status, personality and cultural affiliations, choice of style tells readers whether what we say concerns them, and whether they should read it as serious, humorous, urgent, and so on. In fact, stylistic choices "colour" writing, making the first and longest-lasting impression. Consider these sentences:

(a) In the era of social media, companies have little control over information.
(b) Social media have taken control over information away from companies.
(c) What social media have achieved is to take control over information away from companies.
(d) It is control over information that social media have taken away from companies.

The versions could be multiplied, but what this experiment shows is that you can draw attention to different parts of a topic and modify your tone by reordering parts of a sentence and, similarly, of a larger text. Sentence (a) makes a loose connection between social media and loss of control over information by placing social media in an introductory phrase. Sentence (b) gives much stronger agency to social media by making it the subject of the sentence. It is less equivocal than the first. Sentence (c) also focuses on social media, but in this case, it places social media in the context of its results or achievements. This sentence suggests that the surrounding text would describe social media in terms of its historical or comparative aspects. Sentence (d) emphasizes control over information by implying that it is the most important element that social media have affected in business.

> **TIP**
>
> This brief analysis shows how we create style by orchestrating linguistic units (words, sentences and paragraphs) into different combinations. Assume control over this stylistic manipulation by becoming aware of it in what you write and read.

Sentences and style

The best way to create an effective style is by knowing the values, knowledge and interests of your audience, the context in which you write, and the genre. These elements will determine your choice of going formal, impersonal, chatty, hip, "cool" or whatever other tone you think will be most appropriate. Here are four important areas to watch out for when creating style (more on grammatical aspects of style in Chapter 10).

1 **Include variety.** No document is justifiably boring, so introduce rhythm by alternating long and short sentences, using some active and some passive voice, and beginning some sentences with phrases rather than with subject–verb construction. For example, this extract from a report is concise,

grammatically correct and precise. However, stylistically it is displeasing to the reader and monotonous, because of its succession of simple, short sentences and lack of linking words between sentences:

> Email is one of the most common Internet activities in business. Some of the information in emails is of sensitive nature. A technically savvy person can intercept emails. This person then has access to the information. In fact, there is little awareness of email's lack of security among general users.

A less monotonous revision of this text would produce the following:

> Email, one of the most common Internet activities in business, often carries sensitive information. However, email can easily be intercepted by a technically savy person, who then has access to the information. In fact, general users are often unaware of email's lack of security.

In constructing your document, use a variety of simple and complex sentences, with short, simple sentences for information you wish to emphasize. Because they condense meaning in a few words, short, simple sentences have the greatest impact on the reader. The more you expand a sentence, the more dissipated the meaning becomes. For example:

> The project team sent the data to the laboratory for testing. They expect the results back within two hours of dispatch. *It is not always so.* Sometimes they must wait for hours, which means their whole project could be jeopardized. *It is a risky business.*

Notice how the two italicised sentences carry a lot of weight in this passage because they comment on the rest of the information. They are also the shortest of the five sentences.

2 **Think carefully about using main and subordinate clauses.** Information in a sentence can either come in the main clause or in a subordinate clause. The main clause foregrounds information; the subordinate clause backgrounds information. For example, consider this sentence:

> The proposal, which was approved by the Board, will be implemented immediately

The most important information here is in the main clause: "The proposal will be implemented immediately". The subordinate clause, "which was approved by the Board yesterday" gives secondary information, or information that is assumed to be known by the audience and therefore backgrounded. When using complex sentences with one or a number of subordinate clauses, think carefully if what you subordinate should not be given more importance by coming in a separate sentence as a main clause. Remember that what you subordinate is received by your reader, consciously or unconsciously, as secondary in relation to what you give as main information. Subordination and coordination affect balance and emphasis. Consider the re-write of the above sentence:

> The proposal was approved by the Board. It will be implemented immediately.

Here the two items of information are balanced by being placed in two separate sentences – neither item is subordinated.

When writing complex sentences with more than one subordinate clause, be aware that the ways you combine main with subordinate clauses creates different effects. The different combinations are called **loose structure**, **centred structure** and **periodic structure**. Here are examples of each.

> **Loose:** Sharks can be very dangerous when they smell blood, although they may not always be hungry.

Loose structures begin with the main clause and add subordinate clauses at the end. They project a relaxed, informal style imitating a conversation.

> **Centred:** When they smell blood, sharks can be very dangerous, although they may not always be hungry.

Centred structures begin with a subordinate clause, then give the main clause and end with another subordinate clause. They project a tighter and more formal sentence that gives the impression you are dealing with a complicated or serious matter.

> **Periodic:** Although they may not be hungry, when they smell blood, sharks can be very dangerous.

Periodic structures begin with the subordinate clause(s) and lead to the main clause. They suggest that the information in the main clause is conditional to other factors, or that you concede a point to an opponent before asserting your opinion. Use this structure carefully, because, although it may increase the importance of the main clause, it delays it and could annoy the reader. Think about whether leading to a statement with a degree of suspense would be appropriate for the audience and purpose. This structure is more common in texts intended for oral speech, such as documentaries, than in formal report writing.

3 **Use parallel structure.** Parallel structure adds clarity to sentences and paragraphs. Parallel structure refers to the similar grammatical structure of linguistic items that belong to the same category in a sentence, paragraph, set of headings or list of dot points. The more mathematically inclined will recognize the distributive law in mathematics as analogous to parallel structure in language: $x(a+b) = xa + xb$. The common element must work

grammatically with each of the parallel elements; the grammatically parallel elements could be substituted for each other without needing to change the rest of the sentence. Check for parallel structure when you add items in one category, or balance items on one level of information showing equality between them.

Not parallel:	These books are not primarily for reading, but they are used for reference.
Parallel:	These books are not primarily for reading but for reference.
Not parallel:	Not only is he a conscientious worker, but also he is very competent.
Parallel:	Not only is he conscientious but also competent.
Not Parallel:	Don't underestimate the value of defining technical terms. Prior knowledge on behalf of the reader should not be assumed.
Parallel:	Don't underestimate the value of defining technical terms. Don't assume prior knowledge on behalf of the reader.
Not parallel:	Possible solutions for dealing with at-risk youth include implementing programs and support measures through parent and child education, housing and physical, social and economic conditions should be changed.
Parallel:	Possible solutions for dealing with at-risk youth include implementing programs and support measures through parent and child education, improving housing, and changing social and economic conditions.

Parallel structure is very important in instructions, point lists and headings. For example, here are four introductions to a printer user guide:

A. Setting up the printer, maintenance, and what to do if something goes wrong are easy with the step-by-step user guide.

B. Setting up the printer, maintaining it and troubleshooting are easy with the step-by-step user guide.

C. Printer set-up, maintenance and troubleshooting are easy with the step-by-step user guide.

D. The step-by-step user guide will show you how to set up the printer, how to maintain it and what to do if something goes wrong.

Version A is awkward because the three elements that it lists are not parallel. The other three correct this error. Notice also how although all three are grammatically correct, there are slight differences in tone with each choice.

C with its noun emphasis is the most formal version, while D, with its clause structure and second person pronoun, is the most informal.

4 **Use cohesive devices strategically.** Cohesion is the way segments of a text are combined to produce flow and transition from one point to another. In the hands of a competent writer, cohesion consists of a blend of repetition and variation. Cohesion exists within a sentence, between sentences and between paragraphs. In longer documents, such as reports, cohesion is also achieved through a logical sequence of sections. Cohesion between sentences and paragraphs is achieved by means of *referents* and *adverbial conjunctions*.

Referents are words that refer to preceding words without repeating them. *Synonyms* and *pronouns* can act as referents. Synonyms are words of closely related meaning and provide an effective solution to the problem of excessive repetition. If you said "approach" in one sentence and had to repeat the idea, you might choose "method" in the next sentence. If you said "skill", you could then use "ability", and so on. That would give your reader variety without changing the meaning. It indicates to the reader that you are writing about the same topic without needing to repeat the same words.

When using synonyms, however, be careful not to overuse them. Overwhelming the reader with a wide range of words for an object or concept can be confusing and detracts from the clarity of your document. In certain cases, especially with regard to technical terminology, it is better to repeat a term rather than replace it with a synonym.

Pronouns are words that refer to nouns (I, he, she, it, we, you, they, this, that, these).

If two sentences begin with the same subject, it is sufficient to use a personal pronoun in the second sentence instead of the noun.

The report claims that the new incentive to include all financial figures in Intranet documents has not led to an increased interest in the company's economic development. *It* adds that most stakeholders do not know how to access Intranet information.

However, guard against ambiguity: sometimes the use of a pronoun instead of a noun can be confusing, especially if there are several nouns in the previous sentence to which the pronoun might refer. In this case, it is better to repeat the noun or use a *demonstrative pronoun* (this, that):

Incorrect: The report claims that the new incentive to include all financial figures in Intranet documents has not led to an increased interest in the company's economic development. Although

> *they* (?) are now available, most stakeholders do not know how to access Intranet information.
>
> **Revised:** The report claims that the new incentive to include all financial figures in Intranet documents has not led to an increased interest in the company's economic development. Although *these figures* are now available, most stakeholders do not know how to access Intranet information.

Demonstrative pronouns refer to a noun in the previous sentence or to the whole previous sentence, especially if followed by a noun:

> **Repetitive:** The popularity of social media in business communication is increasing. The popularity of social media has been observed by many researchers and is a growing area of study.
>
> **Revised:** The popularity of social media in business communication is increasing. This (popularity) has been observed by many researchers and is a growing area of study.

Pronouns do not only refer to a preceding noun; if this noun refers to a person, the pronoun activates aspects of identity. The use of pronouns to designate gender has come under scrutiny in recent years, after social developments have challenged the belief that gender is binary. English, in contrast to some other languages, does not have gendered nouns, but it does indicate gender in the third person singular pronouns "he", "she", "his", "him", "hers", "her". So, what to do in order to avoid gender bias and recognize the existence of transgender and other gender varieties?

In many cases, using a plural noun solves this problem. For example, consider these sentences:

> **Gender bias:** The reader expects clarity in journalistic writing. She values the writer's attempts to explain clearly complex issues.
>
> **Transgender bias:** The reader expects clarity in journalistic writing. He or she values the writer's attempts to explain clearly complex issues.
>
> **No gender bias:** Readers expect clarity in journalistic writing. They value writers' attempts to explain clearly complex issues.

Using "they" to refer to a singular noun is ungrammatical. However, there is a move towards acceptance of this use in some contexts because of sensitivity to gender issues. This is especially the case when a name does not specify gender or the writing context is gender-sensitive (such as in universities, government departments and socially prominent institutions). For example,

Contextually appropriate although grammatically incorrect:	*Lee Watkins* has made important contributions to the debate on transgender issues in public institutions. *They* proposed constructive changes to style guides regarding pronoun use.

To avoid using the plural "they" to refer to a singular individual, some have proposed the third person singular pronoun "zie" and "hir" which are non-gender specific (see the Gender Neutral Pronoun Blog, 2019).

Adverbial conjunctions are "signpost" words that connect two sentences and show the relationship between ideas or points. Your train of thought will usually seem so obvious to you as not to be worth stating. But if you do not make it clear, you will force your reader to laboriously reverse-engineer your writing to discover your meaning. In professional writing, your reader may not have the time or inclination to do that.

If, for instance, the sentence you are writing is meant to contradict the meaning of the previous sentence, you can signal actively to the reader that you intend a contradiction, by using "however", "nevertheless", or some similar adverb. If one sentence contains the result or consequence of a previous sentence, again, do not leave the reader to infer that you are talking about a result or consequence. Signal it by using "consequently", "as a result", etc. Remember to use signpost words if the relation between ideas is not obvious. Overusing such words can be tiring for the reader and can at times produce a condescending or harsh effect that may be detrimental to the quality of your document.

Table 2.1 shows some adverbial conjunctions that provide cohesion, and the relationships they express.

Table 2.1 Adverbial Conjunctions and their Functions	
Function	**Examples**
Listing	First, Second, Next, Then, Subsequently, Finally
Adding	Also, Moreover, Furthermore, In addition
Showing similarity	Equally, Likewise, Similarly, Correspondingly, In the same way
Emphasizing	In fact, Actually
Showing results or effects	As a result, Consequently, Hence, Therefore, Thus
Explaining	In other words, That is to say
Illustrating	For example, For instance
Showing alternatives	Alternatively, On the other hand

Function	Examples
Contrasting	Conversely, On the contrary, By contrast, However, Nevertheless
Evaluating	Surprisingly, In the final analysis, Paradoxically, Interestingly

Example One: Cohesion

The following extract is analysed in terms of its cohesive devices.

Provides a supportive explanation.

Summarizes an important point in the paragraph.

Repeats the concluding sentence of the previous paragraph and indicates the topic of this paragraph.

Refers to the features mentioned in the previous sentence.

Evaluates this sentence in relation to what was said before.

Understanding the shape of the tree of life and the details of its branches is more than a quaint sideline of biology, even though the science of this quest – known as systematics – has come to be regarded by many biologists as dowdy and old fashioned, little more than stamp collecting. *But such an understanding is probably the best foundation for a larger appreciation of life, including evolution, ecology and behaviour. As Co*lin Patterson, a palaeontologist at the Natural History Museum of London, says: "To retrieve the history of life, to reconstruct the evolutionary tree, is still the aim of evolutionary biology." *Getting it right is therefore important.*

Getting it right, however, is much harder than might be imagined. Inferring an evolutionary relationship from morphology rests on identifying anatomical features, or characters, that are shared by two species because of their common descent. *Such features* might include the shape of teeth, the form of a particular nerve canal, the number of certain flower parts, and so on. *Ironically,* the thing most likely to confound the well-intentioned systematist in identifying such characters is the power of natural selection itself. Many shared characteristics do not reflect a common ancestry, but *instead* are the result of distantly related species independently adapting their bodies to meet the demands of similar lifestyles (Lewin, 1998, p. 37, my emphasis).

This is known as a parenthetical definition. It is used within a sentence to provide a brief definition of a term and is placed between brackets or dashes. It acts as a cohesive device in allowing for explanation without compromising flow as would happen if a separate sentence was inserted to explain the term.

Shows transition of contrast. Note that 'but' and 'and' at the beginning of a sentence makes the writing informal and should be avoided when a higher degree of formality is expected.

Emphasizes contrast.

The three "golden rules" of professional writing

Regardless of genre and style, effective professional writers follow three basic rules: *be clear, be accurate and be concise.* In professional writing, these rules can be traced back to the 1970s when the Plain English campaign that was launched in most English-speaking countries helped to re-conceptualize business and government communication. The main claim underpinning the Plain English campaign was that documents intended for the broad public should be easily understandable. The campaigners criticized the existing belief that formal writing should be technical, impersonal and passive, in order to sound respectable and authoritative. Instead they emphasized the importance of communicative value: if readers cannot understand what a document says, how can they be persuaded by the content or be expected to follow the regulations described?

Since then, audience research has refined the guidelines for professional writing, and this research informs the way in which many corporate and governmental style guides are designed. Writers spend a lot of time researching and thinking about the best words and sentence structures to create the desired effect on target audiences. To be successful as a writer, and especially one with a serious public responsibility, you must have an eye for detail. As novelist Stephen King (2000) advises, to create compelling writing that impacts on readers' perceptions, "you must take your objective one bloody word at a time" (p. 136).

Be clear

Clarity encompasses precision and conciseness. In most cases, the more precise and concise your writing is, the clearer it is. Obscure expression and verbosity are not, generally, conducive to clarity. Clarity should be assessed from the point of view of the reader, so attempt to take the reader's perspective when composing a document. Although in the planning stage you are writing for yourself, to clarify your ideas and give direction to your writing, when revising adopt the reader's point of view.

> **TIP**
> Write as a writer and revise as a reader.

One way to assist clarity is to be as specific as possible. This is achieved by knowing exactly what you want to communicate and to whom, and by choosing relevant information to convey your message. Make sure each piece, section or chapter is about one topic only and that all information you give relates to that topic. Avoid changing the topic or including irrelevant information. Also, avoid writing in a way that forces the reader to waste time by re-reading the document to decipher "hidden meaning" or to reverse-engineer your thinking. For example, the following notice on an office building undergoing renovation would have been very clear to those who wrote it, but very confusing for passers-by and visitors:

> Due to renovations, the first floor will be on the second floor, half the third floor will be on the second floor and half will remain on the third. Second floor will move to the third.

Revising this notice from a reader's perspective could include adding a visual representation of the building or naming the offices that have moved to different floors.

Clarity can be achieved on the text level and on the sentence level. When structuring your document, follow a logical pattern of organization that will be easy for the reader to understand. Usually, this means going from the more general to the more specific, from assumed shared knowledge to new knowledge, from "big picture" to details, or from definition of a problem to its analysis and then to its proposed solution. When revising the document, keep in mind that the reader should not have to go backwards or forwards to understand your message but can continue reading in a linear order.

> **TIP**
>
> One test of the quality of professional writing is the ease with which it can be summarized. If you find a document is hard to summarize, chances are that it needs revising to refine it of digressions, ambiguities or inconsistencies. Use this test on both your and other people's writing.

On the sentence level, clarity is often achieved in these ways:

1 **Favour topic-action structures.** This means focusing your intended meaning on the central parts of the sentence, the subject, verb and object. The topic of the sentence is the main idea that the sentence develops. It does not have to be the subject of the verb but can be the object in passive voice sentences. Ask yourself "what is this sentence about?" and place the answer first or as close to the beginning as possible. Proceed by specifying the action, what this main idea or topic does or is. For example, the following sentence, on the costumes of players in a game, has "the first player" as the topic of the first part of the sentence and "the keeper" as the topic of the second. This is misleading, however, because the topic is actually each player's costume and not the players themselves.

Confusing:	The first player wears a special leather suit that is designed for fast movement and the ability to slip through the opponent's clutches, while the keeper wears a heavily padded suit to protect him from aggressive attacks.
Revised:	The first player's special leather suit is designed for fast movement and slipping through the opponent's clutches, while the keeper's suit is heavily padded to protect him from aggressive attacks.

Also, the following sentence includes the redundant and confusing ideas of "design" and "ability" when the aim is to describe what a prototype does:

Confusing: The prototype is designed to ensure that it would be able to maintain consistency among all products of the same series.

Revised: The prototype ensures consistency among all products of the same series.

2 **Avoid more than two nouns in a row.** Sometimes writers try to make their writing more concise and technical by eliminating prepositions (in, of, etc.), and linking nouns in a chain. Unfortunately, this is often done at the expense of clarity and accuracy. Make sure that elegant style and clarity win over brevity and the tendency to repeat jargon indiscriminately.

Confusing: He designed a new graphics construction language.

Revised: He designed a new language for constructing graphics.

Confusing: The project includes a long-term failure prevention programme.

Revised: The project includes a long-term programme to prevent failure, or The project includes a programme to prevent long-term failure.

3 **Break up long sentences**, especially if they contain more than one piece of information. Usually, sentences that contain one piece of information, even if this includes details on that item, are clearer to grasp in one reading.

Confusing: Although this methodology has been tested worldwide on different formats and has been hailed as the most effective currently available, we have decided not to use it in this experiment because the present situation requires more rigorous techniques of controlling testing procedure.

Revised: This methodology has been tested worldwide on different formats and has been hailed as the most effective currently available. However, the present situation requires more rigorous techniques of controlling testing procedure. Consequently, in this experiment, we have decided not to use it.

Confusing: This is a science fiction action film set in the year 2325 about a self-centred superstar of a world sport phenomenon called Destruktion, which has eclipsed the popularity of all sports, who is targeted by a terrorist group.

Revised: This is a science fiction action film, set in the year 2325, when a world sport phenomenon called Destruktion has eclipsed the popularity of all other sports. The film is about a self-centred superstar of this sport, who is targeted by a terrorist group.

4 Position phrases correctly. When you order words and phrases in a sentence, make sure that nouns agree with all their subject positions. It can be especially misleading when the noun immediately following an opening phrase cannot be identified with the noun of the phrase. This has the effect of confusing agents and actions and potentially leading to incorrect attribution of responsibility.

Confusing: As an experienced manager, my boss gives me little supervision.
Revised: Because I am an experienced manager, my boss gives me little supervision.

Be accurate

To make your writing more accurate, follow these guidelines:

1 Favour quantification. If you can give measurements and numbers, instead of ambiguous words, then do so.

Vague: This policy has been effective for several years.
Revised: This policy has been effective since 2010.

Vague: Many people attended the event.
Revised: About 200 people attended the event. Or: Attendance for the event this year was 20% higher than last year.

2 Avoid words with many meanings. Think of a word that is specific to the meaning you intend in the sentence. For example, consider how we use the word "over" with different meanings:

During – The experiment must take place over the winter
Onto – The fertilizer was spread over the field
More than – This disease affects over 10% of the population
From – We collected data over three locations
Of – Apply two replications over six dilutions
To – Statistical sampling was applied over the data
Across – Sampling was stratified over taxonomic groups
Through – Dust accumulates over time
With – The company policies changed over time

Now consider some examples with the word *wrong*:

Vague: The decision was wrong.
Revised: The decision was financially costly for the company.

Vague: This number is wrong.
Revised: This number is incorrect.

Vague: Cheating is wrong.
Revised: Cheating is unethical.

Vague: He was wearing the wrong clothes.
Revised: He was dressed inappropriately.

Words that have many meanings include also evaluative adjectives whose meaning is relative to the speaker's judgment – "nice", "terrible", "good", "big", etc.

Vague: This team contains good members.
Revised: This team contains conscientious and hard-working members.

Vague: The manager's decision was terrible.
Revised: The manager's decision was irresponsible. Or: The manager's decision was based on short-term profit only.

3 **Define terms** and favour specific words instead of phrases, where possible. This sharpens your writing, making it more direct. However, be careful not to offend readers by putting them in categories and labelling them.

Vague: Clear documentation pleases people and may increase the people who buy our software.
Revised: Clear documentation pleases users and may increase our clients.

Vague: Strict regulations are in place to protect against people who break into computers and steal information.
Revised: Strict regulations are in place to protect against hackers.

Be concise

The above sections show that, to be clear and accurate, you sometimes need to expand on a point, and use more words. This does not condone verbosity, however. Being direct is important in professional writing if for no other reason than "time is money", and readers want to know if a document answers their question or addresses their need without having to analyse it in detail. Some writers believe that by including as many details as possible and repeating information they become clearer. Trying to "drill in" information, however, may draw attention away from the main message and confuse readers. In most cases, by stating clearly and directly your point at strategic points in the document you have a better chance of getting your intended meaning across.

You can make your writing concise by avoiding long, crowded and wordy sentences, especially if they are in succession. If you write one or two long sentences, make sure the next sentence is short to break the density. Also, following these tips will help:

(a) **Favour the active voice where possible.** Passive sentences are wordier and can also be confusing if they do not reveal the agent of an action.

> **Wordy:**   The work was finished by the engineers before the deadline was reached.
> **Revised:**   The engineers finished the work before the deadline.

> **Wordy:**   The policy decision was met with disapproval by the public.
> **Revised:**   The public disapproved of the policy decision.

(b) **Avoid "there is/are" at the beginning of sentences, where possible.** In many cases, we overuse these words, even when they are not necessary.

> **Wordy:**   There are several conclusions that we can draw from these results.
> **Revised:**   We can draw several conclusions from these results. Or: From these results, we conclude…

> **Wordy:**   There are several organizations that belong to the union.
> **Revised:**   Several (number?) organizations belong to the union.

(c) **Use *modals* (may, might, could, should, must) where possible.** Some writers harbour suspicion that modals are informal; however, this is not true. Modals modify verbs and have a clear place in language.

> **Wordy:**   It is possible that the project will be funded.
> **Revised:**   The project may be funded.

> **Wordy:**   It is imperative that all options be considered before making a decision.
> **Revised:**   All options must be considered before deciding.

(d) **Use verbs where possible instead of nouns.** Besides making sentences concise, verbs are action-oriented and give your writing a more direct tone. Noun-centred sentences, known as *nominalizations*, have a heavy effect that makes the sentence static by reducing elements that evoke movement. Although nominalizations are used in some technical and scientific texts, they should be avoided, if possible, in energetic and people-oriented writing.

> **Heavy:**   The results are not a demonstration of a data breach.
> **Revised:**   The results do not demonstrate a data breach.

> **Heavy:**   A vacuum chamber is not a requirement for this procedure.
> **Revised:**   This procedure does not require a vacuum chamber.

(e) **Avoid weak verbs.** Some verbs, instead of signalling action, depend on a noun to support them. In many cases, such verbs can be replaced by other verbs that do not require a noun. Weak verbs include *take, make, do, give, get* and *reach*.

Wordy: Researchers conducted an investigation of inflation.
Revised: Researchers investigated inflation.

Wordy: This study serves to show the results of the investigation.
Revised: This study shows the results of the investigation.

(f) **Use punctuation strategically.** If you find that your paragraph is getting cluttered with too many wordy or long sentences, it is often possible to use punctuation to cut down on words. This is especially effective when announcing or introducing a list of items.

Wordy: There are many reasons for climatic change, which include toxic pollution, deforestation and volcanic activity.
Revised: There are many reasons for climatic change: toxic pollution, deforestation and volcanic activity.

Wordy: Most professional writing can be divided into three categories. These categories are essays, reports and articles.
Revised: Most professional writing can be divided into three categories – essays, reports and articles.

(g) **Avoid wordy clichés.** Some phrases are so commonly used in spoken language that they have become almost unconscious. Writing, nevertheless, gives you the opportunity to become more conscious of how you use language and allows for elimination of repetitive material. Table 2.2 shows a list of such clichés.

Table 2.2 Common Wordy Clichés

Wordy	Concise
a majority of	many (or number)
a number of	some (or number)
subsequent to	after
due to the fact that	because
for the purpose of	to
have the capability to	can

Wordy	Concise
in the event that	if
so as to	to
in order to	to
with regard to	about
has the ability to	can
give a summary of	summarize
make an assumption about	assume
come to the conclusion that	conclude
take action	act
make a decision	decide
make a proposal about	propose
basic essentials	essentials
end result	result
cancel out	cancel
enter into	enter
completely eliminate	eliminate
at this point in time	now
there can be little doubt	definitely, certainly
in the absence of	without
higher in comparison with	higher than
may be the mechanism responsible for	may be why

A typology of style

This chapter ends with a typology, which shows the stylistic features of different kinds of writing and should help you to decide on style. Classifications and typologies impose sometimes artificial boundaries between elements that are often as inclusive as they are exclusive. Classifications can be useful, however, in highlighting similarities and differences in the composition of these elements. The following typology is intended as a continuum, with writing addressed to a broad audience on one end, and writing addressed to a specialized audience on the other. This typology is based on criteria that are conventionally expected in different genres and contexts. Like it is inappropriate to attend an executive board meeting in your pyjamas, so it would be inappropriate to adopt an informal style for a formal occasion and vice versa.

This typology distinguishes three main types of writing style: *specialist, journalistic* and *creative*. Although some genres are associated with a particular type of style, styles can be mixed depending on the writer's intended purpose and are not strictly bound by genre conventions. The basic criteria for selecting a writing style are the audience you are addressing and your purpose. For example, business reports tend to be written in specialist style, but their degree of formality varies according to the company's "personality" – more "hip" companies would favour a less formal style than more traditional ones. National culture also plays a role in selecting a style. For instance, American, Australian and New Zealand businesses tend to use a less formal, and more direct, style than British companies, while Asian companies tend to use the most formal, and most indirect, style of English. Such factors show that cultural factors are important in analysing differences in stylistic choices (Holmes & Stubbe, 2003; Watts, 2003).

Journalistic style, as the title suggests, is found in journalistic texts such as magazine and newsletter articles. This style is also used in public relations documents and documents that are addressed to the broad public. How "chatty" such documents become depends on the publication and context.

Creative style is arguably the most complex because it can be found in a variety of genres. Fiction genres, especially poetry, are associated with this style, but fictional texts include a variety of styles. For example, some science fiction texts are written extensively in a specialist style that emulates scientific discourse, even though their content is based primarily on imagination. So, what are the distinguishing features of each type of style?

Specialist style

At one end of the style spectrum is specialist style, which is suitable for an audience with a specific interest and some specialized knowledge in the topic. These readers may be managers, technical peers or technically savvy stakeholders. Characteristics of this style are:

- Strong use of quantitative or quantifiable information: where possible give numbers, facts and measurable data – but make sure you explain them.
- Factual tone produced by minimal use of evaluative adjectives: avoid words that show personal response, such as "wonderful", "horrible", "delightful", "heartbreaking", etc.
- Use of abstract entities as agents of actions rather than people: where possible, use words that refer to things as agents in a sentence. This helps to

focus on facts and observable elements rather than people. For example, write "The project is developing on time" instead of "I am developing the project on time", and "Evidence suggests ..." instead of "I think ...".

- Focus on the topic rather than on readers' anticipated response towards it: avoid using direct questions, such as "Don't you think that ...?", or "Wouldn't you ...?" and expressions that attempt to tangle the reader in appeals to common sense, such as "We all feel that ...", "Of course, everybody knows ...". The "you approach" is a feature of journalistic writing, so avoid it in specialist style.
- Description and analysis of topic, presented with critical distance: describe a situation objectively, even if you have strong feelings about it.
- Use of complete words. Avoid the use of contractions (it's–it is, haven't–have not, etc.), as they give writing a "spoken" or "chatty" tone.

Here is an extract from the introduction and conclusion of a report written by the IT manager of an insurance company to department managers, on the dangers of new computer viruses for the functioning of the company's network. Notice the direct approach tackling the main topic immediately, the use of specifics, such as names and dates, and the impersonal presentation of facts.

Example Two: Specialist Style

This report examines the type of computer viruses that are currently circulating and that constitute the greatest threat to the company's network system during 2019. The viruses discussed are Sircam, Love Bug and Code Red. These are especially destructive and attack the operating system. Given the insidious nature of these viruses, prevention is very important. All employees should follow these precautions:

- Make sure the antivirus software installed on all computers is functioning and updated. Check the bottom right corner of screens for an icon of a sealed computer monitor. If this is not there, contact the System Support section immediately.
- Do not open any suspicious email attachments. Open only those attachments that you are expecting or that are clearly justified.
- Make sure all important files are backed up so that information can be retrieved even if a virus attack deletes files.

Journalistic style

Because it addresses a very wide audience, and comes in a variety of formats, journalistic style is more complex and harder to define. The main purposes of documents written in this style are to inform the public of a development or event, to entertain them by presenting a personal commentary on an issue that is of collective concern, or to influence and motivate them to adopt a certain attitude towards an issue. In this respect, anything that popularizes a subject would use journalistic techniques to an extent. Popular science, for instance, is written in this style. In fact, even some academic or professional textbooks, including this one, are written in journalistic style, as they too aim to present specialist information in a readily accessible manner that can be understood by non-specialists.

Journalistic writing can vary from *factual* (such as reporting news stories), to *informative* (such as the scripting of scientific documentaries), to *promotional* (such as marketing products in business publications) and to *demagogic* (such as the opinionated and often polemic style of editorials). The general characteristics of journalistic style are:

- Chatty tone produced by colloquial words and phrases, question-answer format and sentence fragments
- Appeal to emotion and common sense
- Consistent use of generalities and exaggeration
- Consistent use of imperatives (sentences that begin with command words), and exclamations
- Direct address to the reader: "you" and "we"
- Dramatization of events through use of colourful metaphors and visual language.

Here is an extract from a journalistic piece written by the same IT manager that wrote the specialist example of the previous section. This time the manager is writing for the IT column of a local newspaper and dealing with the same topic as his report – computer viruses. Notice the chatty tone, the direct address to the reader and the use of humorous exaggeration:

Example Three: Journalistic Style

Be prepared for Armageddon! Just as you are farewelling last year's unprecedented cataclysm of computer viruses, a whole new army – better, smarter and stronger – is marching in.

What can you do? Sit tight. If you don't already own anti-virus software, invest in some. If somebody sends you a love email, resist the temptation – don't open it. Love Bug is rampant. In case the worst happens, make sure you have backups of files, online or on hard drives. Remember, do something before a virus attacks: better safe than sorry!

To better understand the difference between specialist and journalistic styles, compare the following two extracts. Both were written by biologist Frank A. Brown, but for two different publications. The first was written for a specialist scholarly journal, addressed to expert peers, while the second was published in a popular science magazine, addressed to a wider, and therefore less technically versed, audience. Both extracts deal with the same topic but present this topic differently to suit the knowledge and interests of the respective audiences.

A. A deep-seated, persistent, rhythmic nature, with periods identical with or close to the major natural geophysical ones, appears increasingly to be a universal biological property. Striking published correlations of activity of hermetically sealed organisms with unpredictable weather-associated atmospheric temperature and pressure changes, and with day to day irregularities in the variations in primary cosmic and general background radiations, compel the conclusion that some, normally uncontrolled, subtle pervasive forces must be effective for living systems. The earth's natural electrostatic field may be one contributing factor (published in *Biological Bulletin* – Brown, 1962).

B. Everyone knows that there are individuals who are able to awaken morning after morning at the same time to within a few minutes. Are they awakened by sensory cues received unconsciously, or is there some "biological clock" that keeps accurate account of the passage of time? Students of the behaviour of animals in relation to their environment have long been interested in the biological clock question (published in *Scientific American* – Brown, 1954).

Extract A, written in a high degree of specialist style, is almost undecipherable by a lay audience. Some features that produce this effect are strong presence of technical jargon, long sentences, and emphasis on abstract entities and processes with no mention of human agents or personal concerns. Extract B, written in journalistic style, "interprets" the technical information by associating it with personal, everyday experience. Some features that demonstrate this are rhetorical questions, use of metaphor ("biological clock"), and generalization ("everyone knows").

For another example, consider this extract, adapted from an editorial in *New Scientist* (30 June 2001). Its use of personal pronouns is typical of the demagogic variant of journalistic style. The demagogue is the enthusiastic public speaker, who tries to sway audiences with a highly emotive tone. Although fine for an editorial, this style would be highly inappropriate in business writing, say, in a formal report to a client:

So, it turns out that poisonous polychlorinated biphenyls (PCBs) are turning up in our food more often than we thought. Should we panic? PCBs are in everyday food in high concentrations and we aren't even monitoring them. It makes you wonder what else is out there.

Creative style

As noted above, creative style is an umbrella term encompassing a variety of techniques, generally associated with fictional writing – although it is also used in some journalistic genres, such as "creative non-fiction" and in advertising. The main aims of creative style are (a) to draw attention to language processes themselves, rather than to events or objects in the objective world, and/or (b) to evoke images in the reader's mind through linguistic symbolism such as metaphor. Creative style is not covered in this book, but it is useful to include this brief description in order to contrast it to the other stylistic types that we discuss. For an example consider this extract from William Gibson's novel *Neuromancer* (1984), which, incidentally, introduced the term "cyberspace" in the lexicon:

> Cyberspace. A consensual hallucination experienced daily by billions of legitimate operators, in every nation, by children being taught mathematical concepts. A graphic representation of data abstracted from the banks of every computer in the human system. Unthinkable complexity. Lines of light ranged in the nonspace of the mind, clusters and constellations of data. Like city lights, receding… (Gibson, 1984, p. 510)

Although this extract describes an abstract concept, cyberspace, it does so by creating mental images and arousing an emotional response, rather than by detailing the technical specifics of the concept. The features that create this effect include the use of fragments (the extract has no complete sentences), the strategic use of metaphor ("consensual hallucination"), analogies to common experiences ("like city lights …"), and intensifiers ("every nation", "every computer", "unthinkable complexity").

Audience and medium matters

It is worth repeating that the most important considerations in choosing your style are audience and purpose. If writing for complete outsiders or novices, for example, you may find that to be clear you have to use definitions and explanations that lengthen the text. If that is what would ensure reader understanding, then so be it – you cannot be as concise and direct in this situation as would be appropriate in a different situation. Also, when writing about a delicate or controversial topic, you will need to take care to avoid using phrases that are loaded with offensive connotations, especially if the audience is the general public (unless you deliberately want to provoke!). Similarly, it is sometimes impossible to be precise when quantifying a situation. In that case you could give a range, average or approximation. In all cases, choose a style that supports your message and is aligned to the situation in which your writing takes place.

> **TIP**
>
> When reading others' writing, use the guidelines given here to analyse and understand what flatters you, offends you, leaves you indifferent, angers you, enlightens you or seduces you. Then use the insights you gain to control your own writing.

The medium is the channel in which you transmit your message and is a separate decision to choosing genre and style. For example, you can submit a report by sending it through the post or you can attach it as a PDF to an email and send it electronically. The genre (report) remains the same in both cases, but the medium is different. Medium is mostly a matter of access. Which medium would reach your target audience most effectively?

Access, however, is linked to the ways readers process information perceptually. For instance, it is still easier and faster to read script off paper than it is to read it off a screen (although new digital technologies are rapidly changing this). Professional editors, in fact, often print typescripts to proofread them since it is easier to pick errors on a hard copy. With regard to style, this means that journalistic style, with its shorter sentences and words, is more suited to digital writing, especially writing that is generally not printed, such as website content.

Besides mental processing, space is another consideration in different media. Websites have a strict layout and typography, which affects the number of words that can "fit" in a space. This is analogous in many ways to magazine and newspaper layout (in fact, websites were initially modelled on magazines). A rule of thumb states that a business headline should have 5–8 words or 16 characters. This has the added advantage that it fits on a smartphone screen. Websites, magazines and newsletters are often printed in columns, so shorter paragraphs, sentences and words are best. A paragraph can look much longer in a column than across a page, so journalistic style is, again, a preferred choice.

ACTIVITIES

1   The following sentences are grammatically correct. However, they are inappropriate for professional writing because of ambiguity and/or wordiness. Restructure the sentences to make them more suited to a professional context.

   1   This program has a graphics design capability.

   2   The security guards have the responsibility of checking all offices.

   3   We opened the project to suggestions with a view to being able to get some ideas on the improvement of the security of the building.

   4   Since we hired the new technical assistant, the quality of the equipment has improved.

   5   His project will involve a big investigation into how the monetary economy has evolved.

   6   There are several organizations that are concerned with the destruction of rainforests.

   7   The inspecting officer can do a verification of the data when the manager has made a decision on a suitable methodology.

   8   The media could not provide the public with a justification of their manipulation of the information in the news story.

   9   When logging in, the data must be completed fully.

   10   Non-computer background personnel can do this task.

   11   To find the committee room, signs have been posted along the corridor.

   12   A detailed analysis of trends and an evaluation of the relations between state and corporation is the purpose of this report.

   13   Prolonged use of the battery can cause it to become drained of its energy.

   14   Because there is a trend towards fewer and larger offices, it will cause an increase in the demand for computers.

2   The following sentences come from informal genres, such as conversations and email. Rewrite them in specialist style to make them appropriate for a formal business report. You will need to make up some specific information.

   1   The deplorable staff turnover rate could be reduced if those long-awaited fringe benefits could be introduced.

   2   You can hardly imagine the effect of incentive pay on staff morale.

   3   I don't understand why anyone would opt for this outrageous solution.

4 Nobody likes to feel unsafe at home, so these building security measures will help to make people feel more secure.

5 I think the Slick Graphics upgrade is a good, solid way to do what we want and we can also save money.

6 Advertisers feed on people's greed and futile attempt to fill the emptiness of their lives with consumer objects.

3 Rewrite the following sentences so that their structures are parallel.

1 He has the ability both to choose a suitable course of action and he can implement his decision wisely.

2 Walking quickly burns as many calories as you burn when you run slowly.

3 It has been found that homo sapiens have not changed anatomically in the last 10,000 years, and also our intellectual capacities are about the same.

4 The court found him guilty of insurance fraud and he has been sentenced to two years imprisonment.

5 From this report it is recommended that the following initiatives be adopted: links with the Chamber of Commerce and Industry, the viability of an information technology school should be examined and also a scheme, which assists small business with accounting matters, should be established.

4 Improve the cohesion in the following paragraphs by using some of the devices described in this chapter. You may rearrange sentences and add linkers, but do not rewrite the paragraphs extensively. Keep the style and content the same as the original.

(a) Romantic individuality may have something to do with the sport's popularity – the fact that one undertakes a kind of Byronic solo adventure when one jumps. The jumpers do their thing in groups and form little outlaw societies in which they approve of and cheer one another. It could be the illegality of the sport that pumps them up. In an interview last April, Kappfjell said he delighted in playing outlaw and "fooling the authorities" as he gained access to his perches. (adapted from Rosenblatt, 1999 – note that the sport mentioned is base jumping)

(b) Complex systems are particularly good for modelling the complexities of the natural world. During the Gulf War, large quantities of oil polluted the sea. This damaged the ecosystem – but how do you go about measuring that damage and monitoring the ecosystem's recovery? Researchers needed to disentangle a complex web of interrelationships. (adapted from Stewart, 1998, p. 37)

(c) Explorative graphics enable the user to move about a web site by selecting a graphical object. This is an alternative to using text to navigate the web site. They make the web site more attractive while increasing download time. Excessive use of exploration graphics can confuse a user.

References and further reading

Brown, F. A. (1954) Biological clocks and the fiddler crab. *Scientific American*, 190, 34–37.

Brown, F. A. (1962) Response of the Planarian, Dugesia and the Protozoan to very weak horizontal magnetic fields. *Biological Bulletin*, 123(2), 264–281.

DeWitt, S. L. (2001) *Writing inventions: Identities, technologies, pedagogies*. Albany, NY: State University of New York.

Dias, P., Freedman, A., Medway, P., & Paré, A. (1999) *Worlds apart: Acting and writing in academic and workplace contexts*. Mahwah, NJ: Lawrence Erlbaum.

Finkelstein, L. Jr. (2000) *Pocket book of technical writing for engineers and scientists*. New York: McGraw Hill.

The gender neutral pronoun blog (2019). Retrieved 26 July 2019 from https://genderneutralpronoun.wordpress.com/

Gibson, W. (1984) *Neuromancer*. New York: Penguin.

Gunnarsson, B-L. (2009) *Professional discourse*. London and New York: Continuum.

Gurak, L. J., & Lannon, J. M. (2007) *A concise guide to technical communication*, 3rd edition. New York: Longman.

Harper, G. (2012) *Inside creative writing: Interviews with contemporary writers*. London: Red Globe Press.

Harris, R. (2009) *Rationality and the literate mind*. London: Routledge.

Holmes, J., & Stubbe, M. (2003) *Power and politeness in the workplace*. London: Longman.

Kane, T. (1994) *The new Oxford guide to writing*. Oxford: Oxford University Press.

Kaplan, J. (1987) Tom Wolfe on how to write New Journalism. *Rolling Stone*, 5 November.

King, S. (2000) *On writing*. London: Hodder and Stoughton.

Kirkman, J. (1992) *Good style: Writing for science and technology*. London: Spon.

Lewin, R. (1998). Family feuds. *New Scientist*, 24 Jan.

Marsen, S. (2004) To be an actor or to be an observer? A semiotic typology of narrator roles in written discourse. *Semiotica*, 149(1/4), 223–243.

Marsen, S. (2012) Detecting the creative in written discourse. *Writing and Pedagogy. Special Issue on Creativity in Writing*, 4(2), Autumn 2012. 209–231.

New Scientist editorial (30 June, 2001). *Here we go again*, n.p.

Orwell, G. (1953) *Why I write*. London: Penguin.

Petelin, R., & Durham, M. (1992) *The professional writing guide: Writing well and knowing why*. London: Longman.

Pinker, S. (2012) *The sense of style: The thinking person's guide to writing in the 21st Century*. New York: Penguin.

Rosenblatt, R. (1999) The whole world is jumpable. *Time*, 19 July.

Stewart, I. (1998) Rules of engagement. *New Scientist*, 29 Aug.

Stott, R., & Avery, S. (2001) *Writing with style*. London: Longman.

Strunk, W. Jr., & White, B. (2000) *The elements of style*, 4th edition. New York: Allyn and Bacon.

Watts, R. (2003) *Politeness*. Cambridge: Cambridge University Press.

Williams, J. M., & Cizup, J. (2016) *Style: Lessons in clarity and grace*, 12th edition. New York: Pearson.

Wisse, J. (2007) 'The riddle of the *Pro Milone*: The rhetoric of rational argument' In J. Powell (ed.) *Logos: Rational argument in classical rhetoric.* London: University of London Institute of Classical Studies, 35–68.

Woolever, K., Trzyna, T. N., & Batschiet, M. (1999) *Writing for the technical professions.* Boston, MA: Addison-Wesley.

Yagoda, B. (2004) *The sound on the page: Great writers talk about style and voice in writing.* New York: HarperCollins.

3

Short Business Documents

Focus:

- Everyday communication genres
- Bullet points
- Presentations

This chapter looks at the writing that professionals do every day, and the formats of short business genres, such as memos, email and oral presentations.

The amount and kind of writing that professionals do every day varies greatly, depending on the industry, the size of the company and the person's position in it. For example, in a routine and relatively uneventful week, a Public Relations Officer in a mid-range high tech company would need to write about ten press releases about two pages long each, one proposal about four or five pages long (a topic could be to get approval and funding to conduct a media trip to a new site of the company), one presentation or speech to be delivered by a senior manager or the CEO, one press conference or media-addressed statement and about two newsletter articles addressed to stakeholders. In addition, every day s/he would write several statements and responses, to media and stakeholders, sent mainly through email and instant messaging. If the company does not have a social media specialist, the PR Officer would also need to update the company's social media communication daily.

Although different genres have their own conventional formatting conventions, there are certain writing principles that are relevant for all business genres since they reflect the rhetorical situation of workplace communication in general. Table 3.1 describes these principles:

Table 3.1   General Business Writing Principles

1 **State your purpose close to the beginning of the document:** business writing is 'top heavy'. This means that the beginning of a document is a prominent position and important information should be placed there. Don't let the reader wait for the main point – suspense is not a desirable quality in business writing.

2 **Respond to the brief/establish a link with previous exchange:** remind readers why you are writing this document. Is it in response to a request? Is it an answer to a question? Is it a follow-up from a decision reached at a meeting? Establishing a link between your document and a previous communication is especially important in short documents, such as memos and email, because readers receive a number of these daily and would need some context.

3 **Present information in order of its importance to the readers:** the most effective way to organize information in a business document, regardless of genre, is from most important to least important from the point of view of the reader.

4 **Chunk information into sections with a clear pattern of development:** make sure the logic of organization of paragraphs and sections is clear to the reader and consistent throughout the document.

5 **Use listing and bullet points to condense and highlight information:** if not over-used, bullet points can be a strategic device for summarizing and emphasizing information, as well as a technique for making your document more concise.

6 **Put information of questionable or partial importance into an attachment:** short documents must have one main message. Any additional information should go in a separate attached document. Reports also have the advantage of allowing you to attach appendices with additional information. This is especially important when you have mixed audiences, with some readers having more knowledge of your topic and others needing more detail and explanation.

7 **Where appropriate, state clearly what action you want the reader to take:** if the document requires action, make sure this is explicit and not implied. Action requested of the readers usually comes at the end of a document – in the closing line in memos and email, and in the recommendations in a formal report.

These principles are consistently confirmed in research into corporate communication (Canavor, 2018; Cardon, 2017). For example, management communication researchers John Fielden and Ronald Dulek (1998) analysed over 2,000 documents in a corporate context and found that most were confusing and ineffective because they buried their main message and purpose by placing it in an inconspicuous position. This forced the reader to re-read sections and to attempt to interpret the writer's intention. To remedy this, Fielden and Dulek propose a 'bottom-line' approach to business writing, by organizing information so that the main message and purpose of the document are stated first, before any justifications, explanations or reasoning. All the information that follows becomes meaningful, because it is framed by the main point.

Short reports

The report is the most common genre in business writing, divided into various sub-genres. Many reports are *analytical*, evaluating and interpreting facts and ideas. Other reports are *descriptive*, stating facts without any analysis. Objectivity and good summarizing skills are necessary to produce clear and useful descriptive reports. Here are some types of descriptive reports, the focus of this chapter and their functions:

Agendas

Agendas for business meetings list the items for discussion. An agenda is circulated prior to the meeting to people who are scheduled to attend. Items included are the date, time and venue of the meeting, and the topics to be discussed. After apologies from absentees is a discussion of whether the tasks allocated at the previous meeting have been actioned – this way facilitating continuity in meetings and, by extension, in the progress of a project or the management of a section.

The following is an example of an agenda for a meeting of the Research and Development Committee of a company.

XYZ Company

Research and Development Committee

AGENDA 19 April 2019

Time: 11.00–12.00 pm
Venue: XX Building Block B

1 **Minutes of Previous Meeting (Attachment A)**

2 **Business Arising from the Minutes**

3 **Reports**

    3.1 Chair's Report

    3.2 Creative Arts Project (Attachment B)

    3.3 Report by Project Director

4 **Any Other Business**
Next meeting Friday 10 May, 10.00am–12.00pm in XX Building Block B

Minutes

Minutes contain a summary of discussions held at meetings. The meeting secretary is responsible for taking notes at the meeting, revising them into a minutes document and circulating the document to members. Minutes should include information on tasks allocated to project or section members to action. Here are the minutes of the meeting following the above agenda:

XYZ COMPANY

Product Development Meeting

Minutes of Meeting 19 April 2019

Present: John Amos, Grace Chung, Mary Willis, Steve Johnson, Adam Reeves
Apologies: George Craig, Petar Sladic

1 **Minutes of Previous Meeting**: The minutes were accepted as a true record.

2 **Matters Arising**: Mary Willis contacted the South American representative and arranged a two-day symposium later in the year to discuss possible collaboration on the new electric engine. Dates to be decided.

3 **Reports**

    2.1 **Chair's Report**: Our main concern is developing the new electric engine within the set deadlines and within budget. As this is an international collaboration many of our problems and delays have been in negotiating meetings, deadlines ,and exchange of resources with our international collaborators. At this stage we are still within the assigned timeline and within budget, but we must act swiftly.

    2.2 **Creative Arts Project**: The Creative Arts Department has not yet been established. It was due to be inaugurated in March, but we had to delay the inauguration and prioritize the development of the electric engine. At this stage, the Creative Arts Project is on hold until further notice. However, the Project must start this year.

    2.3 **Report by Project Director**: We spent the last two months contacting collaborators and gauging interest. We made a formal agreement with Dan Jones, CEO of Trademark to obtain all raw material from them. We have not been able to contact Mario Gracci in Italy because he has been away on business. **Action**: By next meeting, 10 May 2019:

        • Adam Reeves to contact Mario Gracci
        • Mary Ho to initiate contact with UC Davis and gauge interest in collaborating
        • Team members to bring prototype of engine for analysis and discussion.

3. **AOB**: None reported.

Next meeting on Friday 10 May 2019

Progress reports

Progress reports state tasks completed to date within a project. Progress reports compare actual progress against planned progress in terms of cost, resource use, and level of performance. Writing progress reports is an essential part of project management. With regular and timely progress reports, problems can be addressed and corrected before they damage the outcome of the project. Ideally, progress reports are written into project design as a formal requirement. For example, a systems analyst might be required to report to the project team or project manager every three weeks. This procedure reduces the risk of confusion, misunderstandings and delays.

When writing a progress report, consider:

Who to report to: Progress reports of projects are typically addressed to both sectors of the project team, the project steering committee who oversee the project and the project implementation group, who put the project design into operation.

When to communicate: Project reports are generally required regularly.

What to communicate: Headings for the report may include the following:

- Major issues
- Key achievements
- Targets
- Progress against schedule (indicate whether the project is progressing according to plan)
- Resource summary against plan (compare the utilization of resources against planned use at this stage)
- Major tasks remaining
- Forecast
- Additional comments/notation (for example, explain any deviations from the project plan).

How to communicate: As with all professional communication, expression in the report should be accurate, concise and unambiguous. It should be formatted using the house style of the company.

Contracts and licence agreements

Contracts and **licence agreements** list obligations and privileges that bind two or more parties and describe the conditions and rules that underlie the transactions of the signing parties. The legal and non-negotiative nature of such documents gives them the highest degree of formality of all descriptive reports.

Here is an extract from a licence agreement:

Disk Manager/Disk Manager Diagnostics (the 'software') is copyright 1990–2000 by ONTRACK COMPUTER SYSTEMS, Inc, and is protected by International Copyright Law and International Treaty provisions. All rights are reserved. The original Purchaser ('You') is granted a licence to use the Software only, subject to the following restrictions and limitations:

1 The licence is to the original purchaser only, and is not transferable without the written permission of Ontrack Computer Systems, Inc.

2 You may make back-up copies of the Software for your own use only, subject to the limitations of this licence.

Everyday communication documents

Business letters

In addition to reports, much professional communication takes place through shorter documents, such as letters and memos. These two documents are very similar in many respects. Their main difference lies in their recipients: letters tend to be addressed to readers outside the writer's organization, while memos are written for colleagues and employees within the organization.

Business letters generally serve these functions:

- They accompany a report (as in a letter of transmittal), a packaged product or advertising material (such as a brochure).
- They confirm a previous communication between writer and reader by stating the decisions or agreements that were made.
- They introduce a candidate's application for a professional position (as in a cover letter to a job application).
- They notify the recipient of the outcome of his/her application.
- They notify the recipient of changes or developments made in an established relationship (such as writing to shareholders to inform them of a new method of accessing financial data, or notifying employers of resignation).
- They carry a formal complaint or warning.
- They congratulate the recipient on a success, such as a promotion, or offer sympathy on a loss.
- They thank the recipient for his/her support or continued support.

The use and frequency of letters in a company depend on the company culture. Letters are more frequent in traditional companies but are being replaced by digital media in many progressive companies. They generally draw attention to something, whether that is an agreement, product or longer document, and should do this succinctly and directly.

The standard length of a business letter is one page. Only under special circumstances should you go to one and a half or two pages. For any situation requiring a longer document, write a short report. The standard order of items in a business letter is as follows:

1 Use a letterhead for the sender company's name and address. If you are writing as an individual and have no letterhead, include your name and address as the first item on the top left of the page.

2 Follow by the date and then by the recipient's name, position and address. Always try to address readers personally. Avoid addressing them by the impersonal Dear Sir or Madam. If need be, phone the company to find out the person's name. If you cannot find the recipient's name, use their title, such as Dear Public Relations Officer, or Dear Human Resources Manager. Use a title (Mr, Ms) and then the recipient's surname. If you don't know the gender of the person or if you are writing in a gender-sensitive context, do not include a title but write the person's full name. Use a first name only if you know the recipient well. Polite forms of address differ worldwide, so, in cross-cultural contexts, it would be advisable to do some "homework" to find out what term of address is expected.

3 The first sentence should state the nature of the letter. The best way is to write a short sentence beginning with "Here is…" or "This is to…". The word Re (short for regarding) followed by a title summarizing the purpose of the letter is also often used.

4 Follow with two or three paragraphs of two to four sentences each, with the main content. Be as concise as possible and avoid repetition and elaborate descriptions or justifications. End with a sentence indicating further action that you or the reader should take.

5 The most widespread courteous close is "Yours sincerely". Although "Yours truly" and "Yours faithfully", and the less formal "Cordially", are also used extensively, "Yours sincerely" is an internationally accepted standard. If the recipient is a close associate, you could go for the friendlier "Regards" or "Best wishes".

6 Type your name after your signature and follow by your position title.

As regards spacing, leave double space between each section. You can leave more space if the letter is short and there is a lot of white space on the page, but make sure you do not leave too many gaps between sections as this gives a fragmented appearance.

Example One is the letter of transmittal of a report investigating career opportunities for law graduates. The report was commissioned by a career consulting company and written by the president of the law students' society.

Example One: Letter

Law Students' Society
4 Gladstone Terrace
X City, Y Country

Note that in the United States, the month comes first, followed by the date, October 24, 2019.

Catherine Hayes
Manager
Bellevue Career Counsellors
Street Address
City

24 October 2019

Dear Ms Hayes,

This being a letter of transmittal, it summarizes the main contents of the report, and connects them with the client's specifications

Please find attached the report regarding the occupational possibilities of Law Majors that you requested on the 1st of October 2019. In accordance with your specifications, the report includes information on employment opportunities, pay rates and trends – areas interesting to graduates. Also, the report incorporates information for prospective students, such as advice on appropriate choice of courses and study planning.

First sentence states directly the purpose of the letter.

The report outlines possible career options for law graduates and examines advantages of the profession such as the wide range of work available, the flexibility within the occupation and the high levels of remuneration. Disadvantages such as high stress levels and competition are also considered.

The second paragraph goes into more detail on report contents.

The body of the letter ends with a note on recommendations. In other types of letters, this would be replaced with action to be taken by either the recipient and/or the writer.

Recommendations include advice concerning appropriate professional development training, membership in professional associations and publicity.

I hope this report will be useful for Bellevue's further work on career advice to students and graduates. Please feel free to contact me if you have questions about the report or require additional information.

The letter ends with an offer to assist further should it be required.

Yours sincerely,

Franziska Federle
President, Law Students' Society

Memoranda (memos)

Memos are internal documents, written to colleagues, superiors or subordinates within a company. There are a few cases where memos are sent to another company, notably when a *Memorandum of Understanding* is written to formalize an agreement between the two companies.

Memos are rapidly being replaced with email. The use and frequency of memos in a company depend on the company's culture. Since memos are an older genre than email, they tend to be associated with more traditional communication. In many cases, memos are considered a little more formal than email. Often they are attached to email as a PDF or Word document, especially in cases where it is expected that they will be printed or saved in a folder and recorded as a formal notification. Memos were the template for email when it was first introduced, so the two can be seen as variants of the same genre transmitted in a different medium. Both memos and email use the same header, known as a *memo header*: To, From, Date, Subject.

Memos are sent for a great range of reasons that involve some form of notification. They generally serve these functions:

- They confirm in writing the results of an oral communication, often also providing some more detail on the issues discussed.
- They inform the recipient of the stage reached in a developmental procedure. In this case, they function as informal progress reports.
- They carry a formal request, reminder (memorandum is actually a Latin word for reminder) or suggestion.
- They notify employees of a change or development in an established course of action (for example, if set hours for coffee and lunch breaks are implemented or changed).
- They accompany and introduce documentation, such as internal reports.

Companies often have house style templates for internal memos. If not, follow these guidelines:

- Always use a "memo header": To, From, Date, Subject.
- As with letters, aim for one page and do not exceed two pages.
- Begin with a personal address, especially if you are writing to one person or to group members with whom you work closely. A memo is still a relatively informal piece of communication, so beginning with "Dear X", or "Dear colleagues" is more palatable than an abrupt beginning. However, if you are writing to many readers who do not fall into one particular category, leave out the personal address.
- Tie your topic to a concern you expect your reader to share or to a subject you have previously discussed. For example, you could start by writing "As

you know..." or "Following our meeting...". Do not begin abruptly with a new piece of information stated out of context.

- If appropriate, include a closing remark indicating further action, such as "Please get back to me on this question as soon as possible." However, a closing tie is not necessary in a memo and you can, in fact, end with your last paragraph.

- A memo is a short text that states facts, so use bullet points and lists to summarize and classify information. Avoid wordiness and detailed specifications and justifications (but you can write a memo to point the reader to a document that gives these detailed specifications and justifications). Optionally use headings, if they assist communication by signposting information.

Example Two is a memo written by the Staff Welfare Officer to the Human Resources Manager of the Ministry of the Interior. The memo informs the manager of the results reached in a feasibility analysis carried out by the Staff Welfare Officer regarding coffee breaks. Note how it also acts as an informal progress report.

Email

Email has one definite quality: it is fast. For professional situations, this is both an advantage and a drawback. The advantage is that your message can reach a number of recipients in different parts of the world in seconds. Also email can make a message public (read by many readers simultaneously) thereby opening it up to more constructive feedback. The drawback is that, because of its ease and simplicity, email often tends to be associated with speech rather than written language, which can lead to bad audience dynamics and miscommunication. When sending email as part of a professional communication, keep in mind these two points:

An email message is a written text. It is, therefore, bound by the conventions of writing, as discussed in this book. That is, your audience and purpose should determine the relative formality, the style and the amount of detail. Contrary to what is sometimes assumed, the Internet does not level status distinctions; you are still writing to someone with a specific position of power and authority in relation to your own. Reflect this in your writing. Also, the ease with which a message can be transmitted and deleted does not justify sloppy composition, with misspelt words and ungrammatical sentences. In fact, a very common complaint with business email is that the writer seems abrupt and disrespectful and the message is hastily put together. Therefore, implement the guidelines for revision and editing given in this book also for email text.

Example Two: Memo

TO: Greg Taylor, Human Resources Manager
FROM: John Masters, Staff Welfare Coordinator
DATE: 25 November 2019
SUBJECT: Coffee Breaks

The second sentence gives more context by stating the overall purpose of the document.

The headings signal the organization of content.

Greg,
As you requested in our phone conversation last Friday, here is a summary of the issue and recommendations developed in relation to the current problem of coffee breaks. These issues and recommendations will be part of the formal report that I will submit to the Human Resources Committee on January 15th.

The first sentence links this communication with a previous one that initiated it. The recipient is, therefore, given context for the memo.

The Issue

Currently there is no provision of morning or afternoon coffee breaks for staff at the Ministry of the Interior. However, recent surveys and monitoring have indicated that approximately 70% of staff take unofficial breaks of between 20 and 40 minutes' duration each day. Other than causing work disruption, this also leaves staff that do not take breaks feeling disgruntled.

The issue for the Ministry of the Interior is whether it should implement an official morning and afternoon break policy, and, if so, on what conditions.

Recommendations

Studies have shown that 20-minute morning and afternoon breaks have a measurable positive effect on labour efficiency. This is reflected in the fact that three quarters of businesses nationwide have daily break policies.

The beginning of this section summarizes the findings that justify the recommendations.

The formal report in response to this issue will contain these recommendations, briefly outlined here:

1. The Ministry of the Interior should implement an official morning and afternoon break policy. This recommendation is legal and within the powers of the commissioners to authorize.
2. No more than half the employees in any department should be on a break at one time.
3. The Ministry should establish a canteen on the premises to provide a facility where staff can purchase food and beverages. There is currently no such facility close to the Ministry. I have obtained the relevant costs and am currently conducting negotiations for final pricing.

The last sentence avoids an abrupt ending by offering further communication.

Please contact me if you have any other questions at this stage.

Regards,
John

Email does not replace signed copy. Signed documents (often printed) are still considered more binding and formal than soft copy in some contexts. For example, although you may email a formal report for fast transmission, send also a hard copy to formalize the communication (unless youve been instructed not to). One reason for this is that it is still easier to lose documents in cyberspace than if they are in tangible form. Another reason is that electronic communication depends on availability of software and hardware, whereas print can fall back on the universality and reliability of paper. Your best option for certain transmission is to send your document in both forms keeping in mind that digital communication is rapidly replacing "snail mail".

Here are some general guidelines on writing effective business email.

1 **Begin with an opening address**: this could be "Dear" for more formal correspondence, or "Hello" for less formal. Omit an opening address if the message is one in a series of reply exchanges on a topic.

2 **Place your main message as close to the beginning as possible.** Do not force the reader to have to read the whole message to understand what it is about. Give as much information as possible about you (if necessary), and your main point at the beginning to put the reader in perspective. Any details you then proceed to give will be more meaningful.

3 **Write in full words and sentences.** Do not use abbreviated words, unless they are acronyms – email is not text messaging.

4 **Do not use upper case to emphasize.** Words and sentences written in upper case fonts are perceived as equivalent to shouting, not emphasis. If you want to emphasize, do so by using appropriate terminology.

5 **End by clearly stating what action you request or expect the reader to take** in response to your message and close the message politely.

6 **Revise the message before you send it**, paying close attention to spelling, word choice and repetition. Also, make sure the tone is appropriate. Never send an email when you are angry with the recipient. Wait till you cool off!

7 **Sign your message** with your name and affiliation as appropriate: often, the e-mail address is not enough for the recipient to know who you are. If you are writing a response to a thread of emails your name is enough to sign off. Delete long signatures from threads as they take space unnecessarily.

8 **Write short paragraphs** (three to four sentences). It is more difficult to read off a screen than it is off paper, so you facilitate communication by making the text as simple as possible.

9 **Do not use headings, tables or formatted text in the body of the email.** The reason for this is that email text is based on code – HTML (Hypertext

Mark-up Language). This means that layout and formatting may not display as you intended. If you want to send graphs and tables, attach them as a Word or PDF document (and don't forget to actually attach the document!).

10 **Think carefully before you copy secondary audiences.** The ease with which email can be sent increases the temptation to copy in a number of recipients. However, some content may be inappropriate, offensive or just irrelevant to some audiences. Similarly, always be discreet when writing about a third party in an email. This person may well be copied in to your message at some stage in the sometimes long and convoluted circulation of email messages. The nature of the digital medium makes it very easy to make private information public.

11 **Think carefully before you blind copy audiences.** If you send marketing or informational emails to groups of recipients, it is best to blind copy them in order to maintain their privacy (recipients cannot see each other's names). Blind copy also helps to avoid headers with long lists of names. However, do not use blind copy to "hide" secondary recipients from your primary audience. Ethical concerns are important in digital communication, as they are in other media. Transparency is a positive value in professional writing, so don't use the perks of digital media to obfuscate. Similarly, when receiving email, keep in mind that there could be hidden audiences. With email, the possibility of people lurking "on the side" is always a risk.

12 **Give informative subject headings.** The reader should be able to understand the topic of the email from the subject heading. Avoid ambiguous or "playful" titles in professional email and be as descriptive as possible in a few words.

In cases where your message is a binding contract, or includes information that should be recorded, consider submitting it in a different document, such as a letter, a contract, a written agreement or a report. Submit these as PDFs or Word documents or in hard copy. For formal, developmental procedures where the actual document is important, and not just the action it recommends, make sure a permanent copy is available, such as a brochure or content on a website – and maybe signal its existence by an email message.

Example Three is the body of an email written by an information analyst of a small-size IT company to her manager to complain about ineffective duty allocation. The email is tactless, unclear and contentious: it's obvious that the writer did not revise it and wrote it while in an emotional state. The email has bad audience dynamics, and the writer is defeating her own purpose to implement changes in duty allocation by confusing and antagonizing the recipient of the message.

Example Three: Email

Positions in the corporation have multiplied to such an extent over the last two years that human resources have no longer any idea who is doing what. I have to do so much that is not directly in my area that I hardly have any time to do my job. Only last week I had to prepare three press releases for new products and to respond to questions e-mailed to me by the marketing department because I didn't know who to refer them to. None of this is stuff I have to do. My job is to produce reports for management and for clients. I should not be at all involved in the selling area. If you want me to do my job properly, you should contact the human resources manager and tell him to do something about it. We should all get detailed job descriptions, our own and other people's so that we can refer requests to the relevant people within the company.

The email is ineffective in these areas:

- It begins abruptly with no introductory statement to define the context.
- It constantly repeats the writer's personal problem but does not show how this problem affects the whole company and how its correction would benefit everybody.
- It focuses on the problem but makes very little attempt to propose solutions.
- It is written in one chunk with no section or paragraph breaks. This makes it even more unpalatable and overbearing.

Example Four is a suggested revision:

Example Four: Revised Email

Establishes rapport with the reader through shared knowledge.

Gives personal situation as an example, not as the main focus of the message.

Concludes with a request for reader action.

Dear Dave,
I would like to draw your attention to a problem that affects staff efficiency as well as time and resource management.

As you know, over the last two years, positions in the company have multiplied. This has led to a confusion in duty allocation, with staff not knowing who to contact for specific tasks. As a result, many staff members divert their time and energy to tasks that are not officially in their area. For example, I often have to deal with the marketing department for sales enquiries, although this is not within the scope of my position. As you can understand, this situation is counterproductive and time consuming, and works against the company's best interests.

I propose that we organize a meeting with representatives from Human Resources to discuss possible solutions.

Please get back to me with your views on this matter, or if you need more information.

Regards,
Anna

States the purpose and main point in the first sentence.

Gives background to the situation that created the problem.

Links personal situation with the company's interests.

Makes a practical suggestion.

Writing in bullets

With the exception of email, the other short business genres described above (as well as longer reports, of course) include bullet points in their layout. This section gives some general advice on using bullet points effectively. Bullet points and numbered lists are a powerful device to condense and highlight information in reports. They make a text more concise while allowing you to cover a wide area. Points also stand out from the rest of the text and draw the reader's attention to the issues you are discussing. They enable you to show your awareness of issues without needing to discuss them in depth.

> **TIP**
>
> Use bullet points for items of roughly equal value; use numbered lists for items with priority ranking.

Bullet points list information that belongs to one logical category. For this reason, they should not list random or unrelated items. If placed within a report or memo, they should follow from a lead sentence, and be structured as endings of that sentence, with each point suggesting an alternative completion of the sentence. The only cases when bullet points can follow directly from a heading, without an introductory sentence, are in CVs and in presentation slides. Headings describe the content of a whole section and should not be used as an introduction to a list of bullet points. Bullet points could be complete sentences or phrases, but in either case, the rule of being part of a logical category would apply: they should present different aspects of the same category of information. They are an additive, not a developmental or procedural technique: they accumulate information on a topic but do not develop the discussion from one topic to another.

Compare the following extracts; the first is written in a block paragraph, and the other uses bullet points. Both are correctly written, so their appropriateness is determined by context and purpose. For example, the bullet-pointed version lends itself more readily to a document where each point is taken up and discussed further in subsequent sections.

(a) The department must make a reasonable effort to make stakeholders aware that information is being collected and the purpose for which it is collected. Also, the department must indicate who the intended recipients are, and provide details on its own structure. Another responsibility of the department is to notify the stakeholders of the legal requirements of the information (that is, whether it is mandatory or voluntary), and the consequences of not providing it. Finally, the department must clarify what access stakeholders will have to the information.

(b) The department must make a reasonable effort to make the stakeholders aware of the:

- Fact that information is being collected
- Purpose for which the information is being collected
- Details of the department collecting the information
- Legal requirement of the information
- Consequences of not providing the information
- Rights of access and correction of that information.

Common problems with bullet points

If bullet points are overused, they can make writing choppy and may leave the reader without a strong grasp of the main message. Other common problems with bullet points include confusing items in a series, using points to develop a sequence of events, and neglecting parallel structure. Example Five is an incorrect list because the first point is a heading, the second is an explanation of the heading and the third is a prescription of what should be done; the points do not list items in a category and should not be formatted as bullet points.

Example Five: Incorrect bullet point list – Mixed points

- Confusing levels of hierarchy
- This disrupts the flow of information
- Points should follow from lead sentence

In Example Six the points actually describe a chronological sequence of events and should be presented in paragraph form.

Example Six: Incorrect bullet point list – Chronological sequence

- The project investigates the high staff turnover in the company
- We collected data from surveys and interviews conducted over a period of two years
- Exit surveys showed a dissatisfaction with promotion opportunities
- It is obvious that measures need to be taken to prevent such staffing issues.

Parallel structure in bullet points

Parallel structure is very important in bullet points because the similar grammatical structure of all points reflects the fact that they belong to the same logical category. For example, in Example Seven the list lacks parallel structure and is incorrect:

Example Seven: Incorrect bullet point list – No parallel structure

Suggestions for improvement include:
- More incentives for initiative should be given
- Salary increase
- we should review current recruitment methods
- developing a mentoring scheme

This problem can be corrected by choosing one structure and keeping it consistent in all points, as in Example Eight (notice also the consistency in using upper case first letter for each point):

Example Eight: Corrected parallel structure in bullet points

Suggestions for improvement include:
- Giving more incentives for initiative
- Increasing salary
- Reviewing current recruitment methods
- Developing a mentoring scheme.

Punctuation in bullet points

Consistency is very important in bullet points and numbered lists, and this extends to the use of punctuation. Companies usually have their own house style on punctuation in bullet points. However, it is becoming increasingly common practice to omit any punctuation at the end of each bullet point and use a full stop after the last one. Semicolons at the end of bullets are becoming outdated and used in more traditional companies. Using upper or lower case for the first letter of each point usually depends on the content of the points: points that complete the introductory sentence tend to take lower case, whereas those that list independent items tend to take upper case. Whichever option you follow, make sure you are consistent throughout your document.

Oral presentations

Presentations are a staple of business communication. Their combination of physical presence with text and visuals enables the presenters to establish a relationship with their audience and to promote their aims. Presentations are a *multimodal* genre, which allows the presenter to showcase the qualities of a product, new idea or service in an appealing and creative manner. They are used in countless business situations, from presenting a business plan to potential investors, to presenting the particulars of a new advertising campaign to management, to presenting progress on a project, to presenting the findings of an investigation – to name just a few situations.

What makes a good presentation? In the final analysis, the best way to answer this question is by attending presentations and seeing which stand out as impressive, which are competent but unexceptional, and which are downright boring and confusing. You can then analyse the characteristics of each, emulate the ones that produce effective results and avoid the ones that lead to failure, while keeping in mind that quality should be assessed according to the criteria of each industry. Being an attentive member of the audience will give you invaluable tips on being a master speaker. The following guidelines are based on tested observations and discussions with seasoned presenters.

The most common digital tools used for presentations are *PowerPoint, Keynote* and *Prezzi*. All have advantages and disadvantages, and all can suffer from two common misuses caused by over-reliance: "Death by PowerPoint" and "PowerPoint Karaoke".

Death by PowerPoint occurs when the presenter relies on the digital tool to carry through the presentation. This happens when the speaker "kills" the topic (not to mention the audience) by relying inordinately on slides. Some speakers have been known to write slides to fill an hour's talk – which can make up about 90 slides!

> **TIP**
>
> The best way to conceptualize a presentation is as a speech genre with the digital tool as an aid in delivering this speech, a means to an end, not the end itself.

PowerPoint Karaoke occurs when the speaker uses the slides as transcripts and reads them out to the audience. In this case, the slides become the centrepiece of the talk, not the speaker. However, although focusing on one or two slides to analyse information is acceptable (especially if the slides contain financial data or other important graphical information), relying on the slides to carry the whole interaction is not. If you expect the audience to read a lot of data during your talk, consider giving handouts or sending out some written information before the talk, to prepare the audience.

TIP

For complex arguments, elaborate explanations and detailed justifications, complement presentations with written material that does not have to be read off a screen.

Speaking and writing

A. **Differences between speaking and writing**
In order to understand the role of business presentations within the general genre of public speech consider some differences between spoken and written information:

1 **Spoken information is more difficult to retain.** This is why listeners need to take notes or be given written material to summarize, highlight and reinforce the main information presented.
2 **Attention tends to fluctuate when listening.** Distractions are more pronounced in oral communication contexts than in written. When reading, one can always reread information; when listening this is not always possible.
3 **Spoken information is coloured by the speaker's physical presence.** The speaker him/herself may be a distraction, which is why speakers should take care to dress, speak and move in ways that complement the content of their speech, not in ways that draw attention away from it. When delivering an oral presentation take care to present a strong and confident presence (unassuming speakers tend to diminish the importance of what they are saying), with enough control over mannerisms and voice projection, so that you do not become the centre of attention (unless that is your intention), drawing attention from the content of your presentation.
4 **Speaker's presence enables clarification.** This is an advantage in speaking because listeners can ask for explanations and otherwise interact with the speaker.

B. Similarities between speaking and writing

At the same time, oral and written information is governed by certain similarities. In both written documents and oral presentations the following guidelines are valid:

1 **Take the audience from what they know to what they do not know.** People become involved in the interaction if the presentation begins with common ground (that is, information that is shared between speaker and audience), and then presents the new information or findings against this background.

2 **Have an overall message sustained throughout.** A presentation is an interactive instance. Therefore, do not try to cram too much information in it, especially if it does not relate directly to the main message of the presentation. If you have a lot to say, produce different documents with a main message in each, or give a series of presentations. At the end of your talk, the audience should be able to clearly summarize what the talk was about.

3 **Establish a pattern of organization.** Be consistent throughout the presentation, so that the audience can recognize your logic of organization and follow it better. For example, if you decide to present a topic in its chronological development, sustain this throughout. Similarly, if going from most important to least important, sustain it and do not suddenly include an important point towards the end where it is more likely to be misunderstood as a minor detail because of its position.

4 **Balance innovation with expectation.** People generally listen and read to learn something new that they can understand. Therefore, make sure your content is original enough to be compelling and interesting, and understandable enough so that the audience do not lose their way.

Designing slides

When designing slides or screenshots, follow these important tips:

1 **Avoid visual clutter:** include ample white space; in fact, five points or fewer on a slide is a good way to go.

2 **Avoid blaring colours and contrasts:** include informative items on your slides, and avoid irrelevant or distractive items, such as ornamental images or intense colours.

3 **Choose clearly visible fonts:** remember that readers need to be able to read your text so make it easy for them. A font of 18 point or larger is advisable.

4 **Take care when designing graphs:** numbers and graphs are harder to read off a slide than text, so if you use graphs ensure that they are clearly visible.

5 Use animation and special effects judiciously: don't get carried away with the different effects you can include in a presentation. Use animation or other effects strategically with a purpose in mind. Special effects are not just ornamental but also communicate, so make sure the ones you use have a meaning that will be clearly understood by the audience.

Ordering information in presentations

What you say and how you say it depends on your purpose, audience and time limits. An analysis of these should give you the background and confidence necessary to create an effective talk that answers the audience's questions and wins them over. Here are some general guidelines that would be valid for many occasions.

1 Begin with the "bottom line" in business contexts and with hypothesis/ objectives in research contexts: this puts the subject into perspective for the audience in and directs their attention – they know why it is important to listen.

2 Give only as much background as necessary: since listeners cannot retain as much information as readers, limit background details to the essential.

3 Avoid an overly linear sequence: especially in longer (one hour or more) presentations, divide your content into sections. At the end of each section, summarize briefly and introduce the next section. This is useful because listeners may get distracted and lose your thread; by including appropriate section endings and beginnings within the talk, you allow them to catch up.

4 End on a high note: the chances increase that the audience will remember your presentation if it ends on a strong point rather than just fading away or ending abruptly, especially if you are competing with other presenters for attention.

ACTIVITIES

1 Here is an email written by a software developer to the Public Relations Manager of a corporation. The email concerns a new networking system, called Wizz, currently on trial at the corporation. The writer has made the common error of "writing as he thinks", which means the email lacks organization and focus. Read the email and make a list of the problems it has in communicating a clear message. Especially, answer these questions:

- Does the email have a main message? If yes, summarize it.
- What is the implied event that triggered the writing of the email? What problem is the email concerned with?

- What action does the writer expect the reader to take after reading the email? Is this action clearly delineated?
- What problems are there with content organization and cohesion?
- What are some problems with style and sentence structure that contribute to the lack of clarity?

After answering these questions, write a revised version of the email.

To: Michelle Lanier
From: David Atkinson
Date: 10 November 2019
Subject: Wizz

The Wizz system is designed to help with the job of managing a large number of company stakeholders' access to the computer resources of the corporation. This includes configuring the network accounts up in the first place and removing the accounts at appropriate times. As it is currently implemented the system is very incomplete and is useful only as a way for any network administration staff to track how they have set up the computers.

We've had great input into developing what Wizz should be, but much less input at how Wizz should do this. Unless we have specific regulation on how to use to use it, unless we give users specific instructions, unless we get specific feedback on what problems there are, we won't know if Wizz is the best solution to the problem. Using someone who is not the designer of a component to implement it, is a test on the correctness of the design as it is likely to show up any shortfalls in it. For this reason the different approaches of a whole team of developers is valuable, based on their different interpretations or scepticism as well as their ability at solving a particular problem.

In general the Wizz software developed may be the highest quality system we have ever used. The process would work better if we had ways to get specific feedback. For this reason I don't regard the system as a total success, but feel it is a valuable experiment.

References and further reading

Alred, G. J., Brusaw, C. T., & Oliu, W. E. (2000) *The business writer's handbook*, 6th edition. New York: St Martin's Press.

Barker, T. T. (2003) *Writing software documentation: A task-oriented approach*, 2nd edition. New York: Allyn and Bacon.

Canavor, N. (2018) *Business writing today*, 3rd edition. London: Sage.

Cardon, P. W. (2017) *Business communication: Developing leaders for a networked world*, 3rd edition. New York: McGraw Hill.

Fielden, J. S., & R. E. Dulek (1998) How to use bottom-line writing in corporate communications. In K. J. Harty (ed.) *Strategies for business and technical writing* (pp. 179–188). New York: Allyn and Bacon.

Harty, K. J. (ed.) (1999) *Strategies for business and technical writing*, 4th edition. New York: Allyn and Bacon.

Long, K. (2003) *Writing in bullets: The new rules for maximum business communication*. Philadelphia, PA: The Running Press.

Van Alstyne, J. S., & Tritt, M. D. (2001) *Professional and technical writing strategies: Communicating in technology and science*, 5th edition. New York: Prentice-Hall.

Research Methods

Focus:

- Types of research
- Types of sources
- Legal and ethical issues in using sources

In many cases, creating professional documents means finding information, assessing its relevance for your purpose and integrating it in your text. Analysing the information that you find not only provides you with facts and usable data, but also makes you aware of the effects of different styles and writing strategies on audiences. As all good writers are by definition also good readers, text analysis skills are essential in highlighting the structures and techniques of organization in which a writer presents ideas. Being able to understand facts, issues and arguments is fundamental for successful participation in any kind of professional activity. Correlatively, being able to critically analyse the shortcomings and ambiguities of a document assists in avoiding such problems in your own writing.

This chapter considers the role of research in professional writing and describes how information can be accessed and analysed. It begins with a description of types of research, goes on to explain how sources may be evaluated, and continues with an overview of legal and ethical concerns in using sources.

Types of research

The research process

Regardless of the type of information you require to tackle your project, five steps are essential in the data-gathering process:

1 Identify the information that you require.
2 Identify potential sources of information.

3 Decide upon appropriate search strategies.
4 Evaluate the source and content of the information that you find.
5 Integrate the information appropriately and effectively in your writing.

Primary and secondary research

Research is divided into **primary** and **secondary**. Primary research includes direct observation, preparing questionnaires and interviewing, undertaking fieldwork and conducting experiments. Secondary research includes the consultation of printed and electronically transmitted material. Primary research leads to the presentation of empirical data, has a more applied focus and is, therefore, generally written in an analytical and descriptive fashion. Secondary research searches for historical backgrounds, different points of view on an issue, recorded precedents of a situation and theoretical perspectives. As a result, it generally lends itself to techniques of synthesis, interpretation and evaluation.

Primary research: Focus groups, interviews, user observation and surveys

Primary research consists of the knowledge you have obtained through first-hand experience. It includes research associated with laboratory experiments, marketing research carried out with focus groups and statistical evaluations based on responses to set questions. Here we focus on some points to consider when collecting primary data by conducting interviews.

Focus groups

Because work in professional contexts often means developing products and services for the market, or dealing directly with the public, the ability to detect client needs and responses is very important. An effective way to monitor client reactions to a decision or product is through controlled interviews. In fact, many corporations have the interviewing process built in their marketing and public relations procedures through *focus groups*. These tend to be organized at transitional periods of a product or project's development (known as the lifecycle of product development) and involve inviting a selected sample of the target audience, and discussing with them specific problems, needs and expectations. Focus groups have a *facilitator*, who asks questions and generally leads and monitors the discussion and responses.

Focus groups bring facilitator and group in a face-to-face situation that allows for more negotiation of questions, and enables members of the target group to interact and respond to each other's comments. The company thus receives feedback on the value and usability of a product, on ways that would make the product more appealing and competitive, and on common complaints regarding the product's design. The company can subsequently make alterations that would make the product more functional and/or more attractive, and thereby increase their customer numbers. Famous examples of product change as a result of focus group feedback abound: one of these is the development of the now widespread flip-top for toothpaste tubes to replace the previously common screw top, which, as focus groups revealed, used to annoy consumers.

Interviews

The physical proximity that characterizes the focus group situation brings into play non-verbal communication, such as body language, and conversational aspects such as intonation, turn-taking and silence gaps, all of which contribute to the feedback received during the interaction. However, the success of the discussion depends to a large extent on the quality of the questions asked. Whether in person-to-person communication or in surveys, make the most of questions by taking the following points into account:

- Research your target audience. You should have a clear idea of who you are communicating to before deciding on questionnaires and methods of interviewing.
- Decide whether it is appropriate to administer the questionnaire one-to-one, in a focus group, by mail or by email.
- Decide how you are going to approach the respondents to obtain consent.
- Decide if the information will be confidential or not, and make sure respondents know too. Usually, the researchers do not include the name of respondents in any published findings; however, if they do, they must obtain formal consent, as in a signed release.
- Decide whether the information you seek is best obtained by open or closed questions, or a mixture of both. Open questions start with the 5Ws and 1H (*What? Why? Where? Who? When? How?*) and require the respondent to create a response. Closed questions give only a set number of options; the respondent ticks boxes or ranks items on a scale.
- Make sure that your questions are not ambiguous. Will your respondent understand what you are asking for?
- Make sure that each question asks for one piece of information only.

- Make the questionnaire attractive and easy to use by including headings, a clear layout, and an effective sequencing of questions to enable a linear progression and prevent returning to previous questions in zigzag.
- Keep questions short and try them out on someone first.

When conducting interviews face-to-face or focus groups, keep the following factors in mind:

- Allow the interviewee time to respond. Do not be afraid of silence.
- Maintain eye contact, and be professional and impartial. Do not antagonize your interviewee or make personally intrusive remarks.
- Avoid leading questions (questions that presume an answer in advance, such as "Don't you think it's true that ...?" and "Wouldn't you say that ...?").
- Ask easy questions first to build rapport, trust and connection between yourself and the interviewee. Ask short, impersonal and general questions first. Leave difficult or sensitive questions for the latter part of the interview.

If you are dealing with people or animals, do not launch into your research without considering the ethical consequences of your action. Will you be harming your subjects? Engaging in unethical activities? Dealing with confidential information? In many cases, you may need to submit your proposal to an ethics committee for approval before conducting primary research. In other cases, you may need to obtain releases of information or sign confidentiality agreements.

User observation

In cases where the feedback that you wish to obtain is related to usability of equipment or tools, *user observation* is a popular method of primary research. This involves inviting a sample group of target users of the product to try out the product by following the instructions on the provided documentation. Engineers, designers and communication specialists observe the users and note points of misunderstanding and glitches, as well as the areas where the product was used effectively without problems. They then decide if problematic areas are in design or in documentation (or a combination), and make a plan to amend and revise the product and its documentation.

Surveys

If the information you require involves a large number of respondents and statistical data, *surveys* are a useful method.

Table 4.1 shows the question categories of surveys, with examples of each category:

Table 4.1 Survey Questions

1 An open-ended question – this allows respondents to supply their own answer with little guidance:

> Who would you like to see as the corporation's Chief Executive Officer?

2 A closed-ended question with unordered answer categories – this provides several possible answers and asks respondents to select one:

> Who would you like to see as the corporation's Chief Executive Officer?
>
> 1. Smith
> 2. Jones
> 3. O'Neil
> 4. Robinson

3 A closed-ended question with ordered answer categories – this provides several possible answers and asks respondents to rate each according to degrees of intensity:

> For each of these candidates, please indicate how much you would like that individual to be the corporation's Chief Executive Officer.
>
> | | Strongly favour | Somewhat favour | Somewhat oppose | Strongly oppose |
> |--------|-----------------|-----------------|-----------------|-----------------|
> | a. A | 1 | 2 | 3 | 4 |
> | b. B | 1 | 2 | 3 | 4 |
> | c. C | 1 | 2 | 3 | 4 |
> | d. D | 1 | 2 | 3 | 4 |
> | e. E | 1 | 2 | 3 | 4 |

4 A partially closed-ended question – this provides several possible answers, but also allows respondents to select a different answer if required:

> Who would you like to see as the corporation's Chief Executive Officer?
>
> 1. Smith
> 2. Jones
> 3. O'Neil
> 4. Robinson
> 5. Weir
> 6. Other (specify)

5 Ladder-scale question – this provides a scale on which respondents can rate the performance or degree of probability:

On a scale from 0 to 10, where 0 means you rate the job the CEO is doing as extremely poor and 10 means you rate the job the CEO is doing as extremely good, how would you rate the job CEO X is doing?

Extremely   Extremely
Poor   Good

      0 1 2 3   4   5   6   7   8   9   10

---

6 Lickert-scale question – this asks respondents to evaluate the likelihood of particular actions:

How likely do you think you will be to support the election of X as the corporation's new Chief Executive Officer?

1. Very likely
2. Somewhat likely
3. Neither likely nor unlikely
4. Somewhat unlikely
5. Very unlikely

---

7 Semantic differential question – this asks respondents to give impressionistic answers to a particular object by selecting specific positions in relation to pairs of contrastive adjectives on a scale of one to seven. The aim is to locate the meaning of the object in three dimensions: evaluation (for example, good–bad), potency (for example, strong–weak) and activity (for example, active–passive). This method is useful in studying emotional reactions and attitudes and gauging the differences in outlook between cultural groups.

How would you characterize X as the corporation's CEO?

Good ——————————————————————— Bad

Strong ——————————————————————— Weak

Decisive ——————————————————————— Indecisive

Moral ——————————————————————— Immoral

Intelligent ——————————————————————— Stupid

Secondary research: Print and electronic sources

Secondary research refers to the activity of obtaining information from published sources, including books, journal articles, newspaper and magazine articles, government publications, corporate publications, and online journals. Different sources are valid for different subjects, and professionals know what these are through experience and by being immersed in their fields. Strategies to help you keep up to date with current developments in your field include networking with relevant groups and joining professional associations. In addition, many organizations and professional bodies require their members to regularly update their knowledge and qualifications through professional development training.

Depending on your position in a company, very often the writing you will need to do falls into two broad categories: routine documents, such as press releases and information statements (for PR and communication officers), and urgent responses, such as response to crisis. For both these categories, the first port of call is the company's databases. Companies record their history of document production, their *corporate memory*, so new employees do not have to "re-invent the wheel" by writing everything from scratch; they can recycle existing statements and phrases. In fact, many companies have databases of statements related to scenarios that they encourage, if not require, employees to use in their texts.

For example, if you are a PR Officer or Media Liaison and there's been an accident with a company truck overturning on a highway, you will need to rapidly produce a statement informing the media and the public. The company's database will have some information on how to organize your statement in such a situation. For instance, it might say that you need to begin by specifying that this was "an isolated incident" (if it actually was, of course), continue by describing what happened, then emphasize that there was "no environmental damage or deaths", and end by listing the measures taken to fix this problem and prevent it from happening in the future.

Search methods

Besides recorded corporate memory found in company databases and style manuals, work projects may require you to investigate specific topics and problems. Before identifying potential sources or starting any form of research, you should have a clear idea of your objectives. This comes with audience, purpose and genre analysis. Once this is done, and you have some idea of what you are looking for, adapt the following procedure according to the requirements of your topic:

Search for research journals in your topic. For example, if your research is on surveillance technologies, check journals on video and photographic equipment, on new media technologies, and on privacy issues. Many of these have online access, and most allow you to search inside the publications to see if they have published articles in your topic of interest.

Do a Google Scholar search using keywords associated with the topic. Google Scholar is much more likely to direct you to trustworthy, expert work, as opposed to Google standard, which will give you too many hits, most of which are not likely to be of the quality you require. When searching, use a variety of keywords associated with the topic. For example, if you are researching "smoking", look for "tobacco", "nicotine", "lung diseases", "cigarettes", etc.

Search reference material, such as dictionaries, thesauri and encyclopedias. A considerable number of these can be found online. However if your work consists to a large extent of writing, you will find that building a library of reference material will prove very useful for your tasks. The market abounds in dictionaries of various sorts – quotations, humour, famous speeches, clichés, etc. – and a good collection of these will often prove instrumental in helping you come up with the right idea. Reference material will also point you to the right direction even when it does not itself offer the answer to your question. The online encyclopedia *Wikipedia* (www.wikipedia.org), for example, provides information of varying quality and depth; it can, however, direct you to the sources that may be more suited to your requirements and more credible.

Do a database search: many organizations are affiliated with research institutions and universities that have substantial libraries. Others subscribe to online database services, such as the Online Computer Library Center (OCLC), the Research Libraries Information Network (RLIN) and DIALOG, which cover a wide range of subjects and can be searched by keywords. Search library catalogues for names of experts in your topic; search databases for keywords of the topic. Databases such as *ProQuest* will give you a range of sources, while *LexisNexis* will point you to popular sources, such as newspaper articles.

Get company annual reports, government reports, newsletters and information material from institutions and corporations that are related to your topic. These are often available online, although you may need to subscribe. Even if these documents defend the interests of the issuing organizations, they can still offer valuable factual information.

Follow up articles and books that are included in the references and bibliography sections of published material.

For current information and recent developments, **search press releases and news sections of corporate and governmental websites**. Almost all organizations contain a page on their websites where they publicize their breaking news. This is usually called "For Journalists" or "Press Room," and it is where you can get press releases and information on new products. If you work in the fields of science and technology, a central source of press releases is www.eurekalert.org.

Search social media sites. Most organizations have Facebook, Twitter and YouTube sites and these have updated information on developments, products, etc. that might be useful in your project. The advantage of information found in social media sites is that it is current; the disadvantage is that it is often biased, not well thought out and not detailed.

Contact professionals for advice on major publications and journal titles in specific fields. These professionals include academic staff in university departments, editors of key journals in your speciality, staff in research institutions and public relations representatives of relevant companies. Your networks can be very useful in research. Many professionals belong to online social networks that allow them to connect with other professional in different fields internationally and keep up with developments in their field. For example, www.LinkedIn.com is a major social networking site for professionals.

Browse library bookshelves with the call number related to your topic. You may well serendipitously come across useful material that you would not have otherwise planned to get. Also, **browse the catalogues of publishers** that deal with your topic for recent publications. You can **set up alerts** with most publishers, who will email you updated catalogues with titles of newly published books and journals.

Clearly, sources abound. In most instances, there is a higher risk that you will suffer from information overload than from a shortage of data. The problem now becomes which sources to use and which to avoid – the topic of the next section.

Evaluating sources

In truth, there is no totally foolproof way to establish the credibility of a text. New data constantly emerges that destroys previously accepted "truths", bias is insidious and mistakes are made. One safeguard for credibility is to ensure that the text has been accepted by the community in which it belongs, as happens, for example, with peer-reviewed material. Peer-reviewed articles have been read and approved by experts in the field prior to publication. The peer review process takes place in these stages. First, a writer submits his or her text to the editor of a journal or a publishing company. The editor, in turn, sends it to reviewers who are familiar with the knowledge in the field. If the information provided in the text is acceptable, the reviewers recommend that the article proceed to publication. The reviewers could also recommend revisions and amendments to the text, and they could also advise that the text is not worthy of publication.

This method, however, is also inconclusive. Both Galileo's and Einstein's theories, for example, were rejected by the scientific community when they were first formulated.

In other cases, one *discourse community* (group of specialists who share the same way of writing and talking about things) may find fault with a text where another will not. This is a symptom of the diversification of knowledge and the multiplication of specialities, even within one discipline. An author may send an article to a journal, for instance, and have it criticized and rejected by reviewers. S/he may then send the same article to another journal, where it is accepted without hesitation. This shows that knowledge is regulated according to the cultural values of specific groups, who set the criteria for its assessment. Attaining expertise in a professional or scholarly field, therefore, in many ways means being accepted by the community that is formed around this field. It also means that, as a writer, you should not be discouraged by an initial cold reception to your work but continue looking for your "niche"; and, as a researcher, you should be aware that publications reflect certain perspectives and follow a particular tradition of thought.

Keeping all this in mind, when deciding whether an information source is likely to be accurate and reliable, consider the following factors:

- Has the information been peer-reviewed? This will show you at least if a community of specialists have accepted it as "true".
- How prestigious or credible is the information source? Publications with a reputation for impartiality and rigour would be more selective of their material.
- Does the writer give references for information cited? Are these references accurate? An article that is based on personal opinion only may make a good editorial, but it would not provide a solid basis for an objective and comprehensive assessment of an issue.
- Has the writer considered a range of information sources, or merely relied on just a small number of sources? Are the information sources themselves reliable? Writers should not only show rigour in their own thinking, but also ensure that the sources they rely on have done the same.

- What organization does the writer belong to? What is the reputation of this organization? Non-profit organizations may have ideological biases as "big business" may have financial biases, and the possibility of these biases should be taken into account when assessing the information.
- What organization funded the research? Many funding organizations have vested or political interests in assisting certain forms of research, as opposed to others, come to light. Learn as much as you can about the values and political structure of research funding agencies.
- Did the writer conduct primary research? If so, does the writer state what kind of research was conducted and how it was conducted? Is the sample population typical or exceptional in some way? If a questionnaire was used, was it anonymous? Was the interview conducted face-to-face, by mail or by email? Are copies of the questionnaire included? The results of primary research depend strictly on the methods used.

Types of sources

Following the above discussion and keeping in mind that the boundaries between types are not always clear-cut, here is a following typology of sources, going from most to least authoritative.

A. Scholarly

Scholarly sources include academic or research-based journals, research monographs, university textbooks and anthologies of essays on academic disciplines. Most scholarly journals are published by universities or professional bodies, and scholarly books are published by publishers specializing in "serious" work. These sources are written in language specific to their discipline (insider language, or jargon), and always cite their own sources. Writers of such sources make a conscious effort to make their assumptions explicit and to persuade the readers with logical and systematic reasoning rather than emotive appeals or generalizations. The audience for such documents is peers, and students being initiated into the conventions and language expectations of the discipline. Consequently, the style and terminology of these sources is not "easy" or obvious for outsiders.

Scholarly sources are the most authoritative because their authors, in most cases, have a professional commitment to keeping debates open, while acknowledging and building on previously received knowledge.

B. Specialist

Specialist sources include magazines on science, technology and social topics, and serious non-fiction, such as popular science. The aim of such documents is usually to inform a non-specialist public of technical topics in an accessible way, and thereby to publicize or popularize otherwise daunting or overly complex concepts. The intended audience of this type of source would be an educated and informed reader with no or little expertise on the topic presented, but with a commitment to gaining new knowledge, and, consequently, with a longer attention span than a reader of lower level documents.

Authors of specialist documents attempt to entertain as well as inform, and therefore tend to rely more strongly on analogy, metaphor and dramatization than authors of scholarly documents. They do, however, cite sources, although the technique of integrating these in the text may be different from that in scholarly documents, which use formal referencing styles. Serious non-fiction often uses similar techniques of referencing to scholarly work. Specialist magazine articles, in contrast, name researchers and their professional positions in the body of the articles, rather than in endnotes or end-of-text references. In addition, in magazines of this type, the role of visuals becomes important, with attention paid to aesthetics of layout and design.

Specialist documents are an excellent source of information on a rather superficial level. If more depth or analysis is needed, such documents can refer you to the original, more formal sources.

C. Public

These sources include governmental, corporate and legal documents, such as public statements issued by government agencies, and corporate information, as can be found in organizational websites and public relations material. As these documents are generally addressed to the general public, the language is clear and unambiguous, and concepts are made as simple as possible. This is especially so with government and business documents since the Plain English campaign which foregrounded reader-based aspects of communication and propounded a direct and informal approach to public writing.

Documents belonging to this category tend to assume a low attention span, and do not expand on a topic more than is necessary to get their point across. Many have a promotional edge, and, even when they are not selling a product, they support the issuing organization's interests – as happens with press releases, for example. Public documents are usually a good source of facts (often the only source of facts about a corporation or government policy), but should always be read critically, and interpreted according to the requirements of a specific project.

This category includes (non-tabloid) local newspapers and non-specialized, general interest magazines, as they too address the general public, aiming to appeal to the low common denominator of a community's interests and sensibilities.

D. Sensationalist

Sensationalist sources base their information on rumour, fabrication or exaggeration, rather than on any form of empirical or interpretative research, and are, therefore, the least credible type. In fact, they do not merit to be classified as sources of research at all, unless you use them as examples of the distortion of information in the popularization of knowledge. Many popular magazines, newspapers and social media sources fall into this category, especially the ones that appeal to thrill and sensation as opposed to any form of truth or reflection. These sources should be avoided in business writing, unless your aim is to analyse the way they use language.

The Internet

Today information on any subject can be retrieved in a wide variety of formats and through a range of channels, and the plethora of information can make it difficult for researchers or investigators to decide on which sources to use. The temptation for many is to automatically search the Internet. Although this can be productive, be cautious to avoid potential problems.

It is difficult to estimate how much information, and how many documents are available through the Internet at any one time. Whatever number people might estimate, one minute after the estimation there will be more. The size of the Internet in terms of the amount of information contained is one of the factors that, while making it a strong support for learning, can also limit its potential. Sometimes there is just too much information to be found, which makes assessing the credibility of information difficult, and which can also be extremely time-consuming.

For example, those who received primary and secondary education before the 1990s are accustomed to consulting (and trusting) textbooks and encyclopedias for facts about specific events. This attitude is now being seriously challenged by the quantity and quality of information on the Internet. If you do an Internet search for the answers to seemingly straightforward factual questions such as "Who invented the microscope?" and "In what year was the telescope invented?" you may come up with some surprises. You will probably find a range of names and dates offered as the right answer, depending on such factors as different definitions, different methodologies of research, different interpretations of events – even personal preference! This suggests that, because of its lack of control over what is published, the Internet is not always a reliable source of information – but it can certainly give you alternative views and different sides to an issue that you may wish to investigate further.

One way to avoid such problems is by recognizing that the Internet, besides being a source, is, in fact, a medium. This means that although sources of information may be transmitted through the Internet, they can still be evaluated with reference to the typology proposed earlier, like print sources. The presence of "walled gardens" on the Internet is a case in point. For example, many sites are encrypted, and require a special password to access the information they contain. An example of this is digital libraries, which require subscription for access. In fact, many digital libraries from scholarly institutions or reputable publishers have valuable resources online but limit their access to subscribers or members.

Many scholarly and specialist journals offer the option to access materials both online and in print. This is the case, for instance, with many business publications, such as The Economist (http://www.economist.com/) and Time (http://www.time.com/time/magazine), as well as popular science publications *New Scientist* (www.newscientist.com) and *Scientific American* (www.sciam.com), which have both online and print versions. An interesting additional element to using the Internet as a medium in such cases is the option to open articles to discussion and comment. In fact, often writers of articles enter the interactive discussion to offer clarifications on points they have made in their articles, and to respond to reader feedback.

Similarly, broadcast companies transmit news stories online as well as through the older media of radio and television (see, for example, www.bbc. com and www.cnn.com). Finally, government agencies and corporations publish information on their policies and products online, and these can be very useful when you search for facts and figures, and for contacts from whom to obtain more details.

Other Internet sources include:

Blogs and wikis: these are popular online forums for discussion and collaboration. Easily designed with authoring tools that can be downloaded from sites such as www.blogger.com, blogs enable users to interact in real-time to exchange ideas and opinions, or to produce collaborative documents where all writers contribute and can edit each others' work. Blogs can be very productive in their interactive and collaborative function. However, they should not be used as the sole or main source of information because their informality and experimental nature generally does not lead to definite information, but, rather, to work in progress, or to directions that need more exploring through other means.

Blogs (originally weblogs) are authored by individuals or groups, and have a serial nature, offering commentary on a particular topic. The credibility of this commentary, as in other media, depends on the reputation and expertise of the blogger. In contrast, wikis are not serial, but collaborative. Some wikis are open and some are closed. Wikis generally allow the community to add, edit and restructure contents. High-quality wikis have communities of volunteers to continually check and edit content to ensure credibility. They generally also attribute edits and changes to particular individuals and may also include a change history with comments and discussing showing the rationale of the changes. Wikipedia is an example of this.

Discussion groups: you can find discussion groups on practically any topic imaginable. These can be useful in exchanging information with similar-interest peers, who may direct you to the information you need for a project. At the same time, remember that, however insightful the information you obtain may be, it does not represent all the input the topic can generate, and requires careful scrutiny and balance with material from other sources. For straightforward topics, discussion groups can be useful in encouraging and documenting questions and answers. Also, in finding the answer to a query about a narrow topic, discussion groups may be the best resource.

Personal websites: these are the least credible of Internet sources, and could, in fact, be placed in the sensationalist category. The Internet's decentralized and open structure allows anyone with server space and minimal technical knowledge to set up a site and post whatever they want on it, so the best advice is to avoid personal websites altogether for research purposes (unless personal websites are the topic of your research).

Table 4.2 lists some question to ask when deciding if an Internet source is credible.

Table 4.2 Checklist for Evaluating Internet Sources

1. Is the information presented on the site comprehensive and unbiased? Does it describe clearly where the information came from and what its purpose is? Sites that present opinions based on personal experience or belief should be avoided when credible data is required.

2. What is the style and quality of writing of the site? No organization that takes itself seriously would condone sloppy or ungrammatical writing, so if you find this in the site, be careful. As with other types of written communication, the text of a site should use the terminology and style that are recognized and used by its target audience.

3. Does the site clearly state its purpose? Sites whose purpose is ambiguous or hard to find may be of dubious value.

4. Does the site include author's name and affiliation? Does the author have credentials in the field in which s/he is writing? Suspect anonymous sites unless they are sponsored by a well-known organization.

5. Does the site include a date of updating? Like with all publications, the date that the information was last reviewed is vital in assessing its reliability.

6. Does the site have links to other sites and/or references to other sources? What is the value and reputation of these other sources? Links function like references in printed texts, allowing the reader to obtain further information or different points of view on a topic. A site that is self-sufficient is more likely to be based on personal, unsupported opinion.

Searching the Internet

Search engines

Currently, there are more than 100 search engines that can be used to locate information on the Internet. An important feature of search engines is their increasingly commercial nature. For example, many engines will place prominently paid advertisements related to a search, according to criteria set by advertisers. Advertisements should be distinguished from search results, and some engines make this difficult. Also, some engines are suspected of reducing or eliminating search results for products or services that compete with those owned by the search engine company. Finally, some search engines censor results to appease political authorities in some countries.

Another important issue is that many websites actually exist for the sole purpose of being found in search results. These often have many words that people might search for and contain advertisements or links to other sites. Some of these sites promise their content only to those who register with an email address, which then leads to spam advertising messages.

Therefore, choosing the right search engine can mean the difference between finding a lot of useful information and a lot of useless information. Users should have some awareness of the qualities of the different engines so that they can choose the one that best meets their needs.

Searching tips

The following tips are generally valid for many search engines and searching activities on the Internet.

1 Use multiple words

You will get more refined results from several words than from a single word. For example, "Detective Sherlock Holmes" will yield more relevant results than "Sherlock Holmes" or "detectives".

2 Use similar words

The more similar words you use in a search, the more results you will get back; for example, "restaurant, cafe, bistro".

3 Capitalize when appropriate

Capitalize proper nouns. Capitalized names that are adjacent are generally treated as a single name and not as two separate words.

4 Use quotation marks to set off phrases

Use quotation marks to find words that are part of a set phrase; for example, "deep blue sea". Otherwise, you may get pages that include the word "deep", the word "blue" and the word "sea".

Copyright and plagiarism

The general context

When thinking about research, the terms *copyright* and *plagiarism* come to mind. Plagiarism means copying or in some way reproducing someone else's work without giving them credit or acknowledgement. In many ways, it is a form of stealing – consistent with the etymological root of "plagiarism", which in Latin means "kidnapping". In our era of collaborative writing and digital re-mix, however, things are not as simple as they sound. It is sometimes unclear where the boundaries lie between one's own and someone else's work. This section attempts to shed light on some pertinent issues.

Using another's work without permission and/or credit signals one of three different situations: *copyright breach, plagiarism* or *invasion of privacy* (Branscum, 1991; Howard, 2003; Leval, 1990).

Copyright

Copyright is a legal issue. If you use without permission work that has been published in a tangible medium or patented, you breach copyright and are liable to, often very costly, lawsuits. Any item that has been formally published or registered with a recognized organization is protected by copyright law, and this includes Internet sources. Copyright law originated in England to protect the printing trade. Since then, it has become part of a set of laws, together with *patent law* and *trademark law*, that regulate *Intellectual Property* (IP). Copyrighted items include scientific articles; novels and other literary works; drawings, paintings, photographs, films and other audiovisual work; musical compositions; and software. As copyright laws tend to change regularly, it is always advisable to check the copyright status of an item you want to use.

To complicate matters further, copyright is regulated by the laws of each country, although there are some general international principles. For instance, more than 160 countries have signed the Berne Convention, administered by the World Intellectual Property Organization (WIPO), which sets some basic standards for copyright protection.

Copyright expires after a certain amount of time, when the work becomes part of the *public domain*. Countries set a different timeline for this, but a generally accepted principle is that for works created after 1977, the term of copyright protection is the life of the author with 70 additional years for individuals (known as "life plus 70") and 95 years for corporate authors (Karjala, 1999; WIPO, 2019).

Copyright law was designed to protect the rights of producers of literary and artistic artefacts. After all, these individuals make a living from their products, and these should be protected to encourage their producers to continue creating. However, public access to such artefacts also needs legal protection, so *fair use* or *fair dealing* was created as an amendment to copyright law. This entails using a part of a work for purposes that benefit the public good, such as education. According to fair use or fair dealing, you may use another's work without permission if:

- you are using only a fraction (usually 10%) and not the complete item
- you give credit to the original source
- the item has been published, and is, therefore, not private
- the purpose is educational
- your use of the material will not affect the market value of the original.

Government documents are considered public property (government employees are paid from taxes) and are not copyrighted. This does not mean to say, however, that you can copy material from them without citing the source – this would be *plagiarism*, even though it is not copyright breach.

Plagiarism

If you reproduce a work or part of a work without acknowledging the original creator, and present it as being your own, you are plagiarizing, even in cases when the work is not copyrighted and is in the public domain. For example, Shakespeare's work is now in the public domain; however, if you copy a part of it and present it as your own, you are plagiarizing the work, even if you are not liable to legal action for doing so. With plagiarism we leave the domain of law and enter the domain of ethics.

Copyright protects only the tangible expression of an idea – not the idea itself. In contrast, plagiarism regulations cover the unacknowledged reproduction of the idea itself. Knowledge and ideas are academic and artistic currency: through the exchange of ideas, the academic and artistic communities sustain themselves and contribute to the well-being of society as a whole. Individual scholars and artists produce and publish ideas for their livelihood, and any unacknowledged use of their hard work is both injury and insult. This accounts for the heavy penalties universities impose on students convicted of plagiarism; although legal sanctions may not apply if the work is not copyrighted, the ethical violation carries an equally serious consequence – exclusion (temporary or permanent) from the community.

Plagiarism can be avoided by:

- Summarizing: expressing in your own words the gist of a document, and citing the source
- Paraphrasing: expressing in your own words the gist of a part of an idea, and citing the source
- Quoting: copying the exact words of a section of the original document, putting them in quotation marks to set them off from your own words, and citing the source.

TIP

If you copy more than four words in a row from a document, put them in quotation marks.

All ideas taken from other texts need referencing. The only exception is *common knowledge*. Common knowledge consists of propositions and statements that did not originate with the writer (or speaker), but that are accepted facts in the wider community. Examples include such propositions as "Rome is the capital of Italy", "the Sun is a star" and "two plus two equals four". This, however, is not always so straightforward because knowledge, in many cases, depends on the community in which it is used. A proposition that may be considered common knowledge among quantum physicists, for example, may not be so among another group. This is why, as with other aspects of writing, analysing your audience and purpose will point you to the right direction on ways to integrate knowledge in your document, and on when to cite a source. The general advice, though, is that when in doubt, always cite.

Finally, when using another's work you may also be *invading their privacy* – a legally sanctioned offence. This generally occurs when you publicize information that the originator kept personal or private. If you publish your roommate's journal on the Internet, for example, you are infringing on their privacy. If you publish the journal and present it as your own, you are also plagiarizing. In professional contexts, privacy issues often arise with email and Internet use. It is contestable if a manager has the right to "spy" on employees' email exchanges and the sites they visit on the Internet. For some, the manager does have this right, since the employees are using computers, Internet provision and time supplied by the company. For others, email is private if it is not exchanged for professional purposes, and should not be accessed by employers, even if the employee exchanges it during work hours. The debate continues on such issues.

Plagiarism and copyright in business contexts

As the last example shows, the professional world presents a challenge to conventions regarding plagiarism and privacy. One reason for this is that the Intellectual Property (IP) of a company can be used in different ways by employees. Since companies have the legal status of persons, they can own IP, and this can be used in different texts produced by the company. Employees who write material that finds its way into recorded corporate memory generally do not have ownership of this material. In fact, in many instances new recruits sign contracts releasing all the work they produce to the company, which then becomes the sole copyright owner.

Boilerplate text

One example of text that is considered common property within a company is *boilerplate text* – standardized writing that can be reproduced verbatim, or with minor alterations, for different audiences and documents. For instance, letters sent to clients to inform them of company developments or changes work on the boilerplate model – all recipients get basically the same letter, with only the opening address differing. Similarly, a lab whose members often apply for funding may have a set description of the lab and its operations, which individual members must use, unchanged, in their proposals. In such cases, the individual whose name appears on the document is not the same as the one who wrote a section of the document. This is accepted practice in business and is not considered plagiarism in this context.

Public relations texts

Public relations texts are also often anonymous, attributed to anyone who may be a PR officer at a particular time, or written by someone other than the one whose name appears on the document. For instance, corporate websites and promotional material, such as brochures, often contain segments written by different individuals, and they can be updated by rewriting some sections, reorganizing information by cutting and pasting from different sections, etc. – all without acknowledging the original source. Press releases contain the name of a Media Relations Officer from whom the press can obtain more information, but this does not mean the release was written by that person. Furthermore, speeches and articles of Chief Executive Officers (CEOs) and other senior personnel are more often than not written by the company's professional writers but presented as the CEO's own words. The original writer in these cases has nothing to show but financial reward and secret pride!

In the corporate world, the company takes precedence over the individual in matters of production. This is acknowledged as business convention, so the CEOs who put their name on an article written by their writers are not reprehensible. In such instances, the corporation is seen as a body ("body" being, in fact, the etymology of "corporation") and is acting as an individual. Stepping outside the boundaries of a company, however, would transgress this convention. If a writer of X company, for example, uses material that a writer of Y company wrote, s/he is plagiarizing, not to mention breaching copyright if the work was published. Similarly, circulating published material, such as news stories or scientific articles, among members of a project team constitutes copyright breach, regardless of the fact that the material does not leave the company confines. In such cases, permission should be sought from the copyright owners to distribute the material or, alternatively, the distributor should send out the link or reference to the article for each team member to access individually.

Ongoing writing projects in business contexts are generally open to rewrite and, therefore, have many writers, who most often remain anonymous or are given a group or position title. These projects include style manuals, which are regularly updated and changed. It should be noted that this situation is not unique to companies. The creative industries have similar methods. For example, a Hollywood film can have several writers, and the final product shown on screens could be the result of a rewrite done by someone who had no contact with the original writer of the first version.

However, some business documents, especially those that involve major finalizable projects, follow rules akin to those of academic contexts. For example, proposals to management for funding and/or approval of a project always include writers' names, and so do reports describing the results of an investigation. The accountability involved in such writing makes it necessary to frame the writing in more personal terms and associate it with its actual author. Accordingly, in such reports, the writers also are expected to cite their sources of information and to quote, summarize and paraphrase as appropriate. In such situations, the rules of referencing apply, both for sources within the document and for the document itself when used as a source.

Besides giving credit where it is due, citing sources, in both professional and academic contexts, enhances a writer's accountability. As a researcher and problem solver, refer to sources to:

- show you have consulted relevant material and can advise authoritatively
- support your findings and recommendations by linking them with independent data
- enable readers to follow up material for more information.

ACTIVITIES

1. Watch or listen to a television or radio interview and notice how it was conducted. How did the interview compare with the guidelines given in this chapter? How would a different approach have produced other results? Write a short report with the results of your investigation.

2. Discuss the ways that you could use the following sources of information in a formal business report. Decide what other sources you would need to consult to complement these.

   1. A university textbook on software engineering.
   2. A report on smoking published by an anti-smoking organization.
   3. A *Discovery Channel* documentary.
   4. An article on cosmetic surgery published in *Vogue*.
   5. Information on cosmetic surgery published on a plastic surgeon's website.
   6. An article on globalization written by a left-wing radical.
   7. Data published on an academic's personal web page in a university's website.
   8. A website set up by a special interest community group emphasizing the dangers of Genetically Modified Foods.
   9. A press release published on a major corporation's website.
   10. An interview with a scientist published in *Nature*.

References and further reading

Booth, W., Colomb, G., & Williams, J. (1995) *The craft of research*. Chicago: University of Chicago Press.

Branscum, D. (1991, March) Ethics, e-mail, and the law: When legal ain't necessarily right. *Macworld*, 63, 66–67, 70, 72, 83.

Bunnin, B. (1990, April). Copyrights and wrongs: How to keep your work on the right side of copyright law. *Publish*, 76–82.

Croucher, S. M. (2019) *Understanding communication research methods: A theoretical and practical approach*, 2ⁿᵈ edition. New York: Routledge.

Fishman, S. (2017) *The copyright handbook: What every writer needs to know*. Berkeley, CA: Nolo.

Howard, T. (2003) Who "owns" electronic texts?. In T. Peeples (ed.) *Professional writing and rhetoric*. New York: Longman, 250–263.

Karjala, D. (1999) Copyright protection of operating software, copyright misuse and antitrust. *Cornell Journal of Law and Public Policy*, 9 (1), 161–192.

Leval, P. (1990, March) Toward a fair use standard. *Harvard Law Review*, 1105–1136.

Slauter, W. (2019) *Who owns the news? A history of copyright*. Stanford: Stanford University Press.

World Intellectual Property Organization (2019). Retrieved from https://www.wipo.int/portal/en/index.html

5

Journalism

Focus:

- Types of journalism
- Journalistic style
- Writing feature articles

The ability to develop new products, invent new methods for doing things or discover how the universe works requires also the ability to communicate your results to various groups for support, funding or publicity. In such cases, your audience could comprise people who may not have the same level of technical knowledge as you, but who may have an interest, financial or social, to learn about your findings. This chapter looks at techniques that will assist you to write an appealing and informative article for a specialist magazine or company newsletter.

As opposed to other kinds of journalistic writing that address the wide public or the general consumer, high-level specialist journalism addresses an audience that is more versed in subject-specific terminology, and that is more motivated in acquiring the information presented. Business journalists, for example, present more detailed and accurate information than consumer advertisers.

In advertising jargon, the language directed to the general consumer is *marketese:* direct selling in a sensational and highly emotive tone – the language of television commercial scripts and popular consumer magazine advertisements. Because it addresses the wider public, or the consumer in general, marketese lacks specificity and is characterized instead by frequent use of generalities focused on highlighting the benefits of a product for the lowest common denominator of the population. In contrast, high-quality journalism uses language with a strong informative content, which not only entertains, but also educates. The targeted audience is those who know what their specific needs are, and who can communicate in the jargon of the industry – at least on a basic level.

The value of developing skills in journalistic writing is also attested by the diversification of the contemporary job market. Professionals may occupy a range of different roles in their careers, some of which may involve communicating with the public. Also, the development of freelance journalism, spurred mainly by the proliferation of online venues and social media, provides opportunities to business professionals and experts in technical and scientific fields to popularize their skills and knowledge to a wider audience – and increase their income sources at the same time!

A journalism primer

Types of articles

Journalists divide news into hard and soft varieties. *Hard news* is the information that readers need to know: the "breaking" or "hot off the press" news of events that happen suddenly and affect a great number of people or a whole community. Hard news is ephemeral. Although the information presented may have serious and long-lasting consequences, the actual news itself becomes outdated quite rapidly. Examples of hard news are reports of war outbreaks, earthquakes, terror attacks, transportation accidents or stock market changes. *Soft news*, on the other hand, is the kind of information that people want to hear and its relevance or popularity does not disappear as rapidly as that of hard news. Examples include technological developments, profiles of leaders and fashion research (Batty and Cain, 2010; Garrison, 2004; Hay, 1990).

Below are some major journalistic genres, found in most specialist magazines:

Editorial

This is an opinion article written by the editor(s), dealing with a current news topic, usually one that is covered at more length later in the issue. Depending on the publication, editorials can be provocative and/or strongly opinionated, with a "call to arms" approach intended to increase awareness of an issue. In more formal journals, editorials introduce the theme of the issue and briefly present each of the contributors' articles.

News stories

These present the facts in current events and developments. News stories are generally not long – a one-page story would be long; most news stories take up a quarter to half a page. They describe the facts in the event by following the 5Ws and 1H questions (what, where, when, who, why and how). News stories follow the inverted pyramid format of organization. They begin with the most important information and continue with increasingly less important information.

There are two reasons for this format: one is that research has shown readers of news to habitually focus on the beginning of the article and ignore the rest or skip through it, making the beginning more important; the other is that the length of an article is determined not only by its content but, more significantly, by the amount of space available on the page. Conventionally, editors cut down sentences from the end of the article to make it fit. Journalists are therefore required to write in inverted pyramid format: the most important information in the article is placed first. Non-essential information appears in the middle and end of the news item.

The Inverted Pyramid is shown in Figure 5.1:

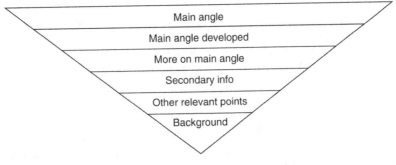

Figure 5.1   Inverted Pyramid Format

Feature articles

These articles elaborate on topics that may have been news stories weeks or months before. They describe the topic in terms of its history, constituent parts, applications, relevant people, and possible benefits and/or dangers. They come in different lengths and are based on secondary research as well as primary research, such as interviews. In magazines, the cover story is a feature, usually located close to the centre of the publication.

Opinion articles

An issue of a magazine may have two to three opinion articles of different lengths scattered throughout the issue. These present an analysis of a topic in terms of the argument(s) it generates. In some cases, a slot where an opinion article appears (a *column*) becomes associated with a particular writer and his/her style (the *columnist*). In other cases, opinion articles are written by scholars who specialize on the topic, and who can, therefore, present an expert opinion.

Interviews

The usual format for this genre is question and answer. These articles focus on the contribution to a topic of an individual and present this topic through the direct words of that individual, spurred by the writer's questions.

Profiles

These articles balance information on a topic with a personal narrative of a key individual associated with the topic. They are similar to interviews in some ways, since, if the profile is of a living person, they are largely based on an interview with that person, with additional or background information from secondary sources.

Reviews

These articles describe and comment on the quality and innovation of a book, film or game. They often compare their object of analysis with others in the field, showing its advantages and drawbacks. For writers, producers and developers, getting a favourable review in a reputable publication is a much-desired achievement.

Layout and page design

Magazine layout is pivotal in editorial decisions about length and presentation of articles. Magazines have a set layout, which determines content choices – not the other way around. In other words, a magazine will not change its layout and the space it assigns to each type of article, to accommodate a particular article, no matter how interesting or how important this article may be. The article will be edited and formatted in the magazine's standard manner. This is analogous to buying furniture. It is unlikely that you would demolish walls and restructure the building to fit particular pieces of furniture. It is much more likely that you would measure the space you have and then buy furniture to fit that space. Printing is costly, and changes to templates make it even costlier.

The following are the main layout considerations:

- **Space**: word limits are required for each article in relation to the space allotted for the article in the magazine template layout.
- **Paragraph length**: magazine articles generally have shorter paragraphs than reports or essays. Paragraphs would need to be even shorter if printed in columns (more on this below).

- **Visuals**: some articles are graphic-intensive, and others are more verbal. In general, visuals complement effectively documents written in journalistic style. Visuals are chosen to convey meaning more accurately to target audiences and are designed with the target audience's assumed needs and expectations in mind.

Page design is divided into four aspects: proximity, alignment, repetition and contrast.

Proximity

This refers to the spatial layout that displays related objects. For example, you should leave more space before a heading than after it. Headings belong to the text that follows them and should be closer to that text. Also, photos and captions should relate to each other and come close to the relevant text. Different elements should be separated by space to create a hierarchy of information.

Alignment

This refers to the horizontal and vertical elements on the page placed in balanced positions in relation to each other – as opposed to thrown together at random. For example, keep unity on a page by aligning every object with the edge of some other object. In a table, for instance, you could align the objects on the left with the left edge of the page, and the objects on the right with the right edge of the page.

Repetition

This refers to repeating elements that tie different sections together. Bullet points, colours and typefaces can be repeated to provide visual impact, and help the reader recognize and scan through the pages quickly and easily. By repeating certain elements, you reinforce the uniqueness, or personality, of a publication, as readers become aware of the characteristic motif of the publication – a bit like a signature.

Contrast

The opposite of repetition, contrast refers to putting together elements that are different and thus creating a visual impression on the reader. The use of contrasting elements acts as an information hierarchy and increases scanning ability. Contrast adds a dimension to the page, introduces an element of surprise and shows that it has depth and variety. Contrast can be used in colours, fonts and direction. To create an effective and impressive publication, ensure a balance of repetition and contrast.

Here is some terminology that journalists use to talk about layout of articles and pages:

Titles and Headlines

Title is used for all articles except news stories; **headline** is used for news stories. Titles can be creative and cryptic; headlines are not: they are structured in sentence form, present tense, leaving out articles. For example, a title could be *Swept Away* (an actual feature article in *New Scientist* on tsunami); a headline could be *Largest Tsunami Ever Recorded Hits Country.*

Pullquote

A **pullquote** is text pulled out of the article and used as a highlighting device – the pullquotes of an article should themselves tell a story (that is, summarize main points of the article).

Subhead

A **subhead** is the text that comes under the title and is used to give more information on the article's topic. Subheads are useful when the title is too enigmatic and needs explanation.

Crosshead

A **crosshead** is a section heading. Crossheads are used, generally, in longer articles as a form of signposting to direct readers' attention. They are also effective in cutting down on transitional sentences and paragraphs and are used when brevity is required. For example, a sentence or even a paragraph can be deleted if space requires it and its content summarized in a phrase that becomes a section heading. As regards organizing content into sections, the general rule for journalistic articles is that they are *top-heavy*, that is, they place important and/or catchy information at the beginning.

Captions

A **caption** is the text that accompanies a visual. Captions can be creative or descriptive and signal to readers the significance of the visual and its relevance to the article.

Organization of content

Paragraphing

The purpose of paragraphs and sections is to divide and prioritize information into meaningful chunks. This helps to highlight points and issues and to encourage a sense of sequence and development. Bear in mind that people assimilate and commit to memory "chunks" of information that comprise between about five and seven items. This should guide your paragraphing style, especially in journalistic documents where a direct and conversational approach is favoured.

Magazine article paragraphs tend to be short, often running to two or three sentences. Most magazine articles are printed in columns: a short paragraph will look longer in a narrow column format than it would if spread across the page. Even one sentence paragraphs are acceptable in articles as long as they do not run in succession. Like short sentences, short paragraphs have a more intense effect than long ones because they concentrate meaning in a few words that stand out from the rest of the text. This is why in magazine articles one-sentence paragraphs are often placed at strategic places to provide a striking effect.

Also, magazines tend to work on the assumption that the reader will have a relatively short concentration span and may not necessarily want to follow an item in detail. In many cases, magazines are read at hours of leisure, coffee and lunch breaks, while riding the bus, etc. Writers, therefore, cannot assume that the reader will invest the time and attention necessary to absorb a complex document. Accordingly, the writer has to present the information succinctly and directly, without elaboration and in-depth analysis. The tone should have a conversational impact rather than conceptual density. Finally, magazine articles also compete for attention. As opposed to a formally commissioned report, which can assume that the reader has a vested interest to read it closely, a magazine article often needs to grab the reader's wandering eye. In this situation, having long paragraphs would be daunting and discouraging.

Organization of information

The order in which information is presented in a text is a strategic device providing the writer with the means to craft information so as to produce the most desired effect. In feature articles, the beginning is very important, so place there information that is likely to attract the readers' attention and not discourage them from reading the rest of the article. If your readers are non-specialists, avoid densely technical jargon in the beginning of the article. For example, the following article on Botox (Example One) is objectively informative and balanced. However, it avoids emphasizing the technical aspects of the drug, and putting off the reader, by describing them towards the end of the article and placing them in an appropriate context.

Example One: Informative feature article

In the Quest for Youth: Understanding Botox®

Creative exaggeration ← In the battle against ageing, Botox® has emerged as the world's favourite weapon to fight wrinkles and fine lines.

Sets the scene ← Botox users are rumoured to include celebrities and politicians. But what exactly is this Botox®? How does it work? And are there side effects that need to be considered before selecting this method for regaining a youthful appearance?

→ *Highlights popularity of product*

→ *Introduces the article by indicating its sections in the form of questions to be answered*

Botox® is an easy and affordable treatment. In fact it is nicknamed the "lunch-hour face-lift," because it is a simple injection costing on average US$400 and taking 10 minutes – very different from the traditional "face-lift," a major and expensive plastic surgery which requires the patient to undergo anesthesia, long recovery time and potential scarring, However, unlike plastic surgery, in order to maintain wrinkles at bay with Botox®, treatments need to be repeated every four to six months.

→ *Description of product showing user benefits. Last sentence acknowledges limitation*

Botox® is Allergen Inc.'s trade name for botulism toxin type A, a neurotoxin produced by the bacterium *Clostridium botulism*. Botulism toxins, of which there are seven distinct types, attach to nerve endings and reduce the release of acetylchoine, the neurotransmitter responsible for generating muscle contractions – and resulting wrinkles. Cosmetic Botox® injections are a diluted form of this neurotoxin, and work by temporarily relaxing the muscles into which they are injected.

Simple scientific description of the Botox process ← In the 1950s, researchers discovered that injections of botulism toxin type A into overactive muscles decreased muscle activity for four to six months. However, it was only in the 1980s that ophthalmologist Alan Scott discovered that the toxin could be used to treat blepharospasm, an eye muscle disorder characterized by uncontrollable contractions. Allergen Inc., then a small pharmaceutical company specializing in eye therapies, bought the rights to the product in 1988. The drug was renamed Botox®. Further clinical trials continued and in April of 2002, Botox® was approved for cosmetic treatments including temporarily eliminating wrinkles, facial lines caused by excessive muscle contraction.

→ *History of the product, linking it with research and experimentation*

Botox® is generally considered safe by medical authorities and has been approved by several international drug authorities. However, side effects are possible, although all known ones are temporary, and no cases have been documented of systemic complications. Clinical trials reveal that the most statistically significant side effect, observed in 3.2% of patients treated with Botox® versus 0.0% placebo, is blepharoptosis, or "droopy eyelid," which results from either

→ *Introduces side effects; emphasizes their low risk*

injection of too much toxin or injection into the wrong facial
area causing paralysis of eyelid muscles. Other common side
effects include headache, respiratory infection, nausea and   *Objectively*
redness at the injection site. ————————————→ *lists side effects*

In the US, the Food and Drug Administration (FDA) also
recently issued a warning against popular "Botox® parties",
at which patients combine Botox® with alcohol in a
non-medical setting. This may be dangerous for two reasons:
(1) alcohol thins the blood, allowing it to more easily pass
into the skin, increasing bruising, (2) since, as with all
medical interventions, complications are possible, the patient
Ends on a   needs to be at a location equipped to handle an emergency.
high note,   *Focuses on one*
suggesting   Today, Botox® is used in over 70 countries, and the   *possible*
the future   popularity of the treatment is growing. Clinical trials   *problem in*
looks good   continue, and novel uses for Botox® are emerging for   *using the*
for the   ← controlling side effects.   *product and*
product   *explains it in*
                                                                                       more depth

Journalistic style

Journalistic writing makes unfamiliar concepts and developments familiar, by
presenting information that is clearly relevant to readers, in a creative and zesty
way. This involves skills of analysis and synthesis: of combining innovation and
the new in a framework that also contains assumed shared knowledge between
writer and readers. When popularizing your topic, choose language and
techniques that are:

Factual: Give as much factual information as possible, while avoiding a "dry"
tone. Use the 5Ws and 1H questions to guide you.

Rational: The business reader is usually interested in making an evaluative
judgement. Therefore, rational descriptions of an economic, technological or
business nature are best. Emotional appeals may fall flat unless they are
supported by a rational basis.

Specific: Give specific examples where possible. People love to read about other
people, so include quotations, success examples and testimonials. Also,
describe experimental data where possible to provide some evidence for your
statements.

Technical: While avoiding tediously technical jargon that may alienate the more
uninformed readers, use the jargon and dominant metaphors of the industry
that you represent. Business and technology journalism should be both
innovative and popular. Show that you can speak as an *insider* who knows
the concerns, strengths and needs of the industry, and with whom your
readers can identify as "one of us".

Example Two compares two (fictional) operating systems: the corporate OpenEye and the open source Salter. The first version of the article is a draft where the writer describes plainly the pieces of information that will make up the final. The second version is an example of how a plain listing of facts can be "spiced up" to produce the creative and energetic style characteristic of "insider" technology journalism. The target audience is IT enthusiasts.

Example Two: Comparative feature article

A: Draft
OpenEye vs Salter

For the last few years, OpenEye has been the strongest company in the computer operating system market. This has been because of a lack of real alternatives, but now OpenEye is being challenged by Salter. This system was created by Mark Salter and is becoming famous. It is based on the source code of an older system, called Marcus. OpenEye beat Marcus, but now Marcus is getting stronger by making another system very similar to it on a basic level. It is cheaper than OpenEye and also has some qualities that OpenEye does not have.

First, Salter costs very little. Its only expenditure is in the side effects of its implementation. It was made this way in order for users to continue developing it as they are using it. On the other hand, OpenEye costs about $700 to start with, and would require much more money if used as an investment.

Second, Salter is faster than OpenEye and it has more functions. Because Salter has been built by engineers all over the world in an open format, it has a variety of functions. For example, it is very easy to network using Salter and this is a serious consideration for IT experts.

The drawback for Salter is that, like Marcus, its predecessor, it is difficult to use. Only specialists with considerable expertise can understand its use, since it uses many of the same commands as Marcus. Also, as Salter was made to run from a command line based shell interface, it is not as visually impressive as OpenEye. OpenEye, on the other hand, uses a graphical user interface, or GUI, as its method of control, which is easy for non-experts to use.

In conclusion, OpenEye is easier and is visually more pleasing than Salter. Salter, on the other hand, is more advanced and gives expert users the satisfaction of control. Increasingly, it is overcoming its weaknesses and becoming more and more competitive for OpenEye.

B: Revision
OpenEye vs Salter – The contest

For the last few years, OpenEye has dominated the computer operating system market. This has been because of a lack of real alternatives, but times are changing and the OpenEye empire may be brought to its knees by a man called Mark Salter. Salter has developed an operating system that has gained mention worldwide. And the name of the new heavyweight? You guessed it – Salter.

Salter was developed from the source code of an older system called Marcus. OpenEye has ruled supremely ever since it overthrew Marcus, but now Marcus is making a comeback with a clone of itself. But why would OpenEye have cause to be afraid? After all, it has already defeated Marcus once. What does Salter have to offer that OpenEye does not?

First in most people's minds is the question of price. How much is this going to cost to implement? Salter has the perfect answer to this question – nothing! Well, almost nothing. There is always going to be some outlay when implementing a new operating system, but Salter takes a long step forward by offering itself for free. Salter was made so that it would be openly available to everyone, thus making it possible for anyone to help develop the system. With this in mind, most applications and other such software are available for free on the Internet, which is more than can be said for the popular OpenEye system. Not only are you looking at a large outlay for the initial purchase of the product, which starts at around US$700, but you could be looking at thousands of dollars being invested in software titles.

A determining factor in whether or not an operating system will be successful, is likely to be the expertise required to use it. This is where Marcus lost out to OpenEye. While Marcus was and still is a more powerful operating system, it required a highly skilled technician to run it. Like Marcus, Salter was originally made to be run from a command line-based shell interface, and so it lacks the lustre of the beautiful graphical interface that OpenEye provides. At first glance, Salter even looks like Marcus as it uses many of the same commands and thus is almost as difficult to use. OpenEye, on the other hand, uses a graphical user interface or GUI, as its method of control. This means that almost anyone can use it, and it provides a great introduction to the world of computers for complete novices.

There is no debate as to which system is faster. Salter is light years ahead of OpenEye as far as speed goes. Functionality? Salter wins the race hands down. Because Salter has been built by engineers all over the world in such an open format, there is almost nothing it cannot do. Networking is a breeze, and anyone in an IT position would have to seriously consider Salter over OpenEye. While OpenEye may be more aesthetically pleasing and simpler to use, it does not have the same degree of mastery that Salter has when it comes to making the computer do what you want it to. The fact remains that until Salter becomes easier to use, OpenEye will still be the juggernaut. But Salter continues to grow in strength, and so the war rages on.

The revised article includes these changes:

A consistent use of the metaphor of contest and fight: "contest", "dominate", "overthrow", "heavyweight" and "juggernaut". This helps to create an image or schema in the minds of the readers with which they will subsequently identify the system.

Rhetorical questions: open questions to the reader, which act as a technique of engagement, and make the writing conversational.

Sentence variety: the revised version includes more variety of sentence structures and lengths, introducing more rhythm in the article.

Writing for the media

In light of the above points, here are some guidelines to follow when writing to popularize a subject or to inform and engage the public.

- Focus on your reader and keep your style simple, direct and clear.
- Focus on your key point. What is the take-home message? You should be able to summarize that message in a sentence and in the space of a headline. Write that sentence and headline first.
- Include in your piece as soon as possible a paragraph that summarizes the crux of what the whole article is about. This is known in journalism as a "nut graf" – the paragraph that contains the story's kernel.
- Provide enough explanation of concepts, companies, events and people so the reader can keep reading without having to puzzle over what something means.
- Be specific in identifying problems and solutions. Your article should communicate clearly what it is arguing for, what is at stake and why it matters. Avoid umbrella statements like "something needs to be done". You're the expert, so tell the reader what needs to be done.
- Avoid scope creep (providing too much detail or introducing complementary subjects). You cannot cover everything in the number of words expected in a magazine article. So be judicious and stick to your key points.

Accuracy in journalism

As a scientist or technical professional, you are faced with a dilemma when popularizing a complex concept: how accurate can you be and also avoid jargon, equations and formulas? How appealing and entertaining can you make your article without betraying the complexity and seriousness of your topic? By creating a lighthearted approach will you not also be sacrificing depth? In short, will you be misleading your readers into thinking there is an absolute truth where in fact there are only conjectures and hypotheses? Such doubts have plagued science writers for a long time. Einstein, for example, describes this situation quite neatly in 1948:

> Anyone who has ever tried to present a rather abstract scientific subject in a popular manner knows the great difficulties of such an attempt. Either he succeeds in being intelligible by concealing the core of the problem and by offering to the reader only superficial aspects or vague allusions, thus deceiving the reader by arousing in him the deceptive illusion of comprehension; or else he gives an expert account of the problem, but in such a fashion that the untrained reader is unable to follow the exposition and becomes discouraged from reading any further. If these two categories are omitted from today's popular scientific literature, surprisingly little remains. (cited in Barnett, 1948, p. 69)

There is no simple answer to this predicament. Three factors, especially, must be considered. First, as noted earlier, space is a major consideration in journalism, and it is impossible to do justice to a complex topic by examining it from different angles and analysing it in depth within such space constraints. In this respect, popular science, non-fiction and travel writing books have an advantage because they have the length necessary to expand and elaborate. Second, audience is another major consideration. People still need and want to be informed about technological developments even if they do not have the same expertise as the initiators of these developments. At the same time, it would be unrealistic to expect them to understand terminology and methods that have taken professionals years to learn. Therefore, an interpretation becomes necessary. Third, the market and general social context should be taken into account. Technology develops hand in hand with the evolution and diversification of society, in which market forces and commercial interests are major factors. Connecting technology and science with its social relevance, the theory with the application, is, therefore, important as is identifying the links between scientific endeavour and commercial practice.

Within this framework, writing for the media can be fruitful if the writers:

- understand that they cannot be as thorough in a popular document as in a specialist or scientific document, and must, therefore, be carefully selective
- have a sense of visualization and narrative and can explain concepts in terms of images and stories, keeping in mind that being simple does not mean being simplistic
- can resist the temptation to exaggerate, generalize or sensationalize in ways that would mislead the reader into thinking that a debatable and inconclusive topic has a clear answer.

Hedging (using terms that mitigate certainty and absolute constructions) is a major difference between academic/scientific writing aimed at specialist, peer audiences, and journalistic/popular writing aimed at a wider public. One of the reasons that academics are often suspicious of journalists is the tendency of the latter to simplify and generalize from inconclusive results, and thereby to discourage or raise the hopes of the public inappropriately. Science writing scholar Jeanne Fahnestock (1986, 2004) gives some interesting examples of this. In the debate whether the sexes are equally endowed with mathematical ability, she quotes scientists' statements and compares them with their interpretations in popular publications.

Here is the scientists' claim:

We favor the hypothesis that sex differences in achievement in and attitude toward mathematics result from superior male mathematical ability, which *may* in turn be related to greater male mathematical ability in spatial tasks. This male superiority is *probably* an expression of a combination of both endogenous and exogenous variables. *We recognize, however, that our data are consistent with numerous alternative hypotheses.* (Benbow & Stanley: Sex differences in mathematical ability: Fact or artifact? *Science* 1980, cited in Fahnestock, 1986, p. 284; my emphasis)

Here is one popularization of the claim:

According to its authors, [...] Benbow and [...] Stanley of Johns Hopkins University, males inherently have more mathematical ability than females. (The gender factor in math – *Time Magazine,* cited in Fahnestock, 1986, p. 285)

And here is another:

The authors' conclusion: "Sex differences in achievement in and attitude toward mathematics result from superior male mathematical ability" (Do males have a math gene? – *Newsweek,* cited in Fahnestock, 1986, p. 285)

Table 5.1 shows some common communicative strategies that characterize the styles and content choices of specialist writing and journalistic writing:

Table 5.1 Stylistic Strategies of Specialist and Journalist Writing	
Specialist Style	**Journalist Style**
Concentrates on objects, events and outcomes. Credibility comes from showing that a claim stands objectively, independently of personal merits of specific persons.	Concentrates on people, their intentions, thoughts, hopes and reactions. Interest comes from showing the human interest aspect of professional endeavours.
Uses jargon and specialist terminology. Shows that writer is a member of the expert community.	Avoids jargon. Instead "translates" technical terms into everyday language. May give examples to illustrate the meaning of specialist terminology. In specialist journalism, writer uses "insider" language to establish peer–audience dynamics.
Uses specific claims or statements that are testable and falsifiable. Supports these claims with specific and detailed evidence, such as facts and figures.	May rely on general observations when explaining a phenomenon. May appeal to imprecise constructs such as "common sense" and "people".
Avoids certainty. Uses "hedging" to modify the certainty aspect of statements ("might," "appears to be," "it seems," "evidence suggests").	Describes events with more certainty. Does not need to look at different sides of a hypothesis, but may present one view only. Uses imperatives (command-type structures).
Avoids emotional evaluation of observations. Instead uses words that specify and quantify. Concentrates on factual information rather than on feelings about this information.	May use evaluative adjectives, such as "terrible," "fantastic," etc. Shows relevance of abstract data for personal experience, for example, through examples of everyday life.
Appeals to scientific community and not to individual readers. Avoids excessive use of personal pronouns.	Appeals to ideal, personalized readers, using techniques such as direct questions and use of pronouns.

As an example of how these strategies work on the textual level, consider Example Three, on the financial crisis of 2008. Both extracts come from the introductions to their respective articles: extract A is taken from a scholarly journal and extract B is taken from a journalistic publication for non-specialist readers. As is the norm, the article from where extract A comes was written before extract B, with the latter being a popularization of the findings presented in the former.

Example Three: Style adaptation

A. Academic/Specialist Style

This paper analyses the narrative and discourse strategies of annual reports of banks from different world regions during the financial crisis of 2008, in order to ascertain if they contain significant patterns or distinctive features. It aims to shed light on how the banks used the annual report genre to construct their role in the crisis, and how these constructions compared with the ways the crisis was represented by independent investigative reports. The paper examines the annual reports of Bank of America (BOA), Barclays, Royal Bank of Canada (RBC), and Australia-New Zealand Bank (ANZ) over four years from 2008 to 2011. The analysis focuses on the narrative sections – the President/Chairman and CEO's letter. The banks were chosen from the 20 largest in the world by market capitalization and by total assets, and were selected to represent major global regions, North America, Europe and Oceania respectively, each of which was affected to varying degrees by the crisis.

Starts by clearly stating the aim of the article.

The second sentence elaborates on the aim.

Provides details of the data analysed with some justification.

The paper examines the annual reports through these research questions:

1 What is the narrative of the financial crisis composed by independent investigations, and how do the narratives created by the banks in their annual reports compare with this? In other words, do the banks identify similar factors in the crisis as do the independent investigations, or do they resist the findings in some way and propose alternative interpretations? Is there a different approach by each bank and does this change over the four years?

2 What Image Repair strategies did the banks employ in their narratives to represent the crisis, and how did they position strategically the events and agents that they describe?

3 Are there any discourse patterns in the ways banks represented the crisis in their annual reports? In other words, are there any recurrent linguistic features used by the banks in constructing the crisis and their role in it?

Itemizes and explains clearly the research questions on which the article is based.

B. Journalistic/Popular Style

During crises, everybody tells stories – the businesses, the media and the public. However, the kinds of stories they tell differ. And sometimes they clash. Understanding what stories are told is a way forward in overcoming crisis.

Different stories were told about the Global Financial Crisis (GFC) of 2008. The banks told some stories while government reports told others. I looked at three government reports and the CEO's letters in the annual reports of four

The lead sets the scene and aims to arouse interest. Note the use of generalizations – 'everybody'. Also, note the short length of sentences and paragraphs compared to the above extract.

States the context of the research in simple terms.

Places the context of the research in a personal narrative of the researcher.

banks: Bank of America, Royal Bank of Canada, Barclays and ANZ. Did they agree or not?

Ends with a direct question.

One way to see storytelling is through the actions of heroes in their struggle towards a goal. These heroes have a motivation, which answers the question "Why is the hero acting this way?" and they are assisted by some elements (helpers), while opposed by others (opponents). Taking banks as the hero, I looked at who the helpers and opponents were in the stories told.

Describes narrative in terms of 'storytelling' and 'heroes', thereby making a link with popular culture.

Continues the researcher's personal narrative.

Developing journalistic texts

This section gives guidelines on how to develop a feature article, non-fiction piece, travel writing or any text where you inform the public of something new and/or important or interpret complex information in an understandable and appealing way (Kaku & Cohen, 2012; Roush, 2004; Starkman et al., 2012). In these genres, you may be doing one or more of the following:

- Describing the parts of your object and their interrelationships
- Tracing the history of the object and describe its changes
- Describing the object's qualities and characteristics
- Analysing the object's value.

To achieve this effectively, use a combination of these strategies:

Definition

Define terms and differentiate them from other similar ones. This is very useful when you are writing about a large topic with many subdivisions, aspects and categories. By defining it, you are specifying the parameters in which you will explain it.

You can give an extended definition of an object or phenomenon, a sentence definition or a parenthetical definition. An extended definition takes one or more paragraphs, and includes explanations of the meaning of terms, as well as a description of the general category in which the defined object belongs.

Be careful that your definition does not contain terms that will themselves be obscure to your target audience. If you have to use such terms, ensure that they too are explained or defined. Lead the audience from the familiar to the unfamiliar. Sentence definitions are condensed versions of this, while parenthetical definitions explain the meaning of a term without disrupting the sentence in which they are found.

Here is a one-paragraph definition of "presence" in virtual reality. Notice how the writer justifies the choice of "presence" in a discussion of virtual reality, by pointing out that it is one aspect of virtual reality when seen in terms of human experience rather than of technology. The writer leads gradually to a one-sentence, precise definition of "presence" by first describing some of the attributes of the term.

> The key to defining virtual reality in terms of human experience rather than technological hardware is the concept of presence. Presence can be thought of as the experience of one's physical environment; it refers not to one's surroundings as they exist in the physical world, but to the perception of those surroundings as mediated by both automatic and controlled mental processes. Presence is defined as the sense of being in an environment (Steuer, 1992, p. 75).

The following is a form of parenthetical definition, using a dash (dashes are generally preferred to parentheses in journalistic articles for layout reasons).

> Dating back to Newton's laws of motion, the equations of physics are generally "time symmetric" – they work as well for processes running backwards through time as forwards (Barry, 2006, p. 36).

Analogy

Give an analogy. This gives the reader the gist of what you are saying and makes complicated terms and processes easier to grasp. In the same light, you can contrast the term to what it is opposite to or different from. This is useful if you think the reader may misunderstand a topic by confusing it with something that looks similar but is actually very different.

Analogies are useful when you are presenting a difficult topic or a topic that the reader has little knowledge of. The advantage of analogies is that they can clarify and explain a topic by tracing a parallel pattern with another topic that may be easier to grasp. The disadvantage of analogies is that, if not used carefully, they can confuse the reader by understating or overstating a topic and creating a false equivalence. You use an analogy by juxtaposing two situations and showing their common features and qualities. Rhetorically, an analogy is equivalent to a simile. For example, here is how writer Flannery O'Connor addressed a class in writing:

> I understand that this is a course called "How the Writer Writes", and that each week you are exposed to a different writer who holds forth on the subject. The only parallel I can think of to this is having the zoo come to you, one animal at a time; and I suspect that what you hear one week from the giraffe is contradicted next week by the baboon (Kane, 1994, p. 89).

Here is the introduction to an article on the spectrograph. The writer begins by defining the spectrograph and then explains the definition by creating an analogy with television. The writer ends the paragraph with a concluding sentence that links the analogy with the definition.

> The spectrograph is the single most important instrument used in astronomical observations. Observing with a spectrograph is like watching a football game on a static plagued television set – you might realize when a team scored a goal, but do not see any of the details of the action. Without spectrographs, astronomy would be nothing more than pictures with no real information.

Examples

Give examples that illustrate the functions or properties of the topic you are explaining. This helps the reader put the topic in context and can relate to it better.

A paragraph of example/illustration could lead off with a topic sentence that states the general principle or idea. Your second sentence will usually contain the phrase "for example" or "for instance" or variations on this. If you have a lot of example paragraphs to write you could introduce variation by employing some substitutes for "for example" and "for instance". You might perhaps write, "An interesting case of X is ...".

Another way to exemplify is to define or describe the object discussed in general terms and then to make it specific by focusing on examples of its uses or applications. The following extract on key cryptography exemplifies these principles. The first sentence gives a general description of cryptography. The following two sentences introduce more terms related to this definition, while the rest of the paragraph elaborates on the object through the use of an example that a non-specialist reader will understand.

Cryptography is a catch-all term for hiding information. It covers everything from the "cryptoquotes" in the newspaper to secret government communication to your financial information. Encryption and decryption are the acts of hiding and un-hiding the information you wish to protect using cryptography. For example, when you buy something on the Internet, your credit card information is encrypted on your computer. Then it is sent using cryptography to the vendor, who has the ability to decrypt it. But how can the vendor read this information if you are the one who encrypted it? The answer is that you and the vendor need to share a key – another piece of information used to hide the information. However, anyone who knows the key or guesses it can read your information; so, now instead of transferring your data securely, you have to find a way to transfer the key securely.

In the following extract, novelist Stephen King explains the importance for writers of reading. To illustrate this, he gives examples of the many occasions available for people to read in the course of a day. Notice that the writer adopts a first-person perspective in presenting his examples. This is effective because the writer is an expert in the field he describes (writing), and so his personal experience is directly relevant.

Reading is the creative center of a writer's life. I take a book with me everywhere I go, and find there are all sorts of opportunities to dip in. The trick is to teach yourself to read in small sips as well as in long swallows. Waiting rooms were made for books – of course! But so are theatre lobbies before the show, long and boring checkout lines, and everyone's favorite, the john. You can even read while you're driving, thanks to the audiobook revolution (King, 2000, p. 114).

Comparison

Compare the topic with others to show its special features or common attributes. Like with analogies, comparisons are useful in helping the readers classify the topic in a category with which they are familiar, and/or to understand the innovation or specific nature of the described object.

When comparing, select some qualities from an object and describe how they compare with qualities of another object. Create a balance between similarities and differences. Two objects that are completely different cannot be compared – it would be like comparing an artichoke and an elephant. Similarly, two objects that are identical do not have enough distance between them to allow comparison – this would be like comparing yourself with your image in a mirror. In such cases, other strategies of description and explanation would probably be more effective.

Adverbs and adjectives of comparison are useful in this strategy. "More", "less", "fewer", and words ending in -er or -est show comparison. In addition, there is a range of signpost words and phrases that express the relation of comparison/contrast, for example, "similarly", "conversely", "also", "in the same way", "after all", etc. The following extract compares two cameras. Notice that the writer chooses to base the comparison on user needs and skills.

> Both model X and model Y are great cameras, containing features for the beginner as well as for the more advanced photographer. However, model X's ease of use and limited extra features mean it is more targeted towards the amateur or novice photographer who occasionally wants to dabble in manual photography, but still needs an automatic camera. Model Y, in contrast, with its more powerful system and additional features is more for the serious photographer who occasionally wants to take photos without setting up the scene. Financially, it sets you back a bit more, especially if you purchase all the extra gadgets, but you can take it further – which is great if you get serious about your photography.

The following extract compares science and art.

> The scientist works mainly at the level of very abstract ideas, while his perceptual contact with the world is largely mediated by instruments. On the other hand, the artist works mainly on creating concrete objects that are directly perceptible without instruments. Yet, as one approaches the broadest possible field of science, one discovers closely related criteria of "truth" and "beauty." For what the artist creates must be "true to itself", just as the broad scientific theory must be "true to itself." Thus, neither scientist nor artist is really satisfied to regard beauty as that which "tickles one's fancy." Rather, in both fields structures are somehow evaluated, consciously or subconsciously, by whether they are "true to themselves", and are accepted or rejected on this basis. So the artist really needs a scientific attitude to his work, as the scientist must have an artistic attitude to his (Adapted from D. Bohm, 1998, pp. 32–33).

Description

Describe the properties/qualities of an object or situation and detail how it works or how it occurs and under what circumstances.

Here you detail the features or aspects of the object. This is a spatial strategy, so remember to chunk qualities in categories, and prioritize information if appropriate. You can list qualities or describe them in paragraph form.

The following example lists some aspects that make up the quality of a virtual reality system. The writer first lists the aspects, and then explains each by asking a question from the user/reader's perspective.

To the layman's eye, the quality of the VR system is based on the following:

1 The details of the graphic. Does he really look like a relatively believable robot? Is this an aesthetically pleasing and compelling environment?

2 The responsiveness of the image. Do objects move in real time to match my gestures? When I reach out, is there a delay before my computer-generated hand reaches out?

3 The safety and comfort of the helmet. Does it fit? Can I get out of it if I get claustrophobic?

4 The ease of use of the input device. How coordinated do I have to be to use this thing? (Adapted from Hawkins, 1995, pp. 178–179)

Causes and reasons

Suggest reasons for a situation or development. This is useful when you think the readers are likely to ask the question "why". It justifies a current state of affairs by explaining what caused it to come into being.

When adopting this strategy, present your topic as something whose existence requires justification or explanation. Then describe one or more possible causes. You can begin by describing the causes leading to a phenomenon and then describe the phenomenon itself, or you can describe the phenomenon and then go to its possible causes. In the following example, Bill Gates speculates on the reasons for revolutionary software. He achieves this by listing several possible causes and leading to his answer.

What does it take to create revolutionary software? Does it mean being first to come up with a new idea, or being first to turn that idea into a product? Does it mean carrying out pioneering research, or making incremental improvements to what's already there until you get it right? Does it mean becoming a giant, or standing on the shoulders of giants? Usually, the answer is a bit of each. Most software blends innovation, inspiration, and incremental improvement in equal measure (Gates, 2002, n.p.).

The following extract presents a reason why roboticists do not build more lifelike robots. Notice how this paragraph also leads to a definition of a phenomenon.

One reason researchers have shied away from building more sophisticated androids is a theory put forward in 1970 by roboticist Masahiro Mori. He proposed that our feeling of familiarity increases as robots appear more and more human-like, but that our comfort level plummets as slight defects in behaviour and appearance repulse us, as if we are watching a moving corpse. Mori called this the "uncanny valley". The term is widely used by roboticists and has spread to the animation industry, where it describes people's reaction to increasingly realistic digital characters (Schaub, 2006, p. 43).

Processes and procedures

Describe a process or procedure. This is a way to show how something is done, a protocol or procedure. Describing processes also comes into play when giving instructions on how to carry out a task.

The principle behind presenting a process is quite similar to the principle behind storytelling. When presenting a process, divide it into stages going from the beginning of the process to its intended result. Sentence openers such as "first", "next", "then" and "finally" are useful in describing processes, and so are numbers and lists. If the process includes technical terms, remember to adapt them to the technical level of your target audience. The following paragraph describes a process for extracting titanium.

The process takes place in an electrolytic cell. The cathode is connected to a pellet of titanium dioxide powder, while the anode is made of an inert material such as carbon. The two electrodes are immersed in a bath of molten calcium chloride, which acts as the electrolyte. When the power is switched on, electrons at the cathode decompose the titanium dioxide into titanium metal and oxygen ions. The ions flow through the electrolyte to the anode, where oxygen is released as a gas (Hill, 2001).

Applications and uses

Describe the application or use of an object. This emphasizes the practical aspects of research, by showing how inventions and discoveries can be used in everyday life.

When describing the applications of a discovery, you are, in effect, listing possible future or present situations where the discovery is put to action. Applications show different uses of a product or method, so you could describe them by listing ("first", "second"), or adding ("also", "another application"). Here is an extract from an article describing how science defines the feeling of love as the result of biochemical and genetic processes. The extract outlines some ways in which such research may be useful.

Is this useful? The scientists think so. For a start, understanding the neurochemical pathways that regulate social attachments may help to deal with defects in people's ability to form relationships. All relationships, whether they are those of parents with their children, spouses with their partners, or workers with their colleagues, rely on an ability to create and maintain social ties. Defects can be disabling, and become apparent as disorders such as autism and schizophrenia – and indeed, as the serious depression that can result from rejection in love. Research is also shedding light on some of the more extreme forms of sexual behaviour. And controversially, some utopian fringe groups see such work as the doorway to a future where love is guaranteed because it will be provided chemically, or even genetically engineered from conception (*The Economist*, 2004, p. 10).

Use visual aids, such as a diagram or photograph. If you choose this strategy, make sure you explain in your text what the visual is intended to show and how it fits in your written explanation. To avoid digressing from your text to explain a diagram, consider using side-bars that contain visuals and text, and provide self-sufficient information that complements the information presented in the body of the article.

Narrative

Tell a story that illustrates your discussion. This is useful in making conceptual information more concrete by describing a "physical" situation where the ideas you are talking about were at play. Stories are very effective in assisting the readers to visualize and, therefore, to better understand your description.

When telling a story, decide how much of your story your target reader is likely to be able to absorb without a break and how much they want to know. Also, make sure that your story clearly relates to the topic that you are attempting to explain, by explicitly making connections between the two. For example, the following extract tells a story to explain why many people find the concept of evolution difficult to understand. Notice how the writer begins the paragraph by stating his main topic. Then he asks two questions constructed from the perspective of "most people". He then recounts a story, which becomes a story within a story, giving "most people's" version of why evolution is difficult to grasp. He ends the paragraph by extrapolating that it is the time element in evolution that "most people" find difficult to conceptualize.

> Most people find evolution implausible. Why is my spine erect, my thumb opposable? Can evolutionists really explain that? Once I attended a lecture by the writer Isaac Bashevis Singer, and one of the many biologists in the audience asked Singer about evolution – did he believe in it? Singer responded with a story. He said there was an island upon which scientists were certain no human being had ever been. When people landed on the island they found a watch between two rocks – a complete mystery. The scientists when confronted with the evidence of the watch stuck to the view that the island was uninhabited. Instead they explained that although improbable, a little bit of glass, metal, and leather had over thousands of years worked its way into the form of a watch. Singer's view differed from that of the scientists – as he summarized, "No watch without a Watchmaker." This story reflects the feeling many people share that random chemical interactions cannot explain the existence of life on earth. The reason it is hard for such people to grasp the evolutionary viewpoint is the difficulty in grasping the immense time a billion years actually is (Pagels, 1983, p. 96).

Ben Stubbs (2012) begins his book on Australian communities in South America by contextualizing it within his own personal story. He frames this personal story in terms of curiosity and the urge to explore by means of the metaphors "itch", "mosquito bite" and "rash", which evoke experiences of travelers in exotic lands. The main topic – Australian communities abroad – is connected to the narrator's own family as one of immigrants. The phrases "putting boats in bottles" and "drawing family trees" further reinforce the themes of travel and genealogy that are expanded in the book.

> I started to feel the itch a few years ago. My father was given our family history by a curious relative who liked putting boats into bottles and drawing family trees. I discovered the story of my great great great grandfather William Peat. His grandfather Charles Peat arrived in Australia as a convict on the First Fleet for highway robbery in London. What began as a mosquito bite became a rash as I learned more (Stubbs, 2012, p. 1).

Example Four: Analysis of feature article

Read the following article on the planet Mars and notice how some of the strategies described above are used in its composition.

Life on Mars

Can Mars contain life? Is there any possibility that we are not alone in this solar system? Close examination of these questions has led scientists to propose that the following characteristics (rare for any planet) are necessary for Mars to support life:

- The planet must have a strong magnetic field which is created by the spinning of liquid metals deep inside. This magnetic field acts like a force-field to prevent the harsh winds and energies of the Sun from stripping away atmosphere and clouds like a gas-powered leaf blower.
- The area in which life evolves must be relatively stable. Life is delicate and would not survive repeated bombardments by meteors and other objects, which would cook any developing organisms in hot gas and magma.
- The planet must contain water. Water is necessary for all life. It dissolves almost any compound and allows organisms to produce energy for their own growth and survival.
- It must have an atmosphere with enough carbon dioxide to allow the surface of the planet to be warmed by trapping the Sun's rays much like the Greenhouse Effect.

Lists qualities necessary for life on a planet

With the explosive growth of spaceflight technology, examining Mars for these planetary characteristics has finally become a reality. The Mars of today, unfortunately, does not meet these criteria. The planet's core is not spinning any more leading to the lack of a magnetic field and an atmosphere. All of Mars's water is either deep underground, out of the Sun's reach, or frozen in the ice caps. Finally, Mars is a very cold planet with frozen carbon dioxide that cannot be used by living organisms.

Gives reasons why Mars cannot support life

Thus, for all you ET fans out there, the chance we find any living organisms on Mars is very small. "What's the point of exploring Mars for life?" you may ask. Mars may be cold and dead now, but it wasn't in the past.

Transitional paragraph leading to a historical report on Mars' atmosphere

About four billion years ago, Mars was a stable planet while Earth was still in its infancy. New data analysed from the Mars rovers shows that Mars had an active core resulting in a magnetic field comparable to present-day Earth – enough to maintain an atmosphere of carbon dioxide, oxygen and water. Analysis of Martian canal-like structures reveals a cloud system similar to Earth's and vast oceans several kilometers deep. During this time, Mars was also volcanically active, theoretically providing organisms with energy that could be harnessed for life. Four billion years ago, Mars met all the criteria for a living world. In fact, many scientists have a difficult time arguing *against* life on Mars! ———————→ *Tells a story about Mars' situation in the past*

Why do we care about fossils billions of years old? Evidence of ancient life on Mars has very important consequences for our understanding of how life begins. In 1984, scientists working in Antarctica discovered a meteorite from Mars approximately 4.6 billion years old. This Mars object created controversy, as many scientists suggested the meteorite contained evidence of bacterial life. If such meteorites indeed contained Martians, as could be confirmed by our expeditions on Mars, all living organisms on Earth may have evolved from Martian hitchhikers. We might be, in fact, the last traces of Martian life. ———————→ *Gives reasons for an interest, and leads to a speculation that further supports the reason*

Integrating quotations

An important difference between specialist and journalistic documents lies in the use of quotations. In formal reports, as in academic writing, quotations have a secondary function: they are there to provide credibility or lend support to an idea. In journalistic writing, on the other hand, ideas or facts are often crafted around quotations, foregrounding the immediacy of spoken language. For this reason, specialist documents avoid extensive use of quotations, which give the document a choppy or fragmented appearance. This is not the case for journalistic articles, however, where it is generally expected to attribute opinions, facts and ideas directly to people by reporting their speech.

This difference in emphasis is highlighted in the way quotations are integrated in the text. In specialist documents, lead to a quotation so that the sentence begins in your own words and ends with the quotation. Reverse this technique in journalistic writing: begin the sentence with a quotation and end it with your comment. Compare these extracts. The first is appropriate for a report and the second for a magazine article.

1 Conservation International, North Motor Company and Nielsen Engineering have agreed to collaborate in three "walkway projects" in the Amazon Valley and Indonesia. These projects involve creating walkways that allow visitors to traverse densely forested areas without the need of roads. This is an important step in promoting both tourist activity and the safety of the forests. As the Public

> Relations Manager of Conservation International points out, "Tourism can boost an economy, but it will bust it if it destroys the environment."
>
> 2 Conservation International recently joined forces with Motor and Engineering companies for a series of ventures promoting tourism in environmentally safe ways. "Tourism can boost an economy, but it will bust it if it destroys the environment," says Tim McIntyre, Public Relations Manager of Conservation International. "Ecotourism can be as, if not more, profitable as a logging-based tourism industry, especially in our era of environmental awareness," he adds.

Another difference in the integration of quotations and attributed knowledge in specialist and journalistic documents is the kind of referencing to sources. In specialist documents, such as reports and academic articles, references follow one of the formal styles, APA, Chicago, etc. This means that the full source is named either at a footnote, or in an end-of-text reference list. In journalistic articles, on the other hand, the convention is to include the person's name and affiliation within the body of the article, preferably in the sentence that includes the quotation. References to journals where research was initially published are placed in brackets at the end of the sentence or paragraph that describes this research.

> According to Jeremy Gruber, legal director of the National Workrights Institute based in Princeton, New Jersey, US companies can legally watch everything employees do – and only two states require employers to tell workers they are under surveillance (Newitz, 2006, p. 30, my emphasis).

Leads, hooks and ties

In contrast to reports, journalistic texts do not develop in a linear fashion. Also, they do not state assumptions and background, or give justifications for assertions. They are subjectively descriptive in that they describe an object from the point of view of the mental and/or physical state of the reader – they tell the readers what they want them to see.

A report would start by describing the background, overview and assumptions, and then go on to detail different aspects of the topic leading to a set of recommendations. Instead, a magazine article plunges straight into the description of the product or discovery that the article discusses, immediately showing its relevance to the interests or needs of the reader. It then goes on to present different facets of the topic, beginning with the most crucial and continuing in diminishing importance. It may end quite abruptly, or it may end with one or two sentences that tie in a comment, opinion or evaluative remark to the preceding discussion.

A corporate client needs less invitation to read a report and expects more precision from the outset. A magazine reader, on the other hand, wants to be seduced into reading the article. The *lead* is the opening statement that should attract the reader to the article. Its job is to relate your main topic to what you believe your reader's general interests and experience are. A *hook* is similar to a lead, although it is usually more "spicy" or provocative. A hook should be well baited, so that your reader is tempted to carry on reading. Avoid abstractions and densely technical language at this point. The following extract from an article on the Kepler telescope, for example, makes a connection between Kepler and popular culture:

> In 1982, E.T. phoned home in his big screen debut. Scientists have been trying to trace the call ever since. While finding E.T. is still a way off, astronomers can now at least see some of the houses in his neighbourhood. They are achieving this with the Kepler space telescope.

Also, John Morrish (2000) starts his description of how the word "geek" is used with a short humorous anecdote that sets the scene for the definition that follows. The writer begins with a play on the phrase "made it into", leading to a direct question to the reader and a hypothetical reply, which piques the reader's curiosity.

> There was great excitement the day "geek" made it into *The Times*. Not the newspaper, you understand, but the offices, where someone directed the word at the editor, shortly before resigning on the spot. But what does it mean? A basic guess would suggest that a "geek" is someone who relates better to computers than to people. A synonym for "nerd", in fact. But this is an oversimplification (Morrish, 2000, p. 73).

The sentences following the lead add background to the topic or issue. As with formal report introductions, you may also add a sentence that states what it is that the ensuing article will do, although this is not necessary. The following extract, for example, leads by stating a fact and asking a question about this fact from the reader's point of view. It then goes on to overview the specifics that the article will discuss in more detail, and ends with a statement on the purpose of the article:

> The two market leaders in non-professional cameras are the Canon X and the Pentax Y, but what makes them so good? The X leads the market by being so jam-packed with features. However, the Y holds its own with its ease of use and a slightly better price. Here we set them head to head and pull them apart for our readers.

If you have more space to expand, you may also consider using a short narrative as the lead. As people respond more strongly to narrative information than to any other form, your chances of intriguing and capturing your audience are increased. For example, the writer of the extract below, on the Turing test, begins with a fictional story that sets the scene and captures attention.

> A group of renegade androids, with near-perfect artificial intelligence, are hell-bent on extracting revenge on humanity for their forced servitude. Only through careful interrogation, aided by a polygraph-like apparatus, can the best-trained detectives distinguish these robots from humans.
>
> Does this sound like science fiction? Fortunately, it is. In this scenario, enacted in the cyberpunk film *Blade Runner*, artificial intelligence has evolved to the point where it can emulate human intelligence, a benchmark that Alan Turing, the father of modern computer science, called "the imitation game".

Below is the lead from Richard Branson's 2012 article, *Why we need more women in the boardroom*. It begins with an example from a personal situation that sets the scene for the paragraph's last sentence, the question that forms the basis of the article. This is also an example of an analogy between trial juries and company executive boards.

> I recently watched *12 Angry Men* – that classic 1957 film about a jury struggling to decide the fate of an 18-year-old man who has been charged with murder. The movie gives you a sense of how the legal system worked in the United States back then, when juries were less diverse. By today's standards, we would find it unsettling if a jury were comprised of 12 middle-aged white men. So why have so many business leaders been slow to take notice when women are absent from the boards of their companies?

The *tie* is an optional device that ends the article with a comment or question summing up the writer's attitude towards the topic. More attention is paid to introductions in articles because of the aim to capture attention, and the fact that most readers look at the opening sentences of an article before deciding whether to invest any more time in it. If space allows, however, a good tie does have the effect of emphasizing the main message of the article and making it more memorable for the reader. For example, Richard Branson's 2012 article, whose lead is cited above, on the lack of women in executive positions in business, also has an interesting tie, which loops back to the lead:

> So take a look at who's sitting around your boardroom table. If you see 12 angry men, it's time to write a new script!

Submitting an article for publication

When you decide to submit an article to a magazine for publication, make sure you are familiar with the topics and styles of your chosen magazine. You have a higher chance of having your article accepted if it fits with the "culture" of the magazine. All magazines have details of the editor, so if you cannot find submission guidelines, contact the editor to request them – this is the editor's job and, besides, most magazines are looking for fresh ideas and new writers. In most cases, you will be required to submit a proposal summarizing your article and noting its significance and the types of readers it is likely to interest.

In order to familiarize yourself with the stylistic conventions of your chosen magazine, follow these steps:

1 Read carefully each article in recent issues of the magazine. Note the basic question or issue that they deal with and trace the ways that they answer it. How do they use the 5Ws and 1H? What new knowledge do you learn from the articles? What facts do you learn?

2 Notice the tone of the articles. Is it humorous? Serious? Technical? Chatty? This will give you a hint on what tone to give your own article.

3 Notice the use of research. Have the writers conducted primary research, such as interviewing people, or are most articles based on secondary research – the consultation of written sources? How many quotations do the articles use? How much information is paraphrased, that is written in the writer's own words? List the sources. Check some of them to see how the writer used them in his/her article.

4 Notice the use of pronouns ("I", "you", "we", etc.). Are articles written mostly in an impersonal, objective style or do they rely heavily on personal comment? How do the writers refer to themselves? Do they use personal pronouns?

5   Notice the leads and ties. How long and snappy are they? Do the articles rely strongly on leads to "bait" the reader, or are other elements, such as pictures or quotations of famous speakers, more prominent?

6   Underline the first sentence in each paragraph. They should form a step-by-step sequence. Then note the cohesion that the writers have used: the linking words and phrases within paragraphs and the transitions from one paragraph to the next. Often the same words or ideas will be repeated in the last sentence of one paragraph and the first sentence of the next.

7   Notice how the articles develop their theme. Is the article structured chronologically, developmentally, by alternating examples, point by point? How did the writer build the organizational structure to answer the title's question?

8   What techniques do the writers use to make the article both informative and appealing? For example, do they use analogies, anecdotal examples, metaphors, personal stories, rhetorical questions, direct questions to the readers, etc.?

9   Notice the title. It may have been changed by the editor; nevertheless, how does it reflect the article? Does it tease, quote or state facts? What technique does the writer use to make the reader want to read the article?

10 Look at *para-textual elements*, such as visuals, pull-quotes, subheads, etc. Although the editor may have produced these, you can still get an idea of the type of "framing" that the magazine requires, and this will give you some tips on what types of information the editors consider important.

ACTIVITIES

1   Research the business or scientific magazines that publish in an area you are interested in. Find out the submission requirements of each magazine and make a style-format analysis of the types of articles each magazine publishes. Then write a memo to your instructor detailing your findings.

2   Analyse a feature following the guidelines presented in this chapter. Bring your analysis to class for discussion. Concentrate on what impressed you about the article and what areas you think could be improved. Did the writers answer the questions you had on the topic? Could they have been clearer and more accurate within the space limitations?

References and further reading

Angler, M. (2017) *Science journalism: An introduction*. London: Routledge.

Barnett, L. (1948) *The universe and Dr Einstein*. London: Doves.

Barry, P. (2006) What's done is done. *New Scientist*, 30 September, 36–39.

Batty, C., & Cain, S. (2010) *Media writing: A practical introduction*. London: Red Globe Press.

Bohm, D. (1998) *On creativity*, ed. L. Nichol. London: Routledge.

Branson, R. (2012) Richard Branson on why we need more women in the boardroom. *Entrepreneur*, September 24. Available at http://www.entrepreneur.com/article/224476

Carroll, B. (2017) *Writing and editing for digital media*. New York: Routledge.

Fahnestock, J. (1986) Accommodating science: The rhetorical life of scientific facts. *Written Communication*, 3, 275–296.

Fahnestock, J. (2004) Preserving the figure: Consistency in the presentation of scientific arguments. *Written Communication*, 21(1), 6–31.

Garrison, B. (2004) *Professional feature writing*, 4th edition. Mahwah, NJ: Lawrence Erlbaum.

Hawkins, D. (1995) The future of fun. In F. Biocca & M. R. Levy (eds.) *Communication in the age of virtual reality*. Hillsdale, NJ: Lawrence Erlbaum, 159–189.

Hay, V. (1990) *The essential feature: Writing for magazines and newspapers*. New York: Columbia University Press.

Hill, S. (2001) Get tough! *New Scientist*, 30 June.

Kaku, M. & Cohen, J. (2012) *The best Americal science writing 2012*. New York: HarperCollins.

Kane, T. (1994) *The new Oxford guide to writing*. Oxford: Oxford University Press.

King, S. (2000) *On writing*. London: Hodder and Stoughton.

Kraft, N. (2019) *Always get the name of the dog: A guide to media interviewing*. New York: Routledge.

Lindgren, S. (2019) *Digital media and society*. London: Sage.

Marsen, S. (2006) *Communication studies*. London: Red Globe Press.

Newitz, A. (2006) The boss is watching your every click ... *New Scientist*, 30 September, 3–31.

Pagels, H. R. (1983) *The cosmic code: Quantum physics as the language of nature*. Harmondswoth: Penguin.

Pirolli, B. (2018) *Travel journalism: Informing tourists in the digital age*. London: Routledge.

Roush, C. (2004) *Show me the money: Writing business and economics stories for mass communication*. Hillsdale, NJ: Lawrence Erlbaum.

Schaub, B. (2006). My android twin. *New Scientist*, 14 October, 42–46.

Starkman, D., Hamilton, M., Chittum, R., & Salmon, F. (2012) *The best business writing 2012*. New York: Columbia University Press.

Steuer, J. (1992). Defining virtual reality:Dimensions determining telepresence. *Journal of Communication* (2), pp. 73–93.

Stubbs, B. (2012) *Ticket to paradise: A journey to find the Australian colony in Paraguay among Nazis, Mennonites and Japanese beekeepers*. Sydney: HarperCollins.

Public Relations Writing

Focus:

- Press releases
- Web writing
- Social media
- Speech writing
- Crisis communication

This chapter looks at some major business genres targeting a public audience and the situations in which they are used. The chapter also includes information and guidelines on writing for the Internet and website design.

Public relations texts

Much of a company's success depends on the perception that the public has of it, and on its reputation in dealing with consumers, clients and the general social context in which it operates. The way a company communicates with its public and the ways in which it creates and sustains relationships become paramount in its continued progress and expansion. The two related business fields that focus on the social status of the company are *marketing* and *public relations (PR)*. The first is concerned with the design, branding and positioning of products, while the second is dedicated to identifying, maintaining and correcting factors that contribute to the company's reputation and public image (Bivins, 1999; Davis, 2004; Kent, 2011; Morris & Goldsworthy, 2012; Theaker, 2008).

Genres that publicize a company's products and services, as well as the company's contribution to social endeavours, include:

- **Press releases:** short documents written for the media, functioning to publicize a new development, product, service or policy. They are sent to media outlets and published on the company's website.
- **Websites:** the company's representative in cyberspace, websites tell the company's story, its mission, organization and products. Currently, they are the first source of information for a company.
- **Brochures and prospectuses:** booklets that describe the company's products and/or services. A prospectus is a larger document than a brochure and includes more detail. These can be delivered in print or in digital medium, depending on audience and purpose. In many cases, large organizations offer both versions.
- **Flyers and posters:** similar to brochures and prospectuses but smaller, these are one-page advertisements of an event or product. These too can be delivered in print and digital medium.
- **Mission statements:** the company's concept of its main goals, objectives and reason for existing, the mission statement is addressed as much to employees and investors as it is to the wider public. Since the mission statement is posted on a company's website, however, it is generally perceived as a public relations text.
- **Newsletters:** in-house magazines that report the company's news to various stakeholders, include clients and members. They can be delivered in both print and digital medium, although digital medium is rapidly becoming the favoured form, especially if the recipients are professionals.
- **Letters:** short texts that carry messages of different kinds to customers, members and other stakeholders. Letters can be part of welcome packs and membership packages, or they can inform of the formal outcome of a procedure, such as rewards. Letters also accompany other texts such as prospectuses.
- **Annual reports:** documents written at the end of a financial year, detailing the successes and failures of the company during the year. An important document for investors, annual reports combine technical and financial details with motivating articles on how the company fulfilled its mission during the year. Annual reports are public documents, and most large organizations include them on their websites.
- **Social media:** contributions to social networking sites such as *Twitter*, *Facebook* and *YouTube*, which update the public of new developments to the minute and enable users to respond or comment.
- **Speeches and press conferences:** texts written for oral delivery, speeches can be addressed to the wider public through the media or to employees and stakeholders through the company's internal communication channels.

When deciding on a public communication strategy, it might be useful to think of possible media in terms of *push* and *pull*. Push media are those that transmit information to the public, who are quasi-passive recipients. Broadcast media, such as television and radio, are examples of push media. Pull media, on the other hand, are those in which a company participates in a community and attracts an audience from that community. The digital media, especially social networks, but also, to a lesser extent, websites are examples of pull media. As Guy Kawasaki (2011), says, "Push technology brings your story to people. Pull technology brings people to your story" (p. 135). Each type of medium has a different degree of control. In pull technology the company has less control and needs to take a more adaptive approach. From a consumer's perspective, pull media allow users to select and combine information that they receive from organizations.

Press releases

Press releases target an audience of news professionals, working either in print, broadcast or digital media, and announce new products or events. Sometimes press releases are sent to specialized audiences, such as convention organizers. At other times, they are placed on the company's website, on the "Press", "Public Relations" or "Journalists" page. Often they are mailed to target press representatives as part of a press kit, which may include testimonials, quotations and product features – anything a journalist would need to know to write an article.

Press releases are structured as news stories and vary in length from half a page to three or four pages, depending on the significance of the announcement and on the number of people or companies involved. Press releases are known as *uncontrolled* news. That is, the writer and issuing organization have no control over the final version in which the news will appear. Therefore, clear organization and adequate facts are important. The first paragraph gives all the information the press wants, structured around the 5Ws and 1H. It states what the situation or product is, who is involved, where and when it was produced, launched or used, why it is interesting or important, and how it is different from others or from its predecessors. The subsequent paragraphs give more background and details in descending order. Being news stories, press releases follow the Inverted Pyramid format (see Chapter Five).

As regards the content of press releases, the focus or angle is very important: depending on your product, event or service, will the most effective means of communicating your message be by detailing qualities, by explaining functionality and application or by showing its novelty with regard to its predecessors in a historical framework? Press releases can be *promotional* or *informative*.

Promotional press releases

When writing a *promotional* press release, apply one of these strategies:

Product-Centred Strategy: This looks at features of the product, event or
service, and builds a message around them. This strategy turns the product
into a desirable object by using signs of value, such as prestige, ease, ethical
standards, high-status, aesthetic appeal or expertise.

Prospect-Centred Strategy: This focuses on needs and wants of the target
audience and turns product attributes into client benefits. It emphasizes the
functional aspects of the product in relation to their practical results or
applications. It usually achieves this by outlining how a product may be used,
or the product's effect on people.

Although the two strategies can be used simultaneously, the need to have a
clear focus or angle means that effective press releases tend to construct their
message around one of the two. Regardless of the selected strategy, a press
release is a promotional genre, so where possible emphasize and highlight the
product's *Unique Selling Point* (USP), describing the qualities that make it
distinctive or unique in relation to predecessors or competitors. Focus on
innovations and on the specific attributes and benefits that make the product a
novelty.

As an example of a product-focused strategy, study Example One on a new
laptop produced by the fictional company Wicked Wisdom.

One way to write a promotional press release is to decide on the image you
want to create of the product and on the customer needs that the product
satisfies, and then to brainstorm some key words, phrases and metaphors that
capture this verbally. Then use these words and phrases at strategic points in the
release. For instance, Example One is constructed around the idea of "light" and
"beautiful", and this is reflected in the use of superlatives (that is, structures that
show the highest level of something, such as – est adjectives) *slimmest, lightest,
unique, the best, the most, the first, sharpest*. Also, the release repeats words that
denote beauty, such as *beautiful, gorgeous, stupendous, magical, wonderful,
dazzling, eye-catching* and *attractive*, in every paragraph as well as in the title.
Such strategic repetitions "drill" the message and create a memorable
impression of the product in the reader's mind. It is also more likely that these
words, because of their prominence in the release, will find their way in the
articles and news stories written by journalists on the product. In fact, one
outcome sought after by press release writers is to encourage journalists to
publish as much as possible of the original release (indeed the ideal is to have it
published verbatim) in their articles.

Example One: Promotional Press Release

The title provides information on appearance and functionality of product and this focus is sustained throughout the release. Notice the use of superlatives 'lightest' 'gorgeous' and 'unique' to suggest the highest quality.

Wicked Wisdom Presents Vision:

Lightest Laptop in the World with 14-inch Screen, Gorgeous Look and Dozens of Unique Features

LONDON – June 27, 2019 – Wicked Wisdom today announced the release of Vision, the slimmest and lightest laptop in the world, with a new design that features a beautiful 14-inch screen, 15-hour battery, the unique performance and ultra-speed of 7-4500U (1.80GHz/3.00GHz), and the dazzling look of HD Graphics 4400. Vision comes with OpenEye 6 operating system and, unlike other slim laptops in the market, it includes a DVD drive and three USB drives – all without adding any weight. Loyal to its promise of giving the best vision ever, it even comes with the option of glossy or anti-glare screen.

Consistent with the top-heavy approach of press releases, the first paragraph summarizes all the important features of the product. It also plays on the word "vision" and the name of the product, Vision.

"Vision is the most beautiful and functional machine that we've ever created," said Andrew Watson, Wicked Wisdom's Vice-President. "We've created Vision with the best balance of innovation and functionality. Weighing only 1 kg, Vision is now the lightest 14-inch laptop available, a product both stupendous to look at and multifunctional to use, with an attractive, custom-built 14-inch screen to suit all tastes. Its 10GB of memory and 600GB hard drive make it also the most powerful laptop of its kind".

The second paragraph elaborates on the features listed in the first, in the form of a quotation.

The third paragraph continues the emphasis on superlatives (thinner, lighter). It also introduces the name of the company and positions it as an agent in the events.

Vision is the lightest laptop in the world, with an all-new carbon fibre construction that is 10% thinner and 20% lighter than other laptops. The 600 GB powerful hard drive was designed by Wicked Wisdom to increase performance and efficiency, and to support all the wonderful new features of Vision. And of course, since fibre construction has no moving parts, Vision tops all others also in durability and long life.

The magical 14-inch screen supports millions of colours, and the HD Graphics 4400 make it the best choice for gamers and photographers alike. It is also the only slim laptop in the world to come with the option of glossy and anti-glare display – respecting the uniqueness of its users. Equipped with GMA technology, Vision gives the sharpest image from any viewing angle – perfect for making that eye-catching presentation or watching a favourite movie.

Paragraph four includes the superlatives "best," "the only" and "sharpest". It also mentions the uniqueness of the users, which creates an association between products and users through "uniqueness".

Paragraph five combines product qualities with functionality, mentions again the company name and emphasizes the company's role in designing these qualities and functions. Also, it introduces a "you" angle, which tilts the release towards a prospect-centred approach. The release ends with a reiteration of the "lightest" message.

Vision supports super-fast wireless standards, so you can surf the internet, download and stream content almost faster than you can think. As for battery life, Vision runs for up to 15 hours, enabling you to word process, email, give presentations or watch movies all day long. With the design of Vision, Wicked Wisdom has ushered in a new era in slim and light laptops that are uniquely beautiful in design, can be adapted to different tastes, are ultra-fast and powerful, and have a long life. And all this in just one kilogram!

Informative press releases

When writing an informative press release, which publicizes an event, development or new policy, describe the events and people involved, add some quotations and explain the significance of the event or development. For example, study Example Two, which contains a university press release describing a project of collaboration between the university and a corporation. Notice how the first two paragraphs contain all the information necessary for the audience to understand what this project is about. The rest of the press release provides additional information and elaboration.

Example Two: Informative Press Release

Professors at XYZ School of Business are collaborating with Big Blue to fine-tune an interactive teaching tool specifically designed for use in universities.

The opening sentence summarizes the project. Notice the nickname Big Blue to refer to IBM.

SocialStudent is an adaptation of Connections, IBM's existing business networking environment. Three faculty members in XYZ's Center for Management Communication are using it to teach online components of the core writing class for undergraduate students – and using data from that experience to help optimize the project for IBM.

Elaborates on the first sentence by providing more details.

"It's a great example of XYZ/corporate collaboration," says Sky Marsen, Associate Professor of Management Communication. "We are working with two other universities on this project, Aalto University in Finland and the University of Netherlands. Our students are learning remote team building and negotiation skills."

A quotation that introduces an individual involved in the project and also continues to develop the description of the project.

Mentions other people involved in the project.

Bob Jones and Malinda Walker, both Associate Professors of Management Communication, are also working on the project with their students.

Focuses on the software used in the project.

SocialStudent includes audio and video meeting functions as well as advanced networking and collaboration functions, such as file-sharing and team editing.

"This is essentially a research project on virtual team collaboration," said Jones, whose work with IBM helped bring the project to XYZ

Students at the three universities are collaborating on a team report on corporate reputation. But instead of going for an A plus, they're working for perhaps a more valuable prize. "We've identified the top five teams," said Marsen. "Now we give them to IBM, who will weigh in and choose the top team. Those team members will be offered internships with IBM."

All students who participated in this semester's project will receive badges certifying their role in the project.

Describes the result of the project.

Some important items in both promotional and informative press releases are:

- Clear presentation of names, dates and titles. If you use acronyms, make sure you explain what they stand for. Do not take for granted the readers will understand them, no matter how famous these acronyms may be.
- Easy-to-find contact details of people that the press can contact for more information. Ideally, include phone numbers, email addresses, fax numbers and physical addresses. These come at the end of the release, like a signature.
- At least one relevant quotation. This makes the release more specific, by focusing on the direct words of responsible parties. It also gives the press an indication of the opinion of key figures and a lead to follow if they want to investigate further. The quotation could also be used directly in news stories and features that media professionals will write following your press release, so you are helping them by including it. Company web pages that contain press releases (and press kits sent to media outlets) also include photos and general information on the company, which journalists can use in their stories.
- A zesty, active and concise style. A press release is still a promotional text targeting publicists (it promotes to the promoters, so to speak). Although marketese, or pompous exaggeration, must be avoided, press releases emphasize Unique Selling Points and can create a memorable image through the use of adjectives and metaphors.

If the press release is broadcast on radio or television, timing is very important. The average reader can read about 150 words in a minute. Broadcasts are on average about 30 seconds. So, for a 30-second announcement, you will need about 60–70 words. Practise reading out your announcement to make sure it fits comfortably within this time frame while providing the main information. Also, note that broadcast press releases tend to begin with location. This is an influence from drama, where a scene is described before the dialogue begins. Unless you have reason to improvise, start your announcement by stating the scene. Because broadcast announcements are spoken, avoid abbreviations and acronyms, unless they are well-known (for example, NASA, USA). Finally, incorporate quotations in your own words (that is, paraphrase them) to fit with the reading voice.

Web writing

An internet primer

High visibility and low cost make websites the fastest and most effective means of publicity. Since the medium of websites is the Internet, an overview of its nature would be useful here. This subsection is quite basic, so those with more experience in digital media can skip it.

Think of your computer as divided into three parts: the *hardware* (also known as the part that you can kick!), the *operating system* and the *software*. The hardware is the actual electronics and wiring of the computer together, and includes memory, hard drive capacity, the presence of different drives and type of screen. The hardware gives the computer its inherent power, so, for example, if you want to run multimedia applications, you need a computer with a certain size of hard drive and a minimum of megabytes (MB) of memory. Otherwise, the computer will not be able to handle the programs you try to feed it.

The next step from hardware is the operating system (OS), or platform, that you choose, and this determines general *functionality* (how the computer works) and *interface* (what the design of the screen looks like). It also determines the kind of software you can install and run. Currently, the most common platforms are Microsoft Windows, Macintosh and Open Source operating systems.

Software refers to the programs, or applications, that you install. There is software for different purposes: for example, Microsoft Word is a very widespread word processing program, and Adobe Photoshop is an equally popular graphics program. Most software programs come in two formats, for either Windows or Macintosh platforms.

To connect to the Internet, you need a *browser* and an *ISP (Internet Service Provider)*. The browser is the software that allows your computer to access data on the World Wide Web, for example, Chrome, Firefox and Safari. The Internet is actually a huge, centreless network of computers connected through individual *servers* – the part of a company's computer network that connects directly to the Internet. If you are an individual user, you need a provider that has a server in order to connect (usually at a set fee). Companies and institutions have their own servers. What is known as a *web address* (or *URL, Uniform Resource Locator*) is actually a link to a server. If you want to publish any material on the Internet, such as a website, you need a server, which will *host* your site.

Everyday talk often confounds the Internet with the World Wide Web. A distinction is, however, necessary. The Internet includes the Web; in fact, the Internet is the infrastructure level of the medium, and includes such services as email. The Web is the public face of the Internet medium, where users access information on products and services by visiting websites (allowing for the existence of secure pages, of course, which make the Web not so public!)

It is important to remember that the Internet is a medium – not a genre. In other words, it provides the means of transmission and exchange of different forms of information presented in different document types. For example, you can send a report via email as an attachment or post it as a *Portable Document Format* (PDF) on a site. The document would still be report genre, regardless of its medium of transmission. In other words, when composing it, you should still follow the conventions and expectations of report writing.

Multimedia

Before anything else, remember that websites are addressed to users rather than readers. This means they must provide information in a way that is consistent with the nature of their medium, and in a way that makes full use of the medium's resources. Digital capabilities are often grouped under the umbrella term *multimedia*, which includes *text, graphics, sound, video* and *animation*. The potential of multimedia is increasingly been recognized and used in most areas of communication: in education, entertainment and business. In fact, new fields of communication have emerged through the use of multimedia applications, such as the creative combination of educational, information and entertainment techniques that has come to be known as *edutainment* and *infotainment* (see also Bateman, 2011; Heskett, 2005; Kostelnick & Roberts, 1998).

The fact that the digital medium is actually a collection of different media capabilities gives the web designer a singular task: to coordinate the different media and produce, through their combination, an effective and compelling result. As the technology for graphics, sound, video and animation is constantly changing, the next section focuses on text.

Digital text

Content is still the most important factor in website development. A website is, in most cases, not just an ornamental piece used for decoration. It should provide specific information that will attract and interest readers and motivate them to take some form of action (such as contacting the company, buying a product, etc.) in response to the information presented. This makes text the fundamental element in website development. Surveys of product marketing on the web, for example, generally find that there are more return visits to sites with substantial text content than to those that rely on other multimedia elements. This suggests that most users still expect the graphic elements to complement the text rather than the other way round (Nielsen, 2000).

The writing strategies outlined throughout this book are valid also for web design. The fundamental principles of clarity, conciseness and accuracy are as important in websites as they are in other types of professional documents. In addition to these, text that is read on a computer monitor requires some other considerations. When writing content for websites follow these guidelines:

Balance text with other media. The visual nature of electronic communication should be acknowledged by blending verbal information with visual or aural components to produce a multisensory effect. Sites that rely too much on verbal language exhaust users and are not likely to have a strong appeal. If you have a lot of written information to communicate, it is best to include PDF files or printable brochures in your site. These can be printed out as complete numbered pages, becoming much easier to read.

Begin with most important information. Although this is valid also for other types of journalistic documents, it is of special significance in websites. Pages load from top to bottom, so the users need to read something compelling in the first eight seconds or they might leave. As graphics take longer to download than text, make sure the users have something substantial to read while waiting – preferably some information on the purpose of the site or on the function of the company hosting it. The most common form of information distribution on the web is the Inverted Pyramid style. The conclusion, or central point, of the document goes first followed by information in descending order of importance.

Organize text into small chunks. Words, sentences and paragraphs should be shorter in electronic format than in print, and they are better presented in columns balanced with other media, rather than across the screen. In all, layout considerations for web writing are more similar to journalism than to other professional writing, such as reports. Visual information is processed faster than verbal information, so try to make electronic text as visual as possible.

Select font, colour and size carefully. Legibility is important, so use reasonably large fonts and allow users to change font size. Fonts are divided into *serif* and *sans serif* (serif fonts have little "tails" on the edges while sans serif fonts have sharp edges). Sans serif fonts are easier to read in multimedia format, which may include colours and graphics. See the section on typography, which follows, for more tips on fonts.

Restrict the use of upper case to major headings. Experiments have shown that upper case fonts reduce the readability of text and increase reading time by about 10%. Reading from a screen increases reading time by about 25%, so text has to be made as easy as possible to read.

Be aware of the style and aesthetic that your audience values. The web is too diverse to be bound by one aesthetic. Online communities develop distinctive styles that are recognized and emulated by in-group members. Since "online" is a medium and not a genre, web content varies depending on the genre: for instance, online news stories are still news stories and follow their genre conventions. There are as many styles in cyberspace as there are cultural communities in the physical world, so audience and purpose analysis techniques are as important here as in other forms of document production. General advice is to target a reading level some steps below your target audience's assumed education level, even when writing for professionals.

Cater for international audiences. One thing to remember when choosing words and phrases for your web content is that your audience will be international. This means that many local terms and symbols may be misunderstood by outsiders. For this reason, most multinational corporations employ technical writers and language specialists to *localize* products; that is, to research and recommend appropriate, inoffensive, memorable and pleasant-sounding terminology for international audiences. *Globalization* is accompanied by *localization*, since users utilize global media but still tend to identify with specific cultural groups.

Use colour effectively. Colour is useful for emphasizing important information, grouping related items, reinforcing site structure, and increasing comprehension and recall. When using colour, be aware that it can change the appearance of objects, including text type. For example, warm and bright colours make things look larger than cool and dark colours, so, for example, if you use a black screen, use bigger text. Also be aware that people cannot look into bright colours for long, so avoid dense text on a bright screen.

Shape also affects the appearance of colours. Use blue for large areas and backgrounds, but not for text type, thin lines or small shapes, as it is difficult to focus on blue. To remember the impact of colour on the user, think of the *colour spectrum* (ROYGBIV) running from the front of the screen to the back. For example, red, orange and yellow will stand out the most; blue, indigo and violet will recede into the background. Keep in mind also that colour and shape carry symbolism that varies from culture to culture. This is of particular relevance if you are aiming for an international audience.

Optimize your website for different devices. The internet is accessed from computers, smartphones, digital tablets and other digital devices, so keep this in mind when writing text or designing multimedia.

Digital writing and cultural studies

Besides its use in business websites, digital writing is attracting attention from text and cultural theorists because of its potential to change the cognitive aspects of writing. For example, linguist and philosopher of language Roy Harris (2000) distinguishes three stages in the understanding of writing: *crypto-literacy*, where writing is seen through the lens of magic and secret knowledge, associated with occult or esoteric practices and beliefs; *utilitarian literacy*, where writing is seen as a practical tool achieving particular ends and being equivalent to speech; and *full literacy*, where writing is considered to be "a particular mode of operation of the human mind and the key to a new concept of language" (Harris, 2000, pp. x–xi). Full literacy has not been achieved by any society yet, although Harris suggests that digital technology could well herald its era because of the extensive experimentation with language that computers encourage and make possible.

Two major factors that contribute to the large scope for experimentation inherent in digital writing are *hypertext* and *collaboration* (see also Landow, 2006). Hypertext challenges the linear perception of the printed text by including links to different sites, thereby connecting content from different fields. Hypertext does not only allow for creative associations, but also changes the ways knowledge is defined. Historically, the last time an invention produced a similar result was the creation of the encyclopedia in the 17th century. Collaboration challenges the notion of sole author, since many digital texts are written by various authors. In some situations, such as wikis, collaborative authoring is the norm. This collaborative element of digital writing also enables professionals from different countries to contribute to a project simultaneously, thereby emphasizing the importance of "expert community" rather than "local community".

All in the (type) family: Fonts

This section looks at typography: the study of writing characters, or fonts. Fonts are arranged in generalized groupings known as "type families". Type families are divided into **individual** and **specific**. For example, Arial is a member of the sans-serif family, which can include specific groups such as 10 point Arial, 12 point Arial Bold, 8 point Arial Italic and so on. Some of the more common families are:

Serif
Serif fonts have little "tails" on the end of letterforms. These "tails" help the eye to quickly define letters and words and are easier to read in print than other families. They have an ancient history: the Romans chiselled serif typefaces on their buildings. One serif font is Century Schoolbook, which was designed in the USA in the early 20th century for use in primary school textbooks.

Century Schoolbook

Sans serif
The art and literary movements of the early 20th century, particularly those following World War I, brought sans serif typefaces. As the name implies, the "tails" are missing, giving a stripped-down, unemotional, nihilist typeface reflecting the ideologies of that era. Today, sans serif fonts are the favourites of advertising designers and transportation signage creators. They are generally the preferred font for electronic writing as they are easy to read on a computer monitor.

Verdana

Script

Originally designed to put feeling back into the mechanical world of printing, scripts are used to imitate handwriting. Never use all upper case letters in a script typeface. It is very difficult to read.

Lucida Calligraphy

Decorative

Some type is not meant to be read in large text blocks. Decorative faces are great for headlines, signage and other uses, but use them sparingly.

Party Let

Engraved

Engraved fonts have a classical, sophisticated and elegant look. They are based on the work of John Caxton, the founder of the British printing and typography industry in the 17th century.

Colonna MT

Black letter (also known as fraktur)

In the 16th and 17th centuries, printing and type design were wrapped up in the political and economic birth of European nation states. A few examples of these "nationalistic" typefaces remain in Cyrillic (Russian alphabet) and Black Letter. This typefont has a Gothic touch to it and is associated with horror movies, prison tattoos and Nazis. Because of these connotations, use with care. Once again, avoid setting words in all upper case in this font.

Lucida Blackletter

Wingdings

Wingdings are symbols masquerading as letters. Use very, very sparingly and only for fun. Definitely avoid, if precision and clarity are your aims!

The decision to use a particulat font type should be taken seriously: fonts affect reader response since they are part of the medium in which information is communicated. For example, Pamela Henderson (2005) and her team conducted a survey to gauge reactions to different fonts and found some interesting results. They found that fonts can be perceived as "emotional", "likeable", "unsettling", "cold", "warm", "feminine" or "masculine", and even "exciting" or "dishonest". For instance, Playbill, Onyx, and Stencil were perceived as the worst (which Henderson suggests makes them suitable to use when describing features of competitors!)

- Playbill
- Onyx
- **STENCIL**

At the other end, some of the most comfortable but unexciting fonts, and therefore the "safest" to use, were Georgia, Verdana, Times New Roman and Century Gothic.

- Georgia
- Verdana
- Times New Roman
- Century Gothic

Checklist for evaluating content, aesthetics and usability of websites

How much credibility you give to a website depends, as do all other genres, on *purpose* and *audience*. For example, if the site was designed for entertainment purposes, factors such as accuracy of factual information and in-depth analysis of topics would not be suitable criteria for evaluation. Similarly, a promotional site should be evaluated according to advertising, as opposed to scholarly, criteria. For example, does the site attract attention through graphic design and text that is appealing to its target audience? Does it provide information that anticipates the users' questions and concerns?

The following is a checklist of the most important aspects of an effective website. Refer to this checklist both when you design your own site and when you evaluate others' sites:

CONTENT
Relevance
- Does the site provide information relevant to its topic?
- Does the content reflect the title of the site, and are all headings and sections useful in determining content?

Timely/current information

- Does the site include a date for the information it presents?

Purpose

- If it is a commercial site, has an exaggerated promotional writing style, or marketese, been avoided?
- Are the language and style used appropriate to the content, purpose and audience?

Scannable

- Do users have the option to scan table of contents, section of summaries, bullets, and boldface, short paragraphs?

Concise

- Is the text clear and concise?
- Is text organized in small chunks?

Writing

- Are spelling and grammar correct?
- Is there introductory text where necessary?
- Do multimedia elements support the task?

AESTHETICS
Audio (if used)

- Does the music evoke an appropriate emotion?
- Does the audio help to set the scene?

Video (if used)

- Is it useful?
- Is the quality adequate?
- Does it load quickly?

Animation (if used)

- Is it useful?
- Is the quantity suitable?

Graphics

- Do they complement the text?
- Are they stored for maximum compression (in other words, do they take the least space possible for their size and therefore decrease downloading time)?

Colour
- Is the choice appropriate for the site?
- Is the number of colours suitable?
- Are colours used consistently?

Typography
- Is the font appropriate to the content of the site?
- Are there sufficient margins?

Layout and design
- Does the page fit on the screen?
- Is the layout consistent throughout the site?
- Does the site appear pleasing?

USABILITY
Download time
- Does the content download fast enough (up to 10 seconds)?

Ease of use
- Are options visible without scrolling?
- Is it possible to compare all options at the same time?

Links/Image map
- Do link names match page names?
- Are link headings easy to understand?
- Do all the links work?
- Is there a clear link to the Home Page?
- Are clickable areas obvious in the image map?

Navigation
- Is the navigation scheme obvious?
- Does each page include information on the site?
- Can the user go from one page to another without returning to the Home Page?

Platform and device
- Does the site work with all major browsers?
- Does the site work on small and large monitors?
- Does the site work on all digital devices?

Social media

As one of the "new" media (in contrast to the "old" *print and broadcast* media), the Internet has modelled its design on preceding forms. For example, email, one of the first uses of the medium, is modelled on the memo genre, and website design is modelled on magazine layout. At its inception in the 1990s and early 2000s, the Internet emphasized its visual quality and borrowed cinematic techniques in how it organized and presented information (Manovich, 2001). With its growth, however, it is changing focus and form, to a large extent because of the development of interactive features, such as the dramatically rapid expansion of *social media*.

Social media started with the launch of *wikis* (collaborative writing systems), which allowed different users to contribute to a writing project. *Wikipedia* (launched in 2001) is a prime example of this. The subsequent years saw the development of other social media sites that allowed the interaction of different users: *Facebook* and *Flickr* were launched in 2004, *YouTube* in 2005 and *Twitter* in 2006. These media have come to be known as *Web 2.0*, and are based on *User-Generated Content* (UGC) – that is, writing produced by users of the Internet regardless of expertise or status (although, of course, access to the Internet and to the particular site, as well as a certain degree of skill, are assumed).

At the same time, the advent of social media saw the development of subgenres, such as *citizen journalism*, where "ordinary" citizens create news content, using devices such as mobile phones, and upload it to relevant news sites. Sometimes, as when the news comes from politically restricted areas, such as war zones, news and images delivered by non-specialist bystanders have become the only timely source of information. In fact, this kind of user empowerment in Web 2.0 led *Time* magazine to name as person of the year 2006 "You" (meaning the individual users of the world). This person of the year was imaged by using a reflective surface mounted on a computer screen and carrying the headline "You. Yes, you. You control the Information Age. Welcome to your world" (Cull, 2011, p. 3).

What is the effect of social media on business, and, in particular, on professional writing? The high popularity of social media has made it almost imperative for businesses to incorporate them in their communications strategy. At the time of writing this book, *all* major international corporations had accounts with social media sites and kept these updated to the minute. In fact, many public relations experts advise companies to make the most of social media by joining sites such as *Facebook*, *LinkedIn* and *Twitter*, contributing to *Wikipedia*, adding content to *YouTube*, and blogging.

Social media have allowed companies to very quickly respond to a relevant event, and to direct users' attention to desirable content. Such entries give writers the opportunity to direct readers to more expansive genres, such as blogs or online articles, and generate more company-controlled data on the Internet. Although they create avenues for discussion and exchange of ideas, they are also means by which to promote the company image.

Social media have also created a new kind of professional, a "social media expert", with a clearly defined company position. The job of social media expert is to keep an eye on what users are saying about the company, to respond to users and to advise management on ways to use social media to enhance the company reputation. Similarly, there are consulting companies whose mission is to advise companies on their social media image – known as *Reputation Management*. These professionals monitor the Internet for potentially damaging information about their client and assist their client in handling such information if it emerges.

Personal interviews with such professionals have revealed some techniques of reputation management. These include posting positive data to cover the damaging material and even contacting reviewers and bloggers who have posted negative feedback about the client, to negotiate the removal or amendment of this information. In one example, whose particulars must remain confidential, a company received a negative review by a popular video blogger, whose entry received thousands of views and comments. After research, the company found the blogger's email and contacted him. Following a discussion, the blogger refused to take down his comments, but agreed to post a new entry describing how the company contacted him and showed interest in his opinion. The situation, therefore, was given a different spin, one more favourable to the company.

Although the ethical concerns revolving around such matters are complicated, the fact remains that social media have increased peer-to-peer feedback and recommendations, as well as support, and have introduced an era where consumer-to-consumer and consumer-to-company communication has increasing influence on social perceptions of the company. In fact, the rise of social media has created another title, "influencer". Needless to say, the most ethically constructive way for a company to use customers' reviews and feedback is to learn what people think and to respond to concerns truthfully.

Writing for social media

As regards writing style and genre considerations, social media, being informal venues of information, tend to follow journalistic conventions. The speed in which entries are written and the small space they occupy do not allow for elaborations, definitions or extensive analyses. In fact, *Twitter* modelled its genre on *Short Message Service* (SMS) text-messaging, or *txtese*, favouring abbreviated words. It is therefore very important to scrutinize every word to ensure it has the appropriate impact, as the risks of miscommunication in social media are maximized.

When using social media for professional communication, keep three features in mind:

1 Social media are a marketplace where you compete for attention. So, your company should stand out in some way. Try creating an image for the company through a distinctive use of multimedia and original content.
2 Timing plays a major role in social media – more so than in all other media. Updating content and responding to comments and concerns quickly are crucial factors in maintaining a successful social media presence.
3 Social media are highly interactive, so much so that others might "kidnap" your content and take it in directions you hadn't anticipated. In the micro-blogging site Twitter, for example, at present, you can write up to 1000 tweets of 280 words each a day. Enough to keep your public updated? Keep in mind that "mentions" of your user name or "handle" in others' tweets can draw attention to you. You can also receive "replies" using your user name, and your tweet can be "retweeted" many times over, often with added comments by the re-tweeter. Furthermore, your hashtag can be used by others in their own tweets. All this can be as beneficial as it can be damaging to your organization's reputation.

For example, in a famous PR blunder, the Australian airline company Qantas grounded its fleet internationally for two days due to an industrial dispute in October 2011. This resulted in thousands of disgruntled passengers left stranded around the world. Instead of using social media to apologize and appease the public, Qantas decided to draw attention away from the strike and onto something more positive. Thus, they started a competition for a luxury holiday and advertised it on *Twitter,* just one day after the strike ended. This decision backfired on them, however, as their hashtag was "hijacked" and they attracted a flood of angry replies. For example, one tweeter wrote, "Qantas Luxury means sipping champagne on your corporate jet while grounding the entire airline, country, customers and staff". "Qantas Luxury is getting my flight refund back after waiting almost a month," wrote another. Another customer suggested the phrase meant "more than 3 mins notice that the whole airline is on strike" (Qantas Twitter contest draws thousands of angry replies, 2011).

In a similar blunder, Amazon CEO Jeff Bezos tweeted from a dog sledding holiday in Norway in April 2018:

> Dog sledding above the Arctic Circle in Norway. Jim Lovell says it's not that you go to heaven when you die, but "you go to heaven when you're born." Earth is the best planet in our solar system. We go to space to save the Earth. @BlueOrigin #NoPlanB #GradatimFerociter #EarthDay

This happened in a year when Amazon was hit by an onslaught of accusations for low wages and employee mistreatment. So, although the tweet was meant as a celebration of Earth Day, it didn't take attention away from the company's PR scandals and didn't go down too well with the public. Comedian Sarah Silverman, for example, responded,

> Why do your employees need to be on food stamps & govt assistance? Be an example of fair payment & take the pressure off the taxpayers who are subsidizing ur lack of fair pay. I KNOW you can do it, Jeff! Don't be like the Waltons of Walmart.

The conversational and informal aspect of social media sometimes leads to an attempt by organizations to create a friendly and approachable image in the public mind. This attempt can have both positive and negative results.
The positive effects are more clearly seen when the company's tweet, blog entry or Facebook post is about a new product, especially one that is likely to be well-received by the public. The negative effects emerge when the company attempts to use social media to deal with an explosive or controversial situation. For example, the tweet below was written by BP on 15 December 2010 while the company was under scrutiny for its oil-spill disaster in the US:

BP Public Relations @BPGlobalPR

The bad news – we're being sued by the United States. The good news – they sue in dollars, not pounds. #1.5538

Given the nature of the event, and the public's reaction, a humorous tone would not be advisable in any communication about this topic – making the above comment sound more self-centred than lighthearted.

Speech writing

A major way in which professionals communicate with the public is through speeches – especially true of top management executives. Speeches can be made during press conferences, followed by Question and Answer (Q&A)

sessions, or through broadcasts (radio, television) and digital (*YouTube,* company website) media. In many cases, the speech becomes available in written form for future reference. In all cases, important public speeches are written first, and then memorized or read aloud. Different occasions call for a speech. Also, the speech could have different audiences and would need to be adapted to suit the knowledge and interests of each. For example, speeches to the wider public tend to contain more general information and a zestier style than speeches addressed to investors and shareholders, which include specific details and a more "bottom-line" approach. Speeches in professional contexts generally fall into five broad categories:

Information: Government officials and company executives keep the public informed of initiatives and developments through speeches. These may be delivered at press conferences, at special events or through broadcast and digital media.

Motivation: CEOs and successful entrepreneurs are often invited to give inspirational speeches where they describe their successes and failures and give advice to new professionals.

Promotion: A speech is often an effective medium to promote the qualities of a new product or service because the physical presence of the speaker can enthuse the audience and create interest. This is especially true if the speaker is charismatic and uses appealing and innovative methods of presentation.

Apology: After an accident or mistake caused by a company, the CEO must publicly accept responsibility and apologize. Apology speeches, part of *crisis management* and *image restoration,* are very important in ensuring that the reputation of the company is not damaged irreparably. Apology speeches must be timely (delays have been found to have negative effects on the company reputation), and constructive (the apology itself is not enough – the speaker must show the company is taking measures to effectively repair the situation). See below for more on crisis communication.

Progress: In large-scale projects that have public significance (for example, when taxpayers' money is used), it is important to keep the public informed of events and developments. Press releases can play this role, but at pivotal stages of the project a speech can personalize the project and create a favourable impression.

When writing a speech, follow these guidelines:

- Write in a conversational style so that the speech doesn't sound like reading. Use contractions and idioms.

- Give the speech a clear structure (for example, problem-solution or big picture to detail) and sustain it throughout. Include stories, analogies and examples to ensure the message is reinforced.
- Include a strong beginning and ending. A well thought-out framing makes the speech memorable.
- Make sure the speech has one main message. Know exactly what you want to say and don't try to do too much in one speech.
- Show sincerity and humility as appropriate in the context: do not claim you know all the answers.
- Perform your role in relation to the audience. If you are an expert delivering a speech on an area of your expertise, don't try to "dumb down" the content. Showing expertise, through the use of appropriate technical terminology, adds credibility to what you say. However, if the audience is composed of non-specialists, give enough explanation for them to understand.
- Give credit where it's due. Name any collaborating companies or government agencies and explain their role. This is a technique of transparency as well as shared responsibility. However, if the speech is delivered during a crisis, handle this with care as it can easily become a scapegoating exercise or appear as a method for displacing blame.
- Pay close attention to the tone of the speech. The tone must respect the circumstances of the context and audience. For example, avoid a humorous tone in cases where the audience is likely to be hostile or concerned about a serious matter.

Interviews

A press interview is an oral communication, similar in many ways to a speech. As successful professionals, you may often be invited to present your work to the public through an interview. As PR practitioners, you may be tasked to instruct managers on the best way to present themselves and the company in a press interview. Table 6.1 gives some useful guidelines in preparing for this.

Table 6.1 Guidelines for Media Interviews

Before the interview:
- Learn as much as possible about the reporter, publication/programme interview format, audience
- Have a clear idea of your goal for the interview
- Know what you want to say: review your key message points
- Write likely questions and appropriate answers.

Interview tips:
- Speak in "headlines": offer conclusion first, briefly and directly, and back it with facts or "proof points"
- Do not "over-answer": short answers are better than long
- Do not be trapped by a question, but "bridge" it to a related point you want to make
- When asked about a problem, talk about a solution
- Do not let false charges, facts or figures offered by a reporter stand uncorrected; interviews are opportunities to correct misconceptions
- Do not repeat a reporter's negative statements: frame your reply as a positive statement
- Speak clearly: avoid technical jargon
- If you do not know the answer admit it (positively, if possible) and assure the reporter that you will find and provide the needed facts in a timely manner, or offer to assist the reporter in finding that other source
- Do not overlap the interviewer's question; begin your answer when the reporter is finished
- Keep cool – do not be provoked, and never lie to a reporter.

For telephone and radio interviews:
- Buy preparation time by asking to call the reporter back if deadline allows
- Establish an "interview atmosphere" and mindset
- Use notes
- Ask questions in order to gain feedback
- For radio, speak visually – use words to paint pictures.

For television interviews:
- Take care with appearance and clothes: the common advice is for women to avoid solid black or white or busy patterns, and for men to wear a dark suit
- Do not wear large, shiny or noisy jewellery, unless this reflects the image you want to project
- Sit upright, but don't be too stiff, slightly forward in the chair
- Unbutton suit jacket when seated
- Resist the urge to shout into the microphone; speak and gesture naturally
- Talk to the reporter/interviewer, not the camera
- Keep a pleasant expression; smile when appropriate
- Hold your "interview attitude" from the moment you are lit until the interview is completely over and the camera is off.

Crisis communication

Crisis communication is a branch of public relations dedicated to the study of communication during and after crises. By analysing case studies of crisis and conducting experiments and surveys on public response, crisis communication experts have classified crises and identified communication strategies to deal with them effectively (Benoit, 1997; Coombs, 2014).

Crises can be preventable (human error, corner cutting) or unpreventable (natural disasters), and intentional (sabotage, terrorism) or unintentional (economic recessions, technical faults). An organization that has suffered a crisis tends to be held accountable to varying degrees depending on the type of crisis. In some instances, the organization can claim to be a victim but in other cases it is closer to a perpetrator. Therefore, being strategic in how the crisis is managed is paramount in safeguarding reputation.

Some situations that could signal a crisis include:

- An accident has occurred that caused deaths and/or environmental damage
- Products have been found to contain technical faults and deficiencies
- A company needs to cut down on jobs and make employees redundant
- A company did not make a profit and is in financial difficulties
- Security has been breached compromising people's personal information
- Corrupt management or employees have caused irreparable financial loss.

The gravity of the crisis varies with each situation: an accident involving equipment malfunction that has caused environmental damage is much more serious, and would require much more justification, than a response to a customer's complaint that the company's retail outlets do not open on public holidays.

In general, the following actions have been found to be effective in most public relations crises:

Respond quickly: Things get quickly out of hand in crises, so a company or government agency facing an accusation or a failure should respond immediately, or as quickly as possible. Research has consistently shown that delays sway public opinion against the company, and it is more difficult to repair reputation damage after time has lapsed.

Accept responsibility: It is important to tell the truth and not attempt to conceal faults, or to deflect responsibility. After a crisis, image restoration becomes essential, so defensive tactics would not help. Claiming responsibility for mistakes enhances the company's damaged integrity.

Avoid laying blame and scapegoating: Similar to the above point, don't focus on finding someone to blame. Instead, focus on facts where possible. Usually crises and damage are the outcome of many individuals' actions and cannot be reduced to one person's decisions. It is more constructive to try to find the causes of the damage, not so as to punish individuals, but so as to revise the system that enabled the problem to occur in the first place.

Apologize: Victims of disasters and the public appreciate an apology. An apology shows recognition and respect for people's feelings and losses and should be an immediate response to a crisis.

Describe measures taken to remedy the situation: Apologies are empty without actions, however. Show that your company is taking measures to fix the problem. In cases where people have suffered loss, compensation is a measure to alleviate the situation. In cases where there is ongoing damage, explain clearly how the company is taking the most appropriate actions regardless of cost.

Be constructive: Fixing a problem is important, but not enough. Show also that the company is taking long-term measures to ensure that the problem is not repeated in the future. Show foresight and the willingness to learn from mistakes. In fact, Renewal Theory is an approach to crisis communication that describes crisis as opportunities to implement constructive changes and renew the system, making it stronger and more resilient for the future (Ulmer et al., 2018).

Risk and issues management

Prevention is better than cure. In addition to having a crisis plan in place to deal with a crisis when it occurs, organizations should have clear communication procedures as a part of their everyday functioning. Good communication has been shown repeatedly to prevent a crisis from developing. Similarly, inefficient communication practices have been found to accompany, and often even cause, the sparking of a crisis. In PR, preventing a crisis is known as "risk" or "issues management".

Below are some tested and widely recommended actions that can prevent a problem from escalating into a disaster:

Do not downplay problems: If you suspect that there is a problem somewhere that will worsen if not fixed, make this known to management. Even if you are not sure the problem is serious, it is better to work on the premise of "better safe than sorry". If a situation seems urgent to you as an expert, do not hesitate to communicate this urgency to decision makers. This approach can help to prevent costly and even fatal outcomes, and is the reason that pessimists generally make better risk managers than optimists.

Communicate your message to the appropriate individuals in the most effective genre and style: When communicating bad news or possible dangers to management or decision makers, make sure you present your reasons in ways that they will understand.

Establish feedback mechanisms to enable free exchange of information: If you are in a management position, make sure that there are communication channels and feedback mechanisms between all ranks of employees, and that employees are made aware of these and are encouraged to use them without fear of penalty.

1   Collect as many public relations documents as you can from two competing companies in the same industry and compare them. What similarities and differences can you find in writing strategy, style and layout? How does the company's image (that is, the desired way the company wants the public to see it) account for the differences? Can you see any differences between push and pull media?

2   Below is an abridged version of BP CEO Tony Hayward's speech on the oil spill accident in the Gulf Coast of the US in 2010. The speech was delivered by Hayward on 17 June 2010, addressing the congressional committee (the full speech text can be found at http://www.guardian.co.uk/business/2010/jun/17/ bp-tony-hayward-oil-spill-statement). Although this is a shortened version, it retains the original organization and sequencing of information. Analyse the speech in relation to the concepts of speech writing and crisis communication discussed in this chapter. In what ways do you think the speech is effective and in what ways do you think it is not and could be improved?

The explosion and fire aboard the Deepwater Horizon and the resulting oil spill in the Gulf of Mexico never should have happened – and I am deeply sorry that they did. None of us yet knows why it happened. But whatever the cause, we at BP will do what we can to make certain that an incident like this does not happen again.

Since April 20, I have spent a great deal of my time in the Gulf Coast region and in the incident command center in Houston, and let there be no mistake – I understand how serious this situation is. This is a tragedy: people lost their lives; others were injured; and the Gulf Coast environment and communities are suffering. This is unacceptable, I understand that, and let me be very clear: I fully grasp the terrible reality of the situation.

I want to acknowledge the questions that you and the public are rightly asking. How could this happen? How damaging is the spill to the environment? Why is it taking so long to stop the flow of oil and gas into the Gulf?

And questions are being asked about energy policy more broadly: Can we as a society explore for oil and gas in safer and more reliable ways? What is the appropriate regulatory framework for the industry?

We don't yet have answers to all these important questions. But I hear the concerns, fears, frustrations – and anger – being voiced across the country. I understand it, and I know that these sentiments will continue until the leak is stopped, and until we prove through our actions that we will do the right thing. Our actions will mean more than words, and we know that, in the end, we will be judged by the quality of our response. Until this happens, no words will be satisfying.

Among the resources that have been made available:

- Drilling and technical experts who are helping determine solutions to stopping the spill and mitigating its impact, including specialists in the areas of subsea wells, environmental science and emergency response;
- Technical advice on blowout preventers, dispersant application, well construction and containment options;
- Additional facilities to serve as staging areas for equipment and responders, more remotely operated vehicles (ROVs) for deep underwater work, barges, support vessels and additional aircraft, as well as training and working space for the Unified Command.

Working under the umbrella of the Unified Command, BP's team of operational and technical experts is coordinating with many federal, state, and local governmental entities and private sector organizations. These include the Departments of Interior, Homeland Security, Energy, and Defense, the National Oceanic and Atmospheric Administration (NOAA), US Fish & Wildlife Service (USFW), National Marine Fisheries Service (NMFS), EPA, OSHA, Gulf Coast state environmental and wildlife agencies, the Marine Spill Response Corporation (MSRC) (an oil spill response organization), as well as numerous state, city, parish and county agencies.

Our efforts in response to this incident are focused on two critical goals:

- Successfully stopping the flow of oil; and
- Minimizing the environmental and economic impacts from the oil spill.

These are without a doubt complex and challenging tasks. While we have had to overcome hurdles, we are doing everything we can to respond as quickly and effectively as we can.

The investigation team's work thus far suggests that this accident was brought about by the apparent failure of a number of processes, systems and equipment. While the team's work is not done, it appears that there were multiple control mechanisms – procedures and equipment – in place that should have prevented this accident or reduced the impact of the spill. The investigation is focused on the following seven mechanisms:

1 The cement that seals the reservoir from the well;

2 The casing system, which seals the well bore;

3 The pressure tests to confirm the well is sealed;

4 The execution of procedures to detect and control hydrocarbons in the well, including the use of the blowout preventer (BOP) and the maintenance of that BOP;

5 The BOP Emergency Disconnect System, which can be activated by pushing a button at multiple locations on the rig;

6 The automatic closure of the BOP after its connection is lost with the rig; and;

7 Features in the BOP to allow ROVs to close the BOP and thereby seal the well at the seabed after a blowout.

I understand people want a simple answer about why this happened and who is to blame. The truth, however, is that this is a complex accident, caused by an unprecedented combination of failures. A number of companies are involved, including BP, and it is simply too early to understand the cause.

References and further reading

Bateman, J. (2011) *Multimodality and genre: A foundation for the systematic analysis of multimodal documents.* London: Palgrave Macmillan.

Benoit, W. (1997) Image repair discourse and crisis communication. *Public Relations Review*, 23 (2), 177–186.

Bivins, T. H. (1999) *Public relations writing*, 4th edition. Lincolnwood, Ill: NTC/Contemporary Publishing Group.

Coombs, W. T. (2014) *Applied crisis communication and crisis management.* London: Sage.

Cull, N. J. (2011) WikiLeaks, public diplomacy 2.0 and the state of digital public diplomacy. *Place Branding and Public Diplomacy*, 7, 1–8.

Davis, A. (2004) *Mastering public relations.* London: Red Globe Press.

Eyrich, N., Padman, M. L., & Sweetser, K. D. (2008) PR practitioners' use of social media tools and communication technology. *Public Relations Review*, 34(1), 412–414.

Harris, R. (2000) *Rethinking writing.* London: Continuum.

Henderson, P. (2005) Just my type. *Harvard Business Review*, n.p.

Heskett, J. (2005) *A very short introduction to design.* Oxford: Oxford University Press.

Kawasaki, G. (2004) *The art of the start: The time-tested, battle-hardened guide for anyone starting anything.* London and New York: Penguin Portfolio.

Kawasaki, G. (2011) *Enchantment: The art of changing hearts, minds and actions.* London and New York: Penguin Portfolio.

Kent, M. L. (2011) Public relations rhetoric: Criticism, dialogue and the long now. *Management Communication Quarterly*, 25(3), 550–559.

Kostelnick, C., & Roberts, D. D. (1998) *Designing visual language: Strategies for professional communicators.* New York: Allyn and Bacon.

Landow, G. P. (2006) *Hypertext 3.0: Critical theory and new media in an era of globalization.* Baltimore: Johns Hopkins University Press.

Mangold, W. G., & Faulds, D. J. (2009) Social media: The new hybrid element of the promotion mix. *Business Horizons*, 52, 357–365.

Manovich, L. (2001) *The language of new media*. Cambridge, MA: MIT Press.

Morris, T., & Goldsworthy, S. (2012) *PR today: The authoritative guide to public relations*. London: Red Globe Press.

Nesheim, J. L. (2000) *High tech start-up*. New York: Free Press.

Nielsen, J. (2000) *Designing web usability: The practice of simplicity*. New York: New Riders Press.

Nielsen, J., & Tahir, M. (2001) *Homepage usability: 50 websites deconstructed*. New York: New Riders Press.

Qantas Twitter contest draws thousands of angry replies (2011). BBC News, 23 November 2011. Retrieved 10 January 2019 from https://www.bbc.com/news/world-asia-15852965

Shimp, T. (1997) *Advertising, promotion and supplemental aspects of integrated marketing communications*. Chicago: Dryden.

Taylor, M. (2011) Building social capital through rhetoric and public relations. *Management Communication Quarterly*, 25(3), 436–454.

Theaker, A. (ed.) (2008) *The public relations handbook*. London: Routledge.

Ulmer, R., Sellnow, T., & Seeger, W. (2018) *Effective crisis communication*, 4th edition. Thousand Oaks, CA: Sage.

Reports and Proposals

Focus:

- Proposals
- Business plans
- Problem-solving reports
- Visuals in reports

This chapter looks at longer business document types, in particular proposals, business plans and investigative reports. The guidelines and formats outlined here are based on standard, international conventions where English is the medium of communication. Keep in mind, however, that the format and structure of reports vary to a certain extent to suit the needs of the particular organization, writing situation and audience. As noted before, many companies have in-house templates that should be complied with. In all, however, the framework presented here will alert you to the factors that you should take into account when writing reports, and when creating templates and style guides for others to use.

As a professional in business or industry, the longer documents you will need to produce fall into two broad categories: *reports* on various issues to management and/or clients, and *articles* for professional associations and journals documenting the data you discovered in your experience. If you decide to develop your writing talents further, you might also publish popular interpretations of your work for non-specialist audiences, such as *blogs, essays* for creative non-fiction publications, and *journalistic features* for magazines. This chapter focuses on different types of reports.

Reports

In business contexts, you may be required to produce three types of reports: *descriptive, technical* and *analytical. Descriptive reports* inform the reader of events that have happened in the past or that are planned for the future, and are detailed and factual. *Technical reports* describe and explain specifications, components of equipment and system applications. *Analytical reports* usually deal with a problem by identifying the issues involved, investigating solutions and recommending action. Whereas descriptive and technical reports may be based entirely on facts, analytical reports include elements of persuasion and logical reasoning. Here we consider analytical reports.

Analytical reports

Here are some major types of analytical reports and their functions (see also Bargiela Chiappini & Nickerson, 1999; Bell & Smith, 2010; Kolin, 1998):

Proposals and submissions show the highest level of persuasion. A proposal argues for a particular course of action and often takes the form of a request for funding or formal authorization to pursue a particular project. While an investigative report researches a problem and suggests solutions, a proposal sets out a detailed project and in most cases includes a budget and resource requirements. Submissions argue for or against an issue to be decided by a responsible body. Members of the business community, for example, might make submissions for or against a new taxation bill under consideration by a government select committee.

Problem-solving reports analyse a problem and methodically recommend a specific course of action to solve this problem. They are also known as *investigative reports*. Such reports often require specialist knowledge and are commissioned by a client or management, who requests the writer to expertly judge certain actions and comment in detail on issues and events that relate to a particular situation.

Feasibility studies investigate a possible plan of action and advise on whether the action should be taken. For example, a software company might request a feasibility study to decide whether there is market potential to invest in a new virtual reality application. A feasibility study weighs projected costs against projected income, taking into account such aspects as demographic factors, market demand, the actions of competitors and resource requirements.

To better understand the difference in approach among these types of reports, consider this scenario. Assume you are the Director of Facilities Management in a company, in charge of ensuring security and smooth operation of building facilities. You are confronted with a problem of high electricity costs and inadequate heating. At the moment, the building uses electric heating. You could become aware of the problem in different ways, leading to different forms of communication.

For example, you could become aware of the problem through your own observations and decide to propose a change in heating from electric to gas. In this case, you would communicate your idea in the form of a *proposal*, which would support the claim that it would be more cost effective to replace the current electric heating with gas. Alternatively, you could be led to believe that the problem is serious and long-ranging, and requires more research to find an appropriate solution. In that case, you would undertake an investigation leading to a *recommendation report*, based on the problem that heating costs are high and the building is not warm enough. In your initial stage of research you are aware of the problem, but not the solution: you do not yet know if gas would be more cost effective. Finally, you could begin with the question, "Should we convert to gas heating?" and base your research and analysis accordingly, in order to answer it. Your results would then be presented in a *feasibility analysis*. This would analyse the problem and recommend action but its scope would be more limited than in an investigative report, because you would be considering only one possible solution to the problem.

These alternatives would take the following forms:

Proposal claim:
 It would be cheaper and more effective to replace the current electric heating with gas.

Trigger for investigation:
 Heating costs are high but, at the same time, the building is too cold.

Feasibility analysis:
 Would our heating situation work better if we converted to gas heating?

General guidelines for effective reports

All analytical reports share some common compositional and structural characteristics, so these guidelines are generally relevant to all:

- Include all the information the readers need. Pay special attention to the problem or situation that triggered the report, the methods used to gather information and the findings of the investigation or data-gathering. In design reports, include information about why you made specific design decisions and justify your choices.
- Structure your report so that readers can easily locate the information they want. For example, some readers will be interested in one or several sections. This is why reports are divided into titled and numbered sections. The executive summary and the section headings act as signposting showing the readers where to go to get what they want. Also, it is advisable to include a header or footer with identifying information on each page (such as the

title of the report and your name or the title of the project). Report sections may be distributed, so readers should know where each section came from.

- Write as clearly and concisely as possible without sacrificing content or detail. Keep in mind that clarity comes not only from style but also from the organization of information. The pattern you create in sequencing information communicates as much as the data you present. For example, presenting information in chronological order suggests that time and progression or change are important aspects; similarly, prioritising and listing information show the degree of importance attributed to each item in the list.

Paragraphing in analytical reports

As a researcher and writer, you will find that paragraphing offers a powerful tool for articulating and critiquing your ideas. As a communicator, you will find that paragraphing helps you to keep your reader focused on your topic and line of logic. Paragraphs enable you to divide your material into units that readers can readily cope with and assimilate into their understanding.

Report paragraphs tend to be longer than those in web content or magazine articles, but shorter than in essays. A length of four to six sentences is generally appropriate. By committing yourself to that kind of length you are serving the following objectives:

(i) The paragraphs are sufficiently short so that crucial pieces of information catch the reader's eye. Reports generally contain section headings for this reason.

(ii) But equally, the paragraphs are long enough to allow elaboration and analysis of issues. Enough space should be given so that cause and effect, chronological, comparison/contrast, and other relationships between ideas are clearly and fully expressed.

When composing report paragraphs, follow these guidelines:

1 **Avoid a succession of very short (one to two sentences) and very long (eight sentences or more) paragraphs.** The problem with short paragraphs is that they read disjointedly and present the reader with difficulty in linking your ideas together into a main message. With very long paragraphs, the readers need a pause so as to feel that they have read and understood a unit of the message. If you rush on without a paragraph break, the readers will soon feel overwhelmed and stop assimilating the ideas and interacting with the text.

2 **Present one main point or idea in each paragraph.** Avoid crowding a paragraph with too much vital information. If you have a large amount of reasoning or supporting examples to give for a point, break them into two

paragraphs. Bear in mind that people are adapted to taking in and committing to memory chunks of information that comprise between about five and seven items, so structure your paragraphs in a way that reflects this fact.

3 **Make sure there is enough cohesion within the paragraph.** That is, avoid listing a set of disconnected sentences. Similarly, provide adequate transition signals between paragraphs in one section. Show the reader how the idea of one paragraph is connected to the idea of the next paragraph in that section.

Writers have three main problems when composing paragraphs:

- The paragraph could contain too much information, which can confuse the reader as to what the main point is. This is a bit like a song with discordant rhythm or beat.
- The paragraph could be abrupt, containing incomplete information on the main point. This again loses the reader who may find it difficult to follow through a point and understand its relevance.
- The paragraph could give enough information on the main topic, but the sentences are disconnected and the paragraph lacks unity. This reads like a list of items with no connection and can be quite dull for the reader, who is forced to provide all the links.

Sections and section headings

As opposed to articles and essays, where headings are optional, reports require division of paragraphs into sections and headings for all sections. Headings summarize the point(s) of each section and make reading under pressure easier. Readers can scan a document and find information without having to read all the text. In reports, this is an important asset because, often, different people read different sections of the report. Also, headings give readers some breathing space, as they indicate where a section has ended. Finally, sections give depth and dimensionality to the report by adding levels. The main sections constitute the main level, subsections introduce subordinate levels, etc. When sectioning:

1 **Balance the sections so that information is distributed effectively across the report.** Avoid short, one-paragraph sections; also avoid putting the whole report in one long section. Use subsections for details or subordinate points of the idea of the main section. If information is important, do not bury it in a subsection, but devote a main section to it. On the whole, avoid sub-subsections, for simplicity and clarity. Sub-subsections add layers and therefore introduce more complexity in what could already be a complex report topic. Reduce the layers by analysing information, and thereby spreading it across fewer levels.

2 **Think carefully of the quantity and quality of the information you want to include in a heading.** If a heading is too vague or general, it defeats the purpose of signalling to the reader the content of its section. At the same time, if a heading is too long and detailed, it can slow down the flow of reading unnecessarily.

3 **Make sure all your headings of the same level have parallel structure.** When you choose a structure for all your headings, remain consistent throughout the report. For example, if you begin one heading for a main section with a gerund (an – ing form), the rest of the headings in main sections should also begin with a gerund. If you begin a heading with a noun, all headings should begin with nouns, and so on.

The importance of headings becomes clear in the *report outline*. A report outline lists the sections and subsections that you intend to use in your report. A client or project manager often asks for an outline to monitor the progress of the report, to consider extra funding, and similar reasons. It is important, therefore, that your headings are worded and structured in a way that highlights the content and significance of your project.

Numbering of report sections

Headings and subheadings are conventionally numbered according to **alphanumeric** or **decimal numbering** methods.

Alphanumeric numbering:
I. First main idea
   A. First subdivision of main idea
   B. Second subdivision of main idea
      1. First example
      2. Second example
         (a) First detail
         (b) Second detail
   C. Third subdivision of main idea
II. Second main idea

Decimal numbering:
1. First main idea
   1.1 First subdivision of main idea
   1.2 Second subdivision of main idea
      1.2.1 First example
      1.2.2 Second example
         1.2.2.1 First detail
         1.2.2.2 Second detail
   1.3 Third subdivision of main idea
2. Second main idea

Visuals

Visuals include diagrams, charts, tables, figures, graphs, photographs, drawings, clip art, and other pictorial or schematic representations. Visuals are alternative methods of presenting information and form a useful non-linear complement to the written word. Information presented diagrammatically or in pictorial form is memorable and can simplify, and thereby clarify, complicated data. When including a visual in a document, assess it in relation to two factors: *content,* that is, in terms of how it communicates meaning that is complementary to the meaning presented linguistically; and *design,* that is, in terms of its size and positioning on the page.

As regards content, these points are important:

- The visual should be necessary to clarify a point in the document. Do not include a visual just for decoration. The visual must be the best way to present the particular information you wish to express. It should convey a message more emphatically, more clearly or more concisely than written sentences, or it should clarify the meaning of the sentences.
- The kind of visual you have chosen (pie chart, image, table, etc.) should be the best for your purpose. For example, a line diagram may be inappropriate for discrete data.
- The visual must be introduced, discussed, interpreted and integrated in the text of the document. Remember that raw data is useless unless its relevance to the issue at hand is made clear. The reader should not have to figure out why the visual is included in the document, or what the significance of the data may be.
- The visual must stand alone in meaning. While it should be interpreted in the text of the document, it should also be self-explanatory and complete, and not obscure or confusing.
- All visuals must be numbered consecutively and given a specific, meaningful title. Include the title of a table above the table, and the title of a figure below the figure.
- As with all writing choices, visuals must be designed and formatted in a manner appropriate for the likely audience of the document. Will the visual be clear and appealing from the intended reader's perspective?
- If you have copied the visual from another document or website, remember to credit the source following the formatting required by your referencing style.
- If using a table, make all like elements (the factors to be compared) read down not across.

As regards arrangement and design, these points are important:

- Make the visual easy for your reader to find; the visual should closely follow the reference to it in the text. Where possible, format the document so that visuals do not appear on different pages from where they are mentioned in the text.
- Surround the visual with white space and do not clutter it. This makes it easier for the reader to absorb the information presented.
- Consider whether the visual would be better located in an appendix rather than in the body of the report. If the body of your report is becoming too cluttered, some visuals may be moved to an appendix. Any visual that takes up more than half a page should, ideally, be placed in an appendix.
- As a convention, the visual should take up no less than one third of a page, again, for reasons of clarity and visibility.
- Position the visual in alignment with the text, for balance.
- If using colours, note that by ordering colours from light to dark vertically or horizontally, elements will appear to be next to each other. This is because lighter colours tend to stand out and darker colours to recede (Table 7.1).

Table 7.1   Charts and Graphs

Here is a list of different kinds of charts and graphs with guidelines on their uses in documents.

Line graph

Useful for showing trends and fluctuations over time.

Column graph

Shows clearly comparisons of amounts. It is presented in vertical form.

Bar chart

Indicates proportions as they are related to each other. It is presented in horizontal form.

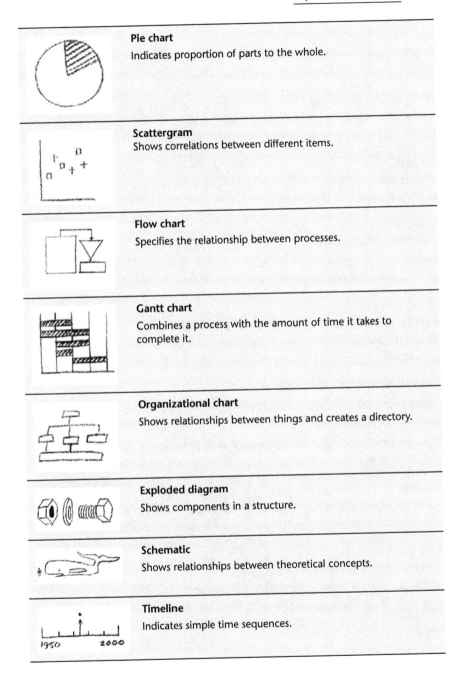

Pie chart

Indicates proportion of parts to the whole.

Scattergram

Shows correlations between different items.

Flow chart

Specifies the relationship between processes.

Gantt chart

Combines a process with the amount of time it takes to complete it.

Organizational chart

Shows relationships between things and creates a directory.

Exploded diagram

Shows components in a structure.

Schematic

Shows relationships between theoretical concepts.

Timeline

Indicates simple time sequences.

Proposals

Proposals are a very common type of document in professional settings. Even if your line of work does not put you in a position to write reports – say, if you are a trade journalist or a computer programmer – chances are that the time will come when you will need to submit a proposal in order to get approval and/or funding for a project. The following guidelines give an overview of the standard format and type of information associated with proposals. Many companies and funding agencies have a house-style template to be filled when submitting a proposal. If that is the case, follow the instructions (they will not be too different from the ones outlined here). If no guidelines are offered, use the model presented here.

Proposals are initiated in two main ways: either you have an innovative idea that you believe will benefit an organization or company and want to sell it to them, or you respond to a request for ideas published by an organization. In the first case, the proposal is *unsolicited*. In the second, it is a *request for proposals (RFP)*. Unsolicited proposals are investigator-initiated, and, therefore, there is often a greater need to sell the concept because it is novel and innovative. On the other hand, an RFP or a programme announcement (PA) calls for research in a defined area or requests an answer to a specific question. In this case, it is a matter of matching one's expertise, ideas and plans to the solicitation.

Preliminary work for proposals

To maximize your chances for success, follow these guidelines (see also Johnson-Sheenan, 2002; Taylor, 2009):

1   **Work on the conceptual framework of your idea** until you have good control over it.
2   **Articulate your conceptual framework.** Sit down with friends and/or colleagues and practise explaining your idea to them in a brief manner. If it is well conceptualized, you should be able to articulate it in a matter of sentences, over three minutes. Entertain their questions and make notes of the questions that occur. Reoccurring questions are probably indicative of problems in your communication or weaknesses in the concept. Use this feedback to improve your concept.
3   **Investigate the current and previous research.** Make sure that no one has already done the work you have in mind, or if they have, that there is something different or necessary about your approach. You are going to have to convince the readers that your activities are unique and justified.

A major "howler" is to be informed that your project has already been done, or that you have missed a fundamental piece of work in the research.

4 **Do your homework on the agency or company.** Make sure that your idea falls within the topics they are interested in (especially if writing externally). Also, get as much information as you can on their required document formats. This will determine what attitude and style you should adopt. Familiarize yourself with the culture of the company and choose your words and expression in tune with this culture. If your proposal is unsolicited, find out about the funding capacity of the agency or company. Remember that small agencies cannot afford to fund high budget projects, so it would be a waste of time submitting ambitious proposals to them.

5 **Assess your need for collaborators.** Sometimes having collaborators can substantially strengthen your proposal. However, it is important that, from the project's inception, everyone understands their role. Make sure that the content of each member's contribution and time allocation is understood and accepted by all.

Proposal components

Table 7.2 shows the body elements that most proposals contain. More or less space is given to each element depending on the nature of the proposal. Therefore, some of these topics would constitute sections in some proposals, and subsections in others.

Table 7.2   Proposal Components
Project description   Identify the problem or question to be addressed and describe its implications. Give some background on the proposed project, including results from prior research. Show a clear connection between the problem, lack or gap that you identified and the role of the proposed project in dealing with it. Visuals that depict the relationship of your work to the current knowledge base or model base are often helpful in getting your message across.
Objectives or specific aims   State concisely and, where possible, in measurable terms the specific aims of the project and the hypotheses that underlie those aims or objectives. Distinguish between short-term plans and long-term goals. It is always useful to describe how the project can evolve and develop if the expected results are achieved (in other words, what the organization is buying in the long run).

Methodology

Describe precisely how you will achieve your objectives. If several outcomes (or result scenarios) are plausible, describe them. Give alternative courses of action in the event that results occurring early lead you away from your original method – anticipate outcomes and have a plan to deal with them.

Evaluation

In certain proposals, especially in those for projects with long-term implications, describe plans for evaluating the project. Explain how you will know if the project is producing positive results.

Personnel and qualifications and facilities

Identify who will perform the various activities or procedures described in the plan. Provide justification for each individual appropriate to his/her level of involvement and include the qualifications of key project personnel. Make clear the reasons that make you or your team the best candidates for the project. Describe the resources that are already available for performance of the project.

Budget and justification

Work out your budget very carefully and give as much detail as possible. Itemize each cost and justify its relevance to the project. The budget is usually presented in cost sheet format. Items commonly included are salaries and wages, fringe benefits, equipment, travel, supplies, publication charges, postage, telephone, consultants, subcontracts and indirect costs. A justification section usually accompanies the budget, which explains how you arrived at your totals. Briefly explain how budget items were estimated and why these items are needed, if not obvious.

Sources cited

If applicable, include a list of the sources cited in the proposal, using a method of referencing that is acceptable in the subject area of your topic.

CV/biographical sketch (optional)

In external proposals, you may need to "sell" yourself as well as your concept. Include some details about your professional background if you think this will influence the reception of your proposal positively. In many cases, attaching a CV is a requirement for proposals.

Appendices (optional)

Possible items include:

- Facilities descriptions
- Letters of support, illustrations
- Maps

- Extensive bibliography
- Other material not easily incorporated into the body of the proposal.

Proposal to an editor

If you decide to submit a feature article for publication in a specialist magazine or have an idea for a book in your area of expertise, you will need to contact an editor for approval. Although similar, in general aspects, to the model outlined above, a book or article proposal differs in some respects.

Publishers' websites include guidelines on how to submit proposals. Table 7.3 gives an outline of the components of a book proposal.

Table 7.3   Book Proposal Components
Description of subject and its position in the market   Describe the topic of the book and explain why it is significant or worthwhile in the current market. Position the book in relation to interests, needs and debates in the wider social context. Propose a title.
Distinctive features   Explain the features of the book that distinguish it and give it a unique identity. Do some homework first to see what is already on offer in the market in order to clearly identify the features that make your book distinctive.
Primary and secondary markets   Describe the target readers of the book. Will they be reading it for entertainment, instruction or other purposes? Will the book interest one particular demographic or psychographic group, or will it have different types of readers? How do you know?
Main competitors   This is a very important section, because it shows that you have researched the topic and know what is available in the market. If the book has direct competitors, you must justify why there would still be a market for your proposed book. Select two or three competing books and describe them in some detail. Explain how your book is different and why this difference is valuable.
Qualifications of applicant   Attach a CV, or give a biographical sketch, highlighting the qualities that enable you to write a book on the proposed topic.
Summary/outline of chapters   Give an outline of the proposed chapters, with a description of each chapter, usually of about half a page. If you have a sample chapter, attach it to the proposal as an example of your approach and style.

Table 7.4 shows the components of a proposal to the editor of a magazine.

Table 7.4   Feature Article Proposal Components

Description of topic

Describe your topic and its scope, explaining the angle, slant or point of view that you will take. Remember to mention the proposed title (although the editor might change it).

Significance and innovation

Explain why your article will interest the target audience of this particular magazine. Why would the magazine benefit by including such an article in its repertoire? Remember that you need to convince the editor that your article will contribute to readers' interest in buying the magazine. Make sure you have investigated the magazine to see if they have already published on the topic.

Sources

List and briefly describe five sources of information that you will use. Justify your choices by explaining the importance of the sources in the relevant field of research. Will you be conducting interviews or primary research, or will your article be based on secondary sources?

Personal information

Describe your qualifications for writing this article, including any special expertise or knowledge in the subject area. Explain also what has spurred your interest in the topic.

Convincing evidence in proposals

The main function of proposals is to persuade. Selecting the most appropriate evidence or reasoning, therefore, is vital. The best way to achieve this is to analyse the funding agency's mission, values, policies and expectations, and to present your project in response to these. A project is acceptable and worthwhile or not depending on particular contexts of reception. Merits of the project are evaluated according to different sets of standards, and knowing these standards maximizes your chances of being successful. Internal proposals have a different scope and impact than external proposals, which may involve the welfare of the public at large. The range and duration the project's impact, and the cost, are decisive elements in the persuasive force of a proposal, and you should take these into account when planning your strategy.

Argumentation theorist Stephen Toulmin (2003), for example, found that "logical" arguments are not universal, and different communities have their own expectations of the reasoning process. What is convincing evidence for natural scientists, for instance, may not be convincing for marketing experts, and what is convincing for marketing experts may not be convincing for engineers. This is corroborated by rhetoric specialists. For example, Gerard Hauser points out that,

> When we seek a project extension, argue for a raise, interview for a job [...] we are involved in acts that require good reasons. Good reasons allow our audience and ourselves to find a shared basis for cooperating [...]. You can use marvellous language, tell great stories, provide exciting metaphors, speak in enthralling tones, and even use your reputation to advantage, but what it comes down to is that you must speak to your audience with reasons they understand. (Hauser, 1986, p. 71)

In addition to learning as much as possible about the funding organization, there are two ways to increase your chances of producing a persuasive document. One is to run your proposal by peers and mentors, who are knowledgeable on the issues covered, especially if they have been successful in obtaining funding by the organization to which you are applying. Since many projects in business and industry are collaborative, it should be easy to exchange ideas and get feedback. The second way is to consider your project from the recipient's point of view, and to brainstorm as many possible objections as you can. Play the "devil's advocate", or get someone to play it for you, and criticize the proposed project from different angles. Table 7.5 lists some common objections to business proposals.

Table 7.5   Common Objections to Proposals

The proposed project is not necessary or is not valuable.

The project is unrealistically ambitious or not well thought out.

The requested budget is not well justified so the result doesn't seem to justify the cost.

The methods are not carefully thought out or are not suited to the objectives.

The applicant doesn't seem well suited to undertake the project.

Table 7.6 lists some common objections to book proposals.

Table 7.6   Common Objections to Book Proposals

The topic is not in the publisher's range of interests.

There are enough books on the market that deal with this topic (or the publisher has enough books on this topic).

The target market is not well defined.

The topic is too specialized to interest a wide audience.

The scope (proposed content) is too broad or too narrow.

Table 7.7 shows the layout of a business proposal.

Table 7.7   Layout of Business Proposals
Title page
Executive summary (for longer proposals)
Table of contents (for longer proposals)
Description of project
Objectives of project
Benefits of project
Proposed method
Evaluation of project (for projects with long-term goals)
Facilities and personnel
Budget
Proposer's CV (for external proposals)

Business plans

When starting your own business, you need to attract investors, high-quality employees, collaborators and other desired relationships. To achieve this, you must persuade those groups that you are well organized, have a clear, realistic and ambitious vision, and are aware of competitors and market needs. The business plan, which many see as a subgenre of the proposal because of its persuasive approach, articulates these elements and reflects your drive and professional competence. Like other important business documents, a business plan involves identifying the target audience, gathering accurate and convincing data, and carefully sectioning and organizing the information in an accessible way (see also Kawasaki, 2011; Nesheim, 2000). The key sections of the body of a business plan are as follows:

Company and product/service description: This covers the company's mission, history, current situation, strategies and plans for the future. The start-up, or new company, is intrinsically linked with the products and/or services that it offers and which define it. Therefore, discuss the vision of the company in relation to what it produces. Divide this into subsections for clarity.

The market and competition: This section defines the company's target market, the industry as a whole, current and potential clients/buyers, and competitors. The section should explain how buying decisions are made, how the market is segmented, what your intended market position is and what your defensive strategy will be to deal with competitors. Show that you are aware of how your product or service is positioned in the local and/or international market, and that you have a clear vision of how it will be distinctive in relation to competitors. Try to formulate your product in terms of a Unique Selling Point (USP), a feature or quality that defines it and distinguishes it from others. Develop a marketing plan and indicate your advertising strategy.

Management and organization: This section describes members of the management team, their backgrounds and qualifications, as well as needs for new recruits. In this section, discuss also key outside advisors and collaborators. Here you are showing how your executive team reflects the vision and mission of the company and the intended stricture of the company. For example, if your product is progressive, it wouldn't help to envision a hierarchical or traditional company structure, as this would conflict with the ideals of the product. Modern, cutting-edge companies are known for their experimental and informal company structure and work environment.

The future and risk management: Show vision for the future by anticipating possible risks and indicating you have contingency plans and ways to avoid these risks. Include some information on investors' exit strategy, showing that you have thought of the best interests of your investors.

Financial information: This presents financial forecasts and is often the most carefully scrutinized section. Here, include detailed balance sheets and statements of cash flow and income. Include a funding request that states how much money is needed and for what purposes. The more organized and well thought out this section is, the more likely it is that investors and potential collaborators will develop respect for your foresight and judgment.

Entrepreneurial "guru" Guy Kawasaki (2004) lists the following points in his advice to those starting out in business plan writing:

- **Do not exceed twenty pages in length**: As noted elsewhere in this book, conciseness is attractive in business contexts.
- **Select one person to write the plan**: Although the plan should reflect the spirit of the management team, the writing of the business plan should be coherent and not patchy.
- **Bind the plan with a staple**: Ornamental presentations do not add any value to the plan. Most readers will be looking for content, not window-dressing. When submitting a hard copy, use simple paper stapled at the top.

- **Simplify your financial projections to two pages**: Investors and other interested parties want to know your financial plans, but not in extreme detail, nor for more than the first five years.
- **Include the key metrics, such as the number of customers, locations, and resellers**: For Kawasaki, this is even more important than actual financial projections because they give a better view of the organization's plans.
- **Include the assumptions that drive your financial projections**: This gives more substance to the projections, because it explains the rationale on which you based them (pp. 70–71).

Table 7.8 shows the layout of a business plan.

Table 7.8   Layout of Business Plan
Title page
Executive summary
Table of contents
List of figures
Company description
Market and marketing plan
Competition and positioning
Management team
Risk management and exit strategy
Financial information
Appendices (optional)

Problem-solving reports

As opposed to a research report, which is usually written to document and publicize research to peers, a problem-solving, consulting or investigative report may be written by a specialist or group of specialists to a non-expert audience. Situations leading to a problem-solving report include consultancies, where an expert, or team of experts, is recruited by an organization to identify issues involved in a problem and to recommend solutions, and commissioned investigations, where an authority puts together an impartial board of investigators to ascertain the reasons of an issue of public concern. Investigative reports may be written internally, when the investigators are members of the organization, or externally, when the investigators are recruited from a "neutral zone".

An investigation follows the specifications of a *brief* or *terms of reference,* and leads to the writing of a report. Like other analytical reports, an investigative report is divided into three main parts, the *front matter,* the *body* and the *end matter.*

Front matter

The front matter includes these components:

Letter/memo of transmittal

The letter or memo of transmittal indicates that the report is being formally delivered to the person or organization that requested it. Write a letter if the report is for someone outside your organization, and a memo for someone within your organization. The letter or memo of transmittal identifies the report topic and scope or extent of the investigation, and communicates key findings.

Title page

This is a single page stating the title of the report, the name and organization of the author and the date of delivery.

Acknowledgements (optional)

This lists the names of people who helped with the investigation of the report and gives a brief description of their contributions.

Executive summary

Most business reports of more than 1500 words include an executive summary. This summarizes the whole report and should be written as a self-contained piece: readers of the executive summary should get a clear idea of the contents of the report. Executive summaries may be written in a block paragraph but may also include bullet points depending on context. Executive summaries are one of the most important and widely read sections in a report. It is important not to confuse the executive summary with the introduction, which introduces but does not summarize the report, and is part of the body. Include these elements in the executive summary of an investigative report:
- A description of the scope and objectives of the report
- A summary of the main results
- An outline of recommendations or solutions.

Table of contents

This lists the sections and subsections of the report with their page numbers. The table of contents acts as an outline of the report.

List of figures

This lists the titles of the visuals (tables, figures, charts, etc.) included in the report and the page numbers where the visuals are to be found in the report.

Body of report

The body of the report is divided into these components:

Introduction

This should lead readers from information they already know to information they need to acquire. The introduction may be only a paragraph long, or it may be a major section in itself, depending on the length of the report. Start with an overview statement indicating the general subject matter and context of the report. Then answer the following questions, adapted as necessary for the specific nature of your report:

- Background: why was the report requested in the first place? What was the change, problem or issue that led people to believe a report was needed?
- Purpose: what are the specific objectives of the report?
- Scope: what issues are covered in the report? Refer to the brief given when the report was requested. Indicate the criteria used for evaluating the problem.
- Research methods: how were the data in the report obtained? What primary and/or secondary data were used? (If your methods were experimental and complicated, a separate section should be devoted to them, after the introduction.)
- Structure: preview the report structure.
- Limitations (optional): what issues are not covered in the report? What are the limitations of the research methods selected? What assumptions have been made?

Discussion

The middle part of the report is the largest and most time-consuming section, and is further subdivided into subsections with headings. Use any one of the following methods, or a combination of methods, for organising the discussion section. Make sure that the method you choose is the most appropriate for presenting and explaining information to the target audience, and that it adheres to the expectations and logical patterns associated with that audience:

- General to specific
- More important to less important

- Comparison and contrast of points
- Classification and analysis of points
- Problems and solutions
- Cause and effect
- Cost and benefits (advantages and disadvantages)
- Chronological
- Spatial

Block and point by point format

When discussing aspects of a topic, issues in a debate, or possible solutions to problems, you can use a *block form* or *point by point* presentation. In the block form, you combine all aspects, issues or problems together, and then analyse them or propose solutions. In the point by point form, you take each aspect, issue or problem and analyse it or propose a solution to it, before proceeding to the next. Table 7.9 shows the two formats.

Table 7.9 Discussion Writing Formats for Reports	
Block form	**Point by point form**
Factor A	Factor A
Item 1	*Item 1*
Item 2	Factor B
Item 3	*Item 1*
Factor B	Factor A
Item 1	*Item 2*
Item 2	Factor B
Item 3	*Item 2*

Conclusion

This interprets the facts set out in the discussion. It answers the question "So what?" Do not introduce new material here; instead, lead straight on to the list of recommendations. In fact, in some reports, conclusion and recommendations are included in one section. In shorter reports, you can omit this section.

Recommendations

Recommendations suggest specific actions. Again, no new material should appear in this section, and recommended actions need not be justified (their justification should be clear from the discussion part of the report). Number recommendations and place them in priority order. This facilitates referring to individual recommendations in subsequent discussions. The executive summary and the recommendations are arguably the most important report sections, so extra attention should be paid to them. Recommendations must be realistic, taking into account factors such as cost, location and current policy or practice within the organization.

Effective recommendations not only state what action ought to be taken, but also specify who should be responsible for implementing it and within what time frame. Recommendations should address *what, where, when, who* and *how* (the *why* having been examined in the discussion section). Make sure all recommendations are grammatically parallel.

End matter

The end matter of the report is divided into these components:

References or Bibliography

These list the sources cited in the report. If a source has been influential, but you have not quoted from it or referred to it, list it under the heading "Bibliography", which should immediately follow the list of references. Use a referencing style suited to your field (APA, MLA, Chicago, etc.).

Glossary (optional)

This defines technical and specialized terms that are not likely to be familiar to readers of the report. Use audience adaptation methods to determine which terms will need to be defined and which will already be known by target readers. Items in the glossary are listed in alphabetical order.

Appendices (optional)

An appendix is a part of your report that is relevant to the main theme of the report, but is not essential. An appendix may include material that is too complex, specialized or detailed to be included in the body of the report. Material that supplements or illustrates points made in the body of the report is also suitable for an appendix. Keep in mind that the reader should be able to understand the main points of the report without needing to read the appendices. At the same time, appendices are useful in cases of primary and secondary audiences that may not have the same level of technical knowledge. In such cases you could include in an appendix specifications or explanations targeted to specific groups.

Examples of documents and data printed as appendices include:

- A copy of a questionnaire used in field research
- A list of questions used in interviews
- Copies of letters or pamphlets
- Maps, particularly if they take up a whole page
- Detailed lists of raw data.

Always refer to the appendix in the body of the report and indicate its relevance to the reader. Letter appendices consecutively (Appendix A, Appendix B, Appendix C, and so on) and start each one on a separate page.

Table 7.10 shows the layout of investigative reports.

Table 7.10   Layout of Investigative Reports
Letter or memo of transmittal
Front Matter
Title page
Acknowledgements (optional)
Executive summary
Table of contents
List of figures
Body
1. Introduction
2. Heading One
1.1. Subheading One
1.2. Subheading Two
2. Heading Two
2.1. Subheading One
2.2. Subheading Two
3. Heading Three
3.1. Subheading One
3.2. Subheading Two
4. Recommendations
End Matter
References
Glossary (optional)
Appendices (optional)

Brief, executive summaries and recommendations

Below is the brief to a problem-solving report. This is followed by the executive summary of the actual report written in response to this brief and the list of recommendations. Notice how each is connected to the others.

Brief

Law Limited, a legal company, has been having difficulties retaining its junior and intermediate level lawyers. This is an industry-wide problem with law firms generally losing more than half of their junior lawyers before they reach an intermediate level (three to four years' experience). The Chief Executive of Law Limited has asked you to prepare a report investigating the problem both within the company and inter-company. Write a report that identifies pertinent issues while taking into account the interests of the company as well as the views of the junior lawyers. Outline a few alternative solutions, evaluate them and propose the best solution justifying your recommendation.

Executive summary

This report examines why Law Limited loses approximately 40% of its junior solicitors before their fourth year at the firm. The results are based on an analysis of current employment practice at the firm, a survey carried out on 80% of junior staff, and comparative material that documents a similar situation within the law industry in other English-speaking countries. The report demonstrates that, for purposes of retention, the solicitors can be classified into three classes: those who will leave regardless of the action taken (30%), those who will stay if action is taken (65%) and those who will stay regardless of whether action is taken or not (5%). Based on these findings, the report suggests that retention strategies should be aimed at making the solicitors feel valued and challenged. Methods proposed include a bonus scheme, a mentoring scheme and a professional development programme.

Recommendations

Following the results of the surveys discussed above, this report recommends the following actions:

1 Implement a bonus scheme rewarding lawyers that surpass a given level of performance. The level of performance and the bonus should be decided by management in consultation with appointed junior lawyer representatives. Both type of bonus and level of performance should be reviewed every three years to ensure their relevance to changing industry standards.
2 Organize a mentoring scheme where senior lawyers are paired with junior counterparts to discuss problems, aspirations and plans.
3 Organize formal briefing meetings with management and junior staff to discuss problems or concerns. These meetings should take place at least twice a year.

4   Make changes to the budget to ensure that enough funds are available to maintain a regular orientation/professional development programme. The recommended time allocated to this programme is 15 hours per year for each staff member.

Examples of reports

Example One: Business Plan

This is a business plan written by the owner of a Fitness Club, Life, to obtain funds in order to expand his business. The plan ends with financial information, and a three-year projection of profit, which is not included here.

Life fitness club

1 Company Description

Life is Berman Park's premier destination for private training, group fitness and functional training programmes. We specialize in offering private training from certified personal trainers in a well-designed, clean, well-maintained and safe facility. **Life** offers yearly and monthly membership packages, a variety of cardio machines, free weights, selectorized machines, locker rooms with private showers, convenient parking that is steps away from the entrance, towel service and flat screen TVs.

Life prides itself on keeping overhead costs low. We have no employees or staff, opting instead to utilize personal trainers on a contract basis, which is standard for the industry. Our only major overhead costs are for rent, equipment leases, utilities and part-time bookkeeping.

Life is a boutique health club with 1,200-plus open memberships and between 20 and 35 private trainers who bring their clients (numbering between 4+ and 20+ clients per trainer) to the facility for private workouts. **Life's** retention rate is high – more than 90% renew their memberships annually. Altogether, there are between 400+ and 700+ private workout sessions at the facility per week, in addition to 100+ individuals per week who use the facilities on their own.

The average age of the health club member is 40.7 years with an average income of $75,000. Most members at **Life** are between 32 and 60 years old. The difference between the demographic of the average health club member and the **Life** member is our retention rate. People who work out at **Life** are serious about working out; they expect a high-energy, social experience.

Now, **Life** is looking to expand and increase our monthly income by offering multiple classes per day, to be taught by highly-qualified instructors. This expansion plan is the result of new-client and continuing-client interest. We get near-daily requests from current members, prospective members and trainers to expand our services into classes. Currently, **Life** offers one boot camp class per week, which is always filled to capacity, and smaller semi-private classes taught by individual private trainers during the week. Because of the success of these offerings, we not only see the need for expansion but feel confident that expanding in this area will create more income and a higher profit margin for the facility.

2 Market Analysis

The International Health, Racquet and Sportsclub Association (IHRSA), a nonprofit trade association serving the global health club and fitness industry, states that the country has 200 health clubs that serve more than two million people. More locally, there are 10 health clubs in the Berman Park area, where **Life** is located, representing nearly 10% of total health clubs in the region.

In Berman Park, there are three large national health club facilities. All are large facilities with spas, classes, child care and state-of-the-art machines. One is open around the clock and is conveniently located in a major retail mall at the corner of Gardenia and Tulip Boulevards. Parking is free but not easily accessible (requiring a long walk, and a lift and/or escalator ride). The second is not quite as large, is in need of remodelling and has limited parking. The third, on the border of Berman Park, is brand new, recently built on a major street, and is the only Berman Park health club to offer a pool. However, all of these facilities are oversold and crowded during primetime workout hours, necessitating wait times for popular machines.

Meanwhile, **Life** attracts a more select clientele than those who frequent the large national health club chains. **Life** members are upwardly mobile professionals living and working in Berman Park. Our members have disposable income and open schedules during the day. Berman Park has among the higher household incomes in the city (rated as $125,000 and up). The average household in Berman Park has a net worth of nearly $1 million and almost 50% of residents have a university degree.

Our plan to offer daily classes would be a success from the start. For example, Barry's Bootcamp, located about a half-mile east of **Life**, at the Queen Centre near the corner of Gardenia and Willow Avenue, offers 64 classes on weekdays, beginning at 5:00 am and continuing to 9:00 pm; and 14 classes at weekends. The cost is $25/class but packages are available (that is, 10 classes for $200.00; 20 classes for $350.00; 50 classes for $700.00).

We have already established the loyalty of the members at **Life** (with a 90+% retention rate) and feel that adding classes taught by expert fitness instructors and private trainers known to the clientele will set us apart from other boutique health facilities in the area. We are not a chain franchise that depends on numbers, and therefore our competitive advantage in this area is the ability to provide smaller, more personalized classes that will give our members the opportunity for higher success.

We anticipate that within six months from renting a new space and marketing classes, we would be offering a significant number of classes. Assuming we initially rented space in July 2020, we would expect to gain a majority of our revenue from classes by 2021. For 2021, on the conservative end, if **Life** offers 5 classes per day @ $20/class, our additional revenue would be as follows:

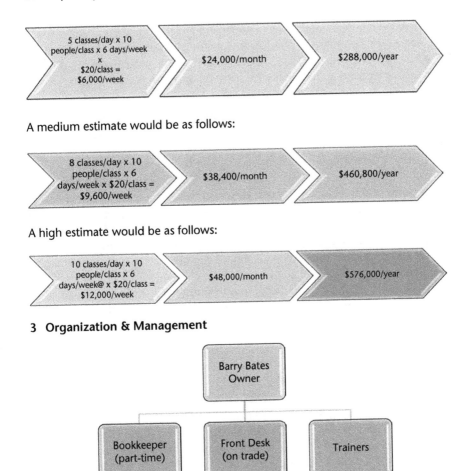

5 classes/day x 10 people/class x 6 days/week x $20/class = $6,000/week → $24,000/month → $288,000/year

A medium estimate would be as follows:

8 classes/day x 10 people/class x 6 days/week x $20/class = $9,600/week → $38,400/month → $460,800/year

A high estimate would be as follows:

10 classes/day x 10 people/class x 6 days/week@ x $20/class = $12,000/week → $48,000/month → $576,000/year

3 Organization & Management

Barry Bates
Owner

Bookkeeper (part-time) | Front Desk (on trade) | Trainers

The **Life** Fitness organizational structure is elegantly simple: there is the owner (Barry Bates), a part-time bookkeeper and private trainers.

4 Organizational Structure

Barry Bates is the sole creator and 100% owner of **Life**. He utilizes the services of a part-time bookkeeper and there is a trainer who watches the facility at night, answering the phones and selling memberships and/or private training. Beyond that, there are 20 to 30 private trainers who pay the facility "rent" to bring their clients in to train at **Life**.

5 Ownership

Information

Barry Bates has been involved with sports and athletics since the age of seven. He was a junior league golfer and an avid wrestler in high school. In 1989, at the age of 17, he began working at Gold's Gym and after accumulating experience working at that facility, he spent the next ten years managing gyms and serving as Fitness Director for many of them.

From 1998 to 2005, Barry owned and operated a successful martial arts training school in Berman Park, which he sold for $500,000 in order to devote his time to **Life**.

Barry is a licensed personal trainer and is certified by many accredited personal training organizations. In addition, he is certified in CPR and other emergency field training techniques. He is also trained for medical emergencies and has educational background in kinesiology, biomechanics, rehabilitating injuries and martial arts. He excels in gym management, gym and fitness consultation, gym and class setup and layout, membership retention, private training organization, gym build-out, equipment purchasing, private training and day-to-day operation of clubs.

In October, 2004, Barry opened **Life** with two trainers and 15 members. Those numbers have climbed considerably in the past 11 years, as **Life** now has between 20 to 35 private trainers and 1,200+ members. In addition, **Life** currently has a database numbering over 7,000 individuals.

6 Service and product lines

Barry would like **Life** to offer fitness classes in Aerobics, Yoga, Spinning, Pilates, Kickboxing and Strength Training. With the success of such facilities as Barry's Bootcamp (see above), and the number of such classes available online through subscription services, we know the demand for classes is there. **Life** would expand conservatively – with five classes a day – and, when interest and demand grows, we will expand to eight classes a day and then to ten classes a day.

7 Marketing & Sales

Life is prepared to hire an outside consultant to help us promote the gym and our new expansion of classes. This consultant will have expertise in best practices for social media. In addition, we will embark on a regional print advertising campaign. We have always had strong word of mouth and we expect this to continue and even grow when we expand to offering classes.

8 Requested Funds

Life requests a five-year loan of $100,000. This amount will allow Barry to lease additional space of approximately 2,600 square feet. Initially, **Life** will need roughly $85,000 for start-up costs. These include a build-out in the new facility for the new fitness classes. New flooring, mirrors, a sound system and other build-out expenses will cost roughly $70,000. During the time of the build-out (approximately two months), **Life** will be paying approximately $6,000 per month in rent.

Barry would like to have roughly $40,000 on top of the initial start-up costs because this represents approximately six months of rent for the new space. This will help alleviate concerns about any delays in getting the build-out completed, obtaining any needed permits and accounting for any other unforeseen delays to running fitness classes.

As you can see in the next section, "Financial Projections", we anticipate that we can build strong returns from this initial $100,000.

Example Two: Consulting Report

This report analysed the market situation of BlackBerry, which, while once the leader in mobile phone technology, was surpassed by competitors Apple and Android in recent years. The report assesses the strategy of BlackBerry, leading to a set of recommendations on how the company could improve its profile. The extract included here begins with the executive summary and ends with the recommendations. The reference list is not included.

BlackBerry: Choosing the vision for a secure future

Executive Summary

This report examines BlackBerry Limited, a mobile communications company founded in 1984 that enjoyed success until 2011 before deteriorating under the pressure of strong competition. BlackBerry provides smartphones and additional technological services and solutions to consumers globally. It has a strong online following but has been unable to translate its social media reach into company sales. The company has operated at a loss since 2012 and needs to make a change in order to survive going forward. BlackBerry's inability to compete with Apple and Google (Android) in the smartphone space calls for a re-focus of company initiative. The company must alter its brand and establish an online presence that properly represents its competitive advantage. By reinventing a mission statement that emphasizes security and device protection, the company can build a brand with a purpose. Once this is determined, BlackBerry can specifically target those who value its strengths, and align its message to enhance its online presence. Ultimately, the company must recreate its identity in order to attract business and secure a future in the industry.

1 Introduction
1.1 Background

Research in Motion Limited (RIM) released its first product in 1999, the same year that the Canadian-headquartered company entered America on the NASDAQ stock market. The product, RIM 850, was one of the first wireless devices capable of sending messages and emails, and effectively connecting users to their corporate lives outside of the office. Three years later, they released the BlackBerry; it was the first in a series of mobile devices that soon expanded to provide cellular phone, wireless email and Internet capabilities (Woods, 2013, n.p.). The BlackBerry phone is widely seen as a pioneer in the "smartphone" market, an industry that has since consumed the world. Recognizing the root of its popularity and successes, the company eventually renamed itself in 2013 to BlackBerry Limited ("BlackBerry" or the "Company").

BlackBerry revolutionized the mobile industry upon its smartphone release at the turn of the century. It quickly established itself as an industry leader, but has been unable to retain its market share since the introduction of the iPhone and Android services in 2007 and 2008 respectively. The strong competition has threatened to run BlackBerry out of business. In 2019, BlackBerry continues to release new phones, but is incapable of drawing the traction that Apple and Google have secured. The loyal following BlackBerry once had is fading, and the message they continue to deliver is not resonating with consumers. In order to survive, the Company needs to make a change.

1.2 Scope & Objectives

The primary focus of this report is to suggest reasons for BlackBerry's recent financial struggle and recommend a plan of action. I chose to focus on the messages spread to consumers, recognizing a failure in translation of marketing outreach to company sales. Space limitations prevent the report from analysing consumer preference and demand. Consumer surveys could provide a better understanding surrounding the public desire for more secure devices and help to establish a more specific target audience. Furthermore, a geographical understanding of the global need for increased security and device protection could be beneficial in determining a worldwide approach for a future marketing campaign.

2 BlackBerry, Then & Now
2.1 Rise of BlackBerry

BlackBerry virtually introduced the smartphone. With its email capabilities and trademark QWERTY keyboard, the phones became an icon in the business world. The devices gained popularity with corporate enterprises and government agencies, as companies offered standardized work phones with practical functions. Increasing its focus towards individual consumers, the brand became a status symbol. With competition still relatively new to the space in January 2010, BlackBerry enjoyed a 43% share in the U.S. smartphone market (De Cagna, 2014, p. 16). Sales grew alongside this market penetration, and in 2011, BlackBerry reported revenues of nearly $20 billion, the highest in company history (Research in Motion Limited, 2012, p. 120). Unfortunately, this trend did not persist, as consumers began to switch preference.

2.2 Financial Fallout

Apple, Google and Microsoft all compete with the BlackBerry platform. It became clear in 2007 that BlackBerry's "first-to-market" advantage was not sustainable. Apple released the first generation iPhone, and the media quickly dubbed it the "BlackBerry killer". BlackBerry tried to respond with its first touchscreen device, The Storm, but its planned release was delayed several months. When it finally entered the market, the public bashed it as inferior to the iPhone's technology. At that time, rather than listen to consumer requests for features similar to the iPhone – "faster browser, more responsive touchscreen, or more diverse applications" – the Company's management suggested they would only lead to more expensive data and a shorter battery life (De Cagna, 2014, p. 24).

Another major challenge that BlackBerry faced was a divide between its two distinct groups of buyers: those who valued design and "coolness" as found in the iPhone and Android, and the "corporate and government technology executives" who did not want unnecessary features, such as a camera or applications that could compromise security (De Cagna, 2014, p. 35). BlackBerry still increased revenues due to international sales to 2011, but because management failed to identify a preferred strategy, the continuing operations lost effect on consumers. As competing devices gained momentum, BlackBerry's share of smartphone subscribers fell drastically (see Figure 7.1).

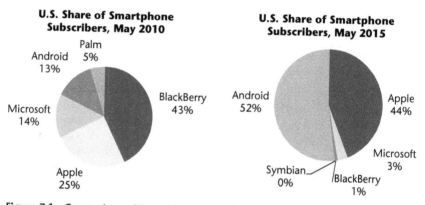

U.S. Share of Smartphone Subscribers, May 2010

Palm 5%
Android 13%
Microsoft 14%
Apple 25%
BlackBerry 43%

U.S. Share of Smartphone Subscribers, May 2015

Android 52%
Apple 44%
Microsoft 3%
BlackBerry 1%
Symbian 0%

Figure 7.1   Comparison of Smartphone Subscribers by Company, 2010–2015

Financial performance declined along with the share of subscribers. Once a 20-billion dollar company (and still $18 billion in 2012), BlackBerry dropped to a measly $3.3 billion in revenue by 2015. The Company reported a net loss in each of the last three years including a devastating $5.8 billion loss in fiscal year 2014. In order to mitigate these losses, in 2018 BlackBerry cut Research & Development by over $400,000 and decreased advertising and marketing spending by 55.4% (BlackBerry Limited, 2018, p. 73). To make matters worse, Apple recently released its new generation iPhone and continues to drive consumer demand.

3 Marketing

In order to determine the proper response to a series of net losses, and develop a strategy for the Company's future, it is important to first understand the relationship between BlackBerry and its consumers.

3.1 Online Presence

In 2019, BlackBerry is active on most forms of social media. Over their years of success, they have amassed a significant following that they can reach on a daily basis. While it is useful to have a strong following, BlackBerry must recognize their current situation. BlackBerry posts on Facebook, Twitter and LinkedIn every day. Typical posts include company news, phone and product reviews, and occasional industry trends and concerns. YouTube is utilized when videos are available. Several videos allow consumers to view features of a new phone or benefits of a BlackBerry product.

If BlackBerry posts frequently and reaches a strong consumer base, why are they underperforming? One explanation might be that they are reaching the wrong audience. While the social media following is large in number, 28,037,751 on Facebook and 4,520,000 on Twitter in April 2019, perhaps it consists of those who considered BlackBerry in the past, but lost interest long ago and ignore all updates coming from the Company. Another explanation could be that BlackBerry is sending the wrong message.

3.2 Message

As management expert J. Rampton (2014) notes, "everything that you do, or want to accomplish, on social media should be based on the values of your business" (p. 3). If a marketing strategy does not align with the company's mission statement, or match its objectives, it is less likely to engage consumers. Simon Sinek (2014) echoes the importance of having a strong brand that sends a clear message to consumers. He describes how great leaders inspire action, explaining that "people don't buy what you do, they buy why you do it" (p. 48). He uses Apple as an example. Apple begins with why: everything that they do, they believe in challenging the status quo. That is why they function as a company. He argues that consumers are more comfortable buying Apple products because they understand the purpose behind its function, rather than just hearing about the features of the product without a strong company message (Sinek, 2014, p. 23). This idea speaks to the importance of branding and determining the reason a company exists before trying to deliver a message.

The BlackBerry website (2019) states that "Today, BlackBerry aims to inspire the success of our millions of customers around the world by continuously pushing the boundaries of mobile experiences" (BlackBerry, 2019, n.p.). While BlackBerry appears to have a mission, we must assess whether they have the strength and ability to produce a product/service that aligns with their mission, and if they do better than the competition. Has BlackBerry been the leader in pushing the boundaries of mobile experiences?

The last time that BlackBerry launched major products was in 2015. In fiscal year 2015, BlackBerry launched four new smartphones. The resulting revenues were less than half of the previous year. A company that wants to establish itself as a leader in mobile experiences, which dedicates time and money towards a focus on smartphone development, must have consumers awaiting the release of a new phone. The sales numbers indicate that this is not the case. Because of this, I suggest BlackBerry consider re-branding altogether.

4 Differentiation

4.1 Competitive Advantage

In the early 21st century, several technology companies have the funding and resources to hire top talent and access technological insight. Most are capable of producing comparable technologies if willing to research and spend. Because of the technological similarities, consumers are more likely to allow intangibles to influence purchasing choices.

In the mobile technology space, a company's brand and the emotional feelings it invokes can drive consumer spending. BlackBerry has failed to change its mission statement or branding outlook, amid major decreases in sales. The Company currently expects a continued decline in BlackBerry users, yet retains its claim as "a global leader in mobile communications" (BlackBerry Limited, 2019, p. 126). It is clear that BlackBerry needs a new direction and a stronger identity. The Company needs to determine its strengths, accept its position, target the appropriate audience, and then market itself.

Aside from smartphones, BlackBerry offers Enterprise solutions, BlackBerry Messaging (BBM), Internet of Things (IoT) platform and applications, and various types of software. As advertised:

- Enterprise solutions – includes 70+ certifications and helps lead to "productivity built on experience and proven security".
- "BBM Protected" – provides an enhanced security model for messaging that "protects corporate data end-to-end with additional encryption".
- IoT platform – manages applications and devices in a "secure, efficient, and scalable way".
- "Business Software" – offers solution "built on the trusted security and reliability we're known for" (BlackBerry, 2019, n.p.).

4.2 Re-Branding

A constant trait among the advertised offerings is *protection, security* and *privacy*. Almost every description includes reference to a secure or safe solution. In fact, the latest smartphone, released in November 2015 is a "BlackBerry *secure* smartphone powered by Android." Its name, "Priv," is short for *privacy*.

The idea of connecting BlackBerry with the concepts stated above would not be new to consumers. The Company began by selling to corporations, government agencies and healthcare companies, targeting those who value privacy and security. President Barack Obama even had a BlackBerry as late as 2015 because the Secret Service could not secure the iPhone as well as they can a BlackBerry. The Company's advantage has been its identity from the onset. The problem is simply that management has failed to advertise the company for what it truly is.

BlackBerry need not remind consumers of their past accomplishments of introducing the smartphone. They should not celebrate the fact that they too sell innovative devices with user-friendly features. Instead, BlackBerry should highlight its ability to secure private information. They should advertise their ability to support the interconnectedness of protected devices. They should move beyond just smartphones and make it apparent that BlackBerry is a leading technology company with a mission to secure and protect data in a data-reliant world.

Once BlackBerry is able to re-brand itself, then it can focus on establishing a target market. As BlackBerry promotes all of its security-driven functionalities, they can approach professionals and businesses that most highly value confidentiality. Furthermore, by aligning the marketing message with the company mission, consumers will begin to recognize the BlackBerry brand and understand the purpose of the business.

5 Recommendations

After analysing the history and recent financial struggles of BlackBerry, it is apparent that the brand and marketing messages do not embody the strengths and identity of the corporation. I recommend that the Company take the following steps:

1 Recognize that company strengths and capabilities revolve around security and protection. Allocate R&D and employee power into building and maintaining these strengths.
2 Refocus the Company mission statement to align the BlackBerry brand with the future of the Company. Establish an identity as a company that is continuously pushing the boundaries of mobile experiences, while strengthening those boundaries to protect and secure the sharing of information.
3 Utilize BlackBerry's social media following, and attract more potential customers by targeting a desired market and sharing the re-enforced BlackBerry brand.
4 Partner with Google/Android (like with the Priv) to cultivate future options for partnerships or a potential merger.

1   You are documentation manager for XXX Software, a growing company, and you supervise preparation and production of all user manuals. The present system for producing manuals is inefficient because three different departments are involved in (1) assembling the material, (2) word-processing and designing, and (3) publishing the manuals. After studying the problem, you decide that greater efficiency would result if the company started using another system for the production of manuals, which would enable everyone involved to contribute during all stages. To achieve this, you must write a proposal to be read by the General Manager, as well as by the three Department Managers.

    Brainstorm some reasons that you think these readers would find convincing for your proposal, remembering that they would have different concerns and interests. What would be your persuasive strategy in this proposal?

2   Here is an extract from a report on the development of a computer game, written by one of the developers to the project manager. The writer follows a "write as you think" approach, which gives the text a muddled and wordy presentation. Also, the style combines specialist techniques (extensive use of technical terminology) with journalistic elements (chatty tone). Revise and edit the text both on a structural and sentence level. Break up paragraphs, include sections, headings and bullet points where appropriate, and reorganize information to make it clearer.

> The game was a drag-and-drop style board game involving one person directing another person's actions using a set list of verbal commands. The game also recorded moves made during a game for reviewing, either as a textual description or as real-time playback. As well as implementation, documentation of the system was a big part of the project with documents on five major aspects of the system produced. P1, the project plan, described the overall project, what was involved in the current system and our plans to implement a new system. P2, the requirements document, detailed the current system and our proposed solution to the problem presented to us by the client. P3, the architecture document, presented how we intended to develop the system and how it met the requirements determined in the previous document. P4 detailed the user interface of the document and also how it met the requirements of P2. P5, the detailed design document, contained the specifics of the implementation of the system and was intended to be used when coding the system. The documentation was intended to guide the implementation process in order to produce better quality software. I think that the software produced during the project was superior to previous software used for the same reason and I think this can be entirely attributed to following the project software development process.

When I say that the software produced during the project was superior to the software previously used I don't mean that the software produced was a superior piece of software. I think the overall design of our project was a good design that could've been implemented successfully but I do think it was lacking in some areas due to not enough time spend during this phase. It was initially intended that the interfaces would respond to users' commands and pass the responsibility of performing the operations on to various other modules. Little consideration was given to how a textual review would be displayed with regard to getting the information from the storage system to the interface so we ended up with the interface extract the information from a stored round object.

3 Below are some verbal descriptions of actions, relationships, steps and trends. Read the description and decide what kind of visual would present this information graphically. Draw the visual to illustrate. There could be more than one option for each description.

Verbal description	Visual
The budget was divided as follows: supplies 20%, salaries 40%, advertising 25%, shipping, 10% and reserve 5%.	
The fuel-mixture container is located on the top-right corner of the engine, and the main valve is located below the injector plug.	
Measured values from the X, Y, and Z plants were 41.2, 50.8 and 20.5 respectively.	
First, check. Then, open. Next, move.	
The engine is composed of A, B, C and D components.	

Verbal description	Visual
The error rate for online help menus was about half of the rate for printed instructions.	
Profits rose continuously in the last five years, even though the number of investors remained constant.	
If X happens, we should do Y; on the other hand, if B happens, we should do A.	

References and further reading

Bargiela-Chiappini, F., & Nickerson, C. (eds.) (1999) *Writing business: Genres, media and discourses*. London: Longman.

Bazerman, C., & Paradis, J. (eds.) (1991) *Textual dynamics of the professions*. Maddison: University of Wisconsin Press.

Bell, A. H., & Smith, D. M. (2010) *Management communication*. New York: John Wiley.

Cornelissen, J. (2017) *Corporate communication: A guide to theory and practice*, 5th edition. London: Sage.

Freed, R. C., Romano, J., & Freed, S. (2010) *Writing winning business proposals*, 3rd edition. New York: McGraw Hill.

Hauser, G. (1986) *Introduction to rhetorical theory*. New York: Harper.

Johnson-Sheenan, R. (2002) *Writing proposals: Rhetoric for managing change*. New York: Longman.

Kawasaki, G. (2004) *The art of the start: The time-tested, battle-hardened guide for anyone starting anything*. London and New York: Penguin Portfolio.

Kawasaki, G. (2011) *Enchantment: The art of changing hearts, minds and actions*. London and New York: Penguin Portfolio.

Kolin, P. C. (1998) *Successful writing at work*, 5th edition. Boston: Houghton Mifflin.

Nesheim, J. L. (2000) *High tech start-up*. New York: Free Press.

Taylor, N. (2009) *Brilliant business writing: How to inspire, engage and persuade through words*. Harlow: Pearson.

Toulmin, S. (2003) *The uses of argument*, updated edition. Cambridge: Cambridge University Press.

Critical Thinking for Management

Focus:

- Principles of critical thinking
- Common fallacies in reasoning
- Uses and misuses of statistics

The ability to reason logically and objectively is considered vital for professional success. In fact, "objectivity", "critical thinking" and "problem-solving" are key words in management positions. Together with skills in leadership, teamwork and communication, a demonstrated ability in dispassionate analysis of critical issues is highly sought after in most professional positions. This chapter addresses this need by describing the main problem areas, especially as they relate to the communication tasks of professional fields.

The terms and ideas presented here form the backbone of all forms of research, investigative writing and objective interpretation of arguments and statements. They also form the basis for professional involvement in corporate policy and public relations. The main value of objective reasoning, as opposed to subjective, or self-focused, opinion, is that it can lead to decisions that benefit a group of people or the wider public. The first part of the chapter describes the cognitive skills related to critical thinking, and follows with a review of the thought processes that lead to faulty reasoning in all forms of communication and decision-making. The second part focuses on a major area of manipulative persuasion, statistical data.

Principles of critical thinking

Critical thinking is not an innate gift or talent: it develops with perseverance and dedication. To sharpen your critical thinking skills, try these strategies (see also Burger & Starbird, 2012; Cottrell, 2011; Hirschberg, 1996; Sagan, 1995):

1 Think independently

Listen to other points of view, but do not follow any particular viewpoint without examining it first from different angles. Especially be cautious not to blindly accept claims and statements just because they are issued by an authority or expert. Everybody can be wrong, and facts can change as knowledge develops. Therefore, develop your own informed opinion.

2 Think objectively

Try to see situations from another person's point of view, beyond your own personal concerns. Do not become too attached to a theory or hypothesis because it is yours, or because you have believed it to be correct up to now. Examine why you believe this theory or hypothesis to be accurate and compare it fairly with alternatives. Play the devil's advocate and find reasons for rejecting it. If the theory survives the test, you will be more prepared to defend it when the occasion arises.

3 Develop intellectual perseverance

Show that you have the persistence to think through all the aspects of a problem. Do not be tempted to give up because a problem is too challenging. Consider more than one hypothesis. If there is something to be explained, think of different ways it could be explained. Then think of how you would test each of the alternatives.

4 Develop observation skills

When you read or listen critically, make sure that you clarify and understand key words, ideas and conclusions. Generate questions about what you read and remember to place the information you read and hear in context, using audience analysis skills. For example, find out about the audience that the information is directed towards, and identify how the needs of the audience influence the selection of information and the manner in which it is presented. Find out who generated the information, and by what methods. From this, ascertain how credible and reliable the information is. In many contexts, such as science, a hypothesis can be accepted only if it is falsifiable. Something that cannot be disproved can also not be proved.

Also, when reading, try to go beyond merely understanding what the writer has said, by asking yourself questions such as:

- What information is missing from the text?
- If I could meet the writer face to face, what questions would I like to ask?
- What further information do I need to know in order to accurately evaluate the information?

5 Trace analogies

How does what you learn in one context apply to other contexts? For example, if you are a computer engineer, you could notice the similarities between computer code syntax and the rules of sentence construction in English. Pay attention to similarities and differences. Many groundbreaking discoveries were made by tracing an analogy between a phenomenon and an idea, or by serendipity, that is, by recognizing connections between seemingly different topics.

6 Establish precision

Precision requires you to be focused and specific in both your ideas and your expression. In your own writing, make a conscious effort to refine generalities and avoid oversimplifications. Distinguish between relevant and irrelevant facts and use technical terminology correctly. If you are considering an argument, remember that all elements must work, not just most of them.

Fallacies of reasoning

One way to study the process of persuasion is to focus on what can go wrong. Many judgements and decisions are based on assumptions made from previous experience, and preconceptions that may be irrelevant to the purposes at hand. Although much innovative thinking also makes use of assumptions, guard against constructing arguments that are based totally on unacknowledged claims and weak reasoning. In the final analysis, persuasion and reasoning depend on the *rhetorical conventions* of particular *discourse communities*. What is valid evidence for one group may not be so for another, so you maximize your chances of producing a convincing case if you know what the expectations and conventions of your audience are.

In addition to audience expectations, ethics is another area that should occupy your thoughts. For example, you may have a workable idea for a new form of plastic, and you may also have convincing evidence that this development will benefit your organization, for example, by increasing its competitive advantage and by reducing costs of production. However, this new form of plastic may produce toxic pollution in its manufacturing, and the organization does not yet have the facilities to recycle such toxic waste. In such a situation, you need to very carefully weigh the organization's advantages with the negative effects on the wider community, and decide if and how the new product should be developed.

Some of the main tactics that lead to fundamentally illogical arguments are outlined below. In rhetorical theory, these are known as *fallacies of reasoning*.

They are extremely common in mass media documents, but also occur in professional and academic contexts:

Appeal to tradition: This occurs when the reason given for following or not following a course of action is that it has always been done this way. This tactic relies on a fundamental psychological trait – the need to trust the legitimacy of a habit. However, as with all forms of persuasion, it can be misused by concealing inherent flaws in the arguments proposed.

Appeal to authority: This occurs when a claim or statement is considered "true" because its source is an expert in the field, or has a respectable and/or popular position in the community. For example, there is an anecdote about a textbook used in a country's universities for many years, even though teaching staff were aware it contained some serious errors. The author was a famous professor whom nobody thought they should correct. In this case, the decision to continue on an erroneous path was based on the assumption that respect for authority should override objective evaluation.

Appeals to tradition and authority are more prominent in some cultures which have a hierarchical structure and a past orientation. However, most people follow such reasoning occasionally.

Appeal to common sense, "everybodiness" and universals: This occurs when, instead of providing a methodical argument that develops specific issues systematically, the writer/speaker proposes a course of action because it "is the right thing to do" or "everybody knows that it is so". Sometimes what appears as "common sense" or "universally acceptable" is nothing but an entrenched belief that has remained unquestioned for such a long time that it has become tradition. This strategy is based on the human need to belong to a group. Many people would be persuaded to follow a course of action because it appears to fall into established but unquestioned universals, such as "justice" or "morality".

Appeal to opposition: This occurs when, in order to support a point of view, the writer/speaker relies on the fact that the opposite point of view has been disproved or is unsubstantiated. For example, some claim that laws prohibiting the use of drugs should be abolished, because there is no substantial evidence to suggest that such laws actually prevent people from using drugs. Although this claim could be a step in the reasoning process, it cannot be the determining criterion for reaching a definite conclusion. A similar example is that of the existence (or not) of God: arguing that there is a God because attempts to disprove his existence have failed (or vice versa) is a claim based on an appeal to opposition. As Carl Sagan aptly puts it, "absence of evidence is not evidence of absence" (Sagan, 1995, p. 213).

Appeal to emotion: Very common in consumer advertising, this occurs when a writer/speaker uses an emotive style when presenting an argument, adding evaluative words and phrases or metaphors that are actually irrelevant to the piece of information presented but that have a strong sensory or emotive effect. Usually adopted to sway opinion on a matter, or to generate a feeling of guilt in the receivers that will induce them to take some form of action, this is what happens when perpetrators of crime are described as "hideous monsters" and their victims as "innocent citizens".

Because of its strong persuasive impact, this is a common device in the mass media. It is also a widespread tactic in some forms of legal reasoning, especially when a lawyer tries to sway the jury's opinion by drawing attention to the defendant's emotional state (traumatic childhood, agitated state, etc.) as a justification of his/her action. This relies on the human capacity for empathy ("What if this happened to you?") and not on logic.

Appeal to extremes and false dichotomies: This occurs when only two options are offered for a complex issue, undermining a balance. A choice between dictatorship or anarchy would reflect this kind of fallacy. This "either–or" device often occurs in emergencies where people need to act urgently and do not have the time to analyse an issue in depth. It tends to occur in very simplistic arguments, for example when an element of physical force or immediate urgency overrides the logical aspects of the argument ("Give me your money or I'll kill you"). "Terrorist tactics" are based on this kind of appeal, reflecting a situation where such a state of disarray has been reached that there are not many choices open for action. This is known as the fallacy of the *excluded middle* in classical argumentation.

Appeal to generalities: This occurs when a writer/speaker abstracts certain properties from some specially selected entities and applies them to a larger number of entities. A typical example is stereotyping ("Politicians are liars"). Another example is when an argument is based on universal terms ("love", "progress") that have not been defined in terms of the requirements of the project at hand. The argument is consequently hidden behind abstract notions. The major problem with this pitfall is that it disregards the specifics of particular circumstances and situations.

Appeal to personal aspects: This occurs when a writer/speaker's ideas are rejected because of this person's status, sex, profession, past record, etc., rather than because of weaknesses inherent to the ideas themselves. Very common in the mass media and in politics, this appeal disregards the issues at hand and, instead, attempts to draw attention away from a claim and onto the personal qualities of the presenter of the claim. This is what happens, for example, when a promising and reasonable idea is rejected by a committee because it was proposed by a junior or inexperienced member. In classical argument, this is known as *ad hominen* (Latin for "to the man" – attacking the arguer, not the argument).

Appeal to the straw man: Related to the previous, this occurs when a writer/speaker caricatures a position by oversimplifying it, exaggerating it or taking it out of context, so that it is easier to attack and demolish. This happens when it is easier to misrepresent an opponent's reasoning in order to dispute it, than to understand it and then present clearly developed objections.

A similar tactic is the use of inappropriate humour. "Straight" humour is a positive aspect of all communication. However, it can become inappropriate, and even sarcastic, when it is used to encourage laughter or ridicule towards an issue that deserves serious attention. If directed at those holding opposing views, this type of humour may reduce their chances of being heard.

Slippery slope: This occurs when a writer/speaker jumps to a conclusion that is not justified by the premises. Associated with paranoid reasoning, this is illustrated by a statement such as "If the government imposes restrictions on the petrol used for cars, what stops them from preventing us from driving cars altogether?" Slippery slope exists when a relatively insignificant event is seen as gaining momentum by inevitably leading to increasingly more serious events.

Special pleading: This occurs when a writer/speaker responds to an objection or observation by claiming that it overlooks some special circumstances. This is usually an evasive or defensive tactic. For example, responding to the observation "Despite the measures we have in place to prevent accidents, accidents have increased in the last month" by the special plea "You don't understand people: they don't follow rules" would be such an appeal.

A more logical response would be to examine the measures and the claim that accidents have increased. Special pleading also occurs when the speaker/writer believes that certain individuals, objects or beliefs are exempt from a general rule. This happens, for example, when one is religious but considers other people's religion as superstition.

Begging the question, or assuming the answer: This occurs when the writer/speaker bases an argument on premises that should in fact be the conclusion, thus producing a circular reasoning. For example, saying that "We must institute the death penalty to discourage violent crime" would fall in this category. This is based on the assumption that the death penalty does in fact discourage violent crime. The logical form of this fallacy, also known as *petitio principii,* is: Claim X assumes X is true; therefore claim X is true.

Card stacking or observational selection: This occurs when the writer/speaker omits what does not support his or her view and concentrates on facts that enhance his or her position. This is a "cherry-picking" fallacy, which is generally associated with propaganda.

False extrapolation: This occurs when a writer/speaker extrapolates a claim from observed facts without considering alternative possibilities. An example would be the statement "We will be successful because we are innovative and law-abiding." This is known in classical argument as *non sequitur* (Latin for "it does not follow").

Statistics and public opinion

Politician Benjamin Disraeli is reputed to have said that there are three kinds of lies: lies, damned lies and statistics (popularized by Mark Twain, 1906). This section focuses on a major trouble area of reasoning: the use of statistical or quantitative information in arguing for or against a course of action, and for justifying decisions. Interestingly, in the history of science, the study of statistics is a recent phenomenon, with origins in the "Enlightenment" era of the 17th century. Prior to that period, the notion that knowledge could be quantified or counted had no substantial hold. Now, however, virtually every facet of nature and society can be expressed in quantitative terms, that is, in terms of numbers, amounts and percentages.

When discussing an issue, people often give statistics to seal an argument and close off any further debate. Also, managers in business and finance, social policy and education routinely support their policies and decisions with numbers and statistics. Statistics can give the appearance of solidity and "hard" evidence; numbers are often thought of as irrefutable, or undeniable. But, actually, the appeal to statistics sets off a whole new set of questions. Where did the statistics come from? What groups in society are excluded from the statistics? If the statistics are accurate, then what decision or action should follow from them? And how can statistical relations and effects be translated into plain English, so that decision makers in business and government can understand them? After all, numbers are meaningless unless they are interpreted.

This section overviews and briefly describes six major areas where statistical support to reasoning is abused in order to manipulate attitudes (Freund & Simon, 1992; Huff, 1993; Paulos, 1996; Sheldon, 1994).

1 Not describing the source of statistics

Statistics are undocumented if the writer does not state their source. Possibly the most common problem with statistical information in the mass media, it makes it very difficult to ascertain whether the conclusions drawn from the statistical analysis are credible, plausible or applicable only to selected cases that cannot lead to general conclusions. Documenting statistics means stating clearly where the statistics came from, where they are published and if they are available to the public.

2 Not describing how statistics were generated

Even if the source of the statistics is documented, we still need to investigate further to verify that the data is valid. Questions to ask in this regard include: What kind of study was done to establish the statistics? What was the size of the sample? How was the sample selected? Is the sample representative of the general population? Were statistics gathered by interview or questionnaire? If they were gathered by questionnaire, was it filled in face-to-face or by self-reporting? What was the response rate? Who commissioned the study, who financed it and who conducted it? When polling results are compared with results from previous years, have key definitions remained the same? Has the margin of error been specified?

3 Not distinguishing between absolute rate and rate of incidence

The *absolute rate* indicates how many items are affected by the issue in question, expressed as a number. By contrast, the *rate of incidence* shows what proportion of the population is affected, expressed as a percentage. The rate of incidence, therefore, gives some indication of statistical significance. On the other hand, the absolute rate sometimes may sound more impressive, but is not as statistically relevant. For example, consider the effect of the statement that 100,000 people died from a kind of cancer in a specific country last year. Scary news? What if you now learn that this number accounts for 0.05% of the whole population of the country? Which rate would alarm readers and which would reassure them?

4 Not making sure that trends are real

Sometimes very slight correlations or changes in occurrence of an event can be blown up to misleadingly huge dimensions. This is sufficient to set off fears or hopes of a trend, particularly in emotional or volatile aspects of human behaviour. In some cases, a typical example being that of financial markets, the perceived trend can become a self-fulfilling prophecy: if small declines in the market are taken to be evidence of a larger trend, panic selling will indeed cause the market to slump or crash.

5 Not distinguishing between quantities given in length or in volume

Expressing quantities in terms of length often sounds more impressive than using volume as a measure. The example given by Paulos (1996, p. 79) is that of a tower and a box: Which contains more five-cent coins, a tower the diameter of a coin rising from sea level to the height of Mount Everest, or a six-foot cubical box? The answer is the box.

6 Not specifying the measure of central tendency

When noting the average of a series of numbers, the writers must indicate whether they have used the *mean, median* or *mode*. For data that falls into a normal distribution, such as human height, these three methods of averaging will produce similar results. However, for other kinds of data spread, mean, median and mode vary markedly. For example, assume a country's average income is $40,000. Does this sound like an affluent and fair-to-all society? What if the range occurs between a high of $200,000 and a low of $10,000?

7 Confusion between causality and correlation

This occurs when a hasty conclusion is drawn from a fact, or when a causal relation is artificially traced between two events that simply co-exist or that follow one another sequentially. This is known in classical argument as *post hoc, ergo propter hoc* (Latin for "it happened after, so it was caused by"). In fact, a major source of misinformation in the use of statistical evidence lies in the frequent confusion between causality and correlation. Two related events that occur simultaneously are said to be in correlation. This does not mean that one event caused the other. For example, consider the high positive correlation between the sale of alcohol and the incidence of crime. This in itself cannot prove that alcohol causes crime. There could be a third factor involved that influences both alcohol sales and crime, for example population growth. Tyler Vigen's humorous book (2015) and website "Spurious Correlations" gives some other examples of the absurdity that can arise when we seek causal relations in coinciding events (http://tylervigen.com/old-version.html). This includes such spurious correlations as per capita consumption of cheese correlating with the number of people who died by becoming tangled in their bedsheets!

In a causal relationship, one factor (the cause or reason) produces another (the result or outcome) only if these three factors are present:

1 There is a clear chronological sequence. A must occur before B does.
2 There is a clear pattern of repetition. To establish that A causes B, there must be proof that every time A is present, B occurs – or that B never occurs unless A is present.
3 There are no multiple causes and/or effects. For example, many factors influence reported crime rates: population distribution (age, wealth, race), crime reporting by citizens, changes to laws and regulations, and changes to police procedures for gathering and reporting statistics. A seeming drop in crime reporting, therefore, would not mean there is less crime.
4 There is agreement in definitions. Often a fact or event seems to cease to exist; however, closer scrutiny reveals that what has in fact changed is the definition of this fact or event.

8 The prosecutor's fallacy

Problems with causality extend to probability. Probability examines the chances of an event occurring, using mathematics and statistics. If not performed expertly, probability errors can cause serious mistakes in policy and action – as well as much heartache for those affected. These errors are called "prosecutor's fallacy" because they underlie faulty reasoning that can lead to legal indictments and prosecutions. If someone happens to be in the vicinity of a crime, for example, in some cases the prosecutor's fallacy can turn them into the culprit. The prosecutor's fallacy is based on the hesitation to accept a sequence or repetition of events as coincidence or random, as well as on the positive value that contemporary culture places on statistical evidence (Mlodinow, 2008).

A famous example is the case of Lucia de Berk, a nurse who was accused of murdering her patients in 2003 (Goldacre, 2010). De Berk was found guilty of four murders and three attempted murders of patients under her care at Dutch hospitals, and sentenced to life in prison. The arguments brought against her were based on probability and statistics. Her accusers, expert witnesses on statistics, claimed that the chances of a nurse working in the same hospitals where unexplained deaths took place, and being present at the scene, are one in 342 million. After her sentencing, other statisticians who were not convinced took up her cause and re-evaluated the evidence. Richard Gill and Piet Groeneboom recalculated the chances that a nurse could experience a similar situation as one in 48, or one in five, depending on the method used (Buchanan, 2007). The case was reopened, a new trial was held and Lucia de Berk was acquitted.

Argument in management

It is often believed that business writing favours numbers and profit rather than complicated argument structure. However, although practical outcomes are indeed a major concern in many management decisions, business ventures are also at the forefront of innovation, cultural change and social justice. Careful consideration of decision implications and ethical consequences of actions is pivotal in the success and social acceptance of business projects. In fact, successful proposals and business plans (documents with a high degree of persuasive impact) demonstrate evidence of what is known as the three Cs of management communication – *credibility*, the writer's foresight, integrity and judgement, *creativity*, the novelty of ideas, and *compliance*, the willingness to follow industry or company regulations and procedures. All three are expressed in writing through stylistic factors, such as choice of words, sentence structure and forms of cohesion.

The Toulmin and stasis models

Argumentation and persuasion theorists have created models of argument structure to show the methods used in constructing systematic arguments. Here we consider two useful models for management professionals: Stephen Toulmin's model and the stasis approach.

According to Stephen Toulmin (2003), particular contexts, purposes and audiences require a different form of argument. These forms of argument are based on different kinds of *claims*, a claim being the statement that requires evidential support. Being aware of the kind of claim your argument is based on helps in following appropriate persuasion strategies. According to this model, we have the following types of claims:

- **Claims of fact** are statements of proposed truth about a person, place, or thing.
- **Claims of worth** propose judgements on the merit of an idea, course of action, or position over a competing set of alternatives.
- **Claims of policy** are statements that set criteria or standards, directly expressing what one ought to do.
- **Claims of concept** either define or describe a proposition or an idea.
- **Claims of interpretation** provide a frame of reference for understanding an idea.

In many ways, this model builds on the ancient rhetorical model of *stasis* (ancient Greek word for "stance" or "position"). According to the stasis approach, we have four main types of argument:

Definition: This looks at the components of the object or issue examined. What is the nature of the problem being investigated? What are its parts and how are they connected? A definitional argument would be based on the question "What is the issue/object?"

Conjecture: This concerns the facts of the situation and the sources used to obtain information. It examines what happened, events and people. A conjectural argument would be based on the question "How did the issue/object get this way?"

Quality: This is evaluative and concerns the value of an object or issue. It looks at how serious an issue is and the strengths and weaknesses of possible solutions. A quality argument would be based on the question "What is the issue/object's quality?"

Policy: This looks at suitable actions needed to solve a problem or to address an issue. Proposal arguments are based on the question, "How to solve this problem?"

As an example, consider these paragraphs from a research article in organizational communication, which looks at naming organizations:

Example One: Developing an Argument

Presents the claim of the argument. ←

Naming signifies an important step in an organization's existence because it is through various incarnations that 'it' can then be made present. For example, there was a time when the Microsoft Company did not officially exist. By inventing the name 'Micro-Soft' in 1976, Bill Gates and Paul Allen could start to act in the name of their organization. Obviously, the organization had started to exist informally through various activities carried out by these two founding fathers, such as the creation of a BASIC interpreter for the MITS platform.

→ *Gives an example of the claim and gives some facts around it.*

Resumes elaboration of the argument after the concession sentence. ←

Adds more support to the claim by developing the example. ←

Concludes the paragraph by linking to the beginning. ←

Nevertheless, in 1976 the organization became a "legal fiction", that is, a juristic person or artificial entity (what Hobbes [1651/1997] called an "artificial person' in Leviathan), when the trade name "Microsoft" was registered. Even more interesting is that by naming something that initially did not exist (at least officially), conditions were created that enabled many different human and nonhuman agents (products, logos, people, etc.) to represent it, make it present or incarnate it, showing the close connection between the process of incarnation and naming. Naming thus allows a social collectivity to refer to itself through its representatives and enables the experience of being united under the same signifier; it creates a "we" that allows people to act or speak in the name of the organization. When Bill Gates speaks nowadays (for example, to announce Microsoft's new strategy to the media), for example, it is not only he who speaks, but also his company (Cooren et al., 2008, p. 1345).

→ *Gives a concession to show understanding of possible objections to the argument.*

→ *Draws a conclusion based on the claim presented above.*

These two paragraphs contain a mini argument based on the claim that naming affects the existence of an organization and signals its existence. This mini argument gives a historical example and elaborates on it to support the claim. Therefore, the claim is one of fact (Toulmin) – what things are – or conjecture (stasis) – how they got to be this way. It does not evaluate or propose solutions.v

A useful writing strategy for constructing an argument in a management context is this:

1 Summarize objectively the opposing argument to show that you have understood it.
2 Acknowledge ways in which the opposing viewpoint is correct.
3 Use a transitional word, phrase, sentence or paragraph indicating contrast or a shift in point of view.
4 State your claim or the different point of view as an alternative to the opponent's proposition.
5 Give evidence supporting your claim, remembering that the value of evidence should be assessed from the audience's perspective.

ACTIVITIES

1 Decide which types of fallacy the following statements would fall under. Some of these are borderline, and some contain more than one fallacy.

1 I suggest that we buy Adidas products, as we have been a loyal customer since they produced their first sports shoes.

2 As it cannot be proved that our new work policy in X country caused the resignations, it should be implemented by other countries.

3 Intelligent shareholders are against the takeover as it is obvious that such mining results in disastrous problems.

4 Given that he is the President of Amnesty International, his opinions on capital punishment should not be published.

5 He enjoys travelling, cooking and mountain climbing. Therefore, he would be suitable for work in public relations.

6 Because you expect to be looked up to by others, you are likely to be preferred in work situations.

7 During WWII, about 375,000 civilians died in country X and about 408,000 members of the armed forces died overseas. On the basis of those figures, it can be concluded that it was not much more dangerous to be overseas in the armed forces during that time than it was to stay at home as a civilian.

2 A current area of debate, where emotions, vested interests and objective evidence meet, is legislation over gun control. Although this is prevalent in the United States,

where the growing number of mass shootings in recent years has exacerbated the situation, the debate has international relevance. Therefore, it provides a fertile ground for the analysis of reasoning strategies and the use of statistics.

One reason for the controversy over the effects of strict regulations on the availability of guns is that no conclusive evidence exists directly linking high crime rates with gun possession. Researchers who study the relation between gun control and homicide rates have not, as yet, come up with any convincing proof that strict gun control laws actually lessen the number of gun killings.

Find an argument against and one for gun control and analyse them using the following questions:

1   How convincing is the reasoning presented here?
2   How credible is the use of statistics?
3   What more information would you need to reach more conclusive results?

3   Give a critical evaluation of the following news article on beans and bowel cancer, by answering the following questions (the article is fictitious, so no need to stop eating beans!)

1   What do you think of the amount and type of information selected in this article?

2   Does the article leave out important data? Does it "dumb down" or over-simplify scientific research? If so, how does it do this, and how could it perhaps avoid doing so?

3   What other information would you need to gather to form an informed opinion of the correlation between beans and bowel cancer?

Then, find another article in the media that presents scientific findings and analyse it following this example.

Beans seen as factor in bowel cancer

Beans, celebrated as the "meat substitute" for vegetarians and the health conscious, could do you more long-term harm than good, says a French study.

The National Institute on Cancer Research in Paris has warned people in middle age to stay off the pulse product or increase their risk of contracting cancer of the bowel.

Vegetarians cherish beans as a non-animal source of protein and iron, and it is sometimes recommended as a health food because it is rich in healthful plant oestrogens and iron. But phytoestrogens do not act like natural oestrogens, especially in our digestive system, nor are they good for us as once believed, say the French researchers into cancer.

Scientists followed the fortunes of 3,500 French men since 2000 to see who developed the disease. They found no positive connection between the disease and alcohol intake, smoking, education or professional status.

Instead, they found that those men who reported eating beans at least twice weekly when first interviewed were 28 times more likely to have developed cancer of the bowel than those that never ate beans. That could be because phytoestrogens are blocking the effect of natural oestrogens in the digestive system, and preventing normal digestive processes, say the scientists.

References and further reading

Buchanan, M. (2007) Conviction by numbers. *Nature*, 445, 254–255.

Burger, E. B., & Starbird, M. (2012) *The 5 elements of effective thinking*. Princeton, NJ: Princeton University Press.

Cooren, F., Brummans, B., & Charrieras, D. (2008) The coproduction of organizational presence: A study of Médecins Sans Frontières in action. *Human Relations*, 61(10), 1339–1370.

Cottrell, S. (2017) *Critical thinking skills: Developing effective analysis and argument*, 3rd edition. London: Red Globe Press.

Freund, J. E., & Simon, G. A. (1992) *Modern elementary statistics*, 8th edition. Englewood Cliffs, N.J: Prentice Hall.

Gardner, H. (2004) *Changing minds*. Boston: Harvard Business School.

Goldacre, B. (2010) Conviction for patients' deaths does not add up. *The Guardian* (9 April).

Hirschberg, S. (1996) *Essential strategies of argument*. New York, NY: Allyn and Bacon.

Huff, D. (1993) *How to lie with statistics*, 2nd edition. New York: Norton and Company.

Mlodinow, L. (2008) *The drunkard's walk: How randomness rules our lives*. New York: Pantheon.

Paulos, J. A. (1996) *A mathematician reads the newspaper*. New York: Anchor.

Sagan, C. (1995) *The demon-haunted world*. Chicago: Chicago University Press.

Sheldon, R. (1994) *First course in probability*. New York: Macmillan.

Toulmin. S. (2003) *The uses of argument*, updated edition. Cambridge: Cambridge University Press.

Twain, M. (1906) Chapters from my autobiography. Chapter Ten. *The North American Review*, 184 (607), 113–119.

Vigen, T. (2015) *Spurious correlations*. New York: Hachette.

Working in Teams

Focus:

- The role of teamwork in business
- Project management
- Cooperation and conflict

Many projects in business and industry require collaboration for their completion. In fact, teamwork is rapidly becoming the norm in many business projects, especially those that entail the cooperation of specialists in different fields. Therefore, a discussion of the concepts and terms that underlie teamwork and collaboration has an important role in a guide to business communication.

As regards the writing component of team projects, two trends are common. One trend, generally the most successful one, is for the team to have a writer, usually the team member with the best communication skills. This person gathers information from other team members and produces the documents that record and report on the project. The other trend, a more problematic option, is for all team members to contribute to the writing component of projects. This trend tends to be effective if all team members have equal communication skills. Even in those cases, however, it is difficult to build coherence in a document that is made up of styles of different writers.

> **TIP**
>
> Where possible, select a writer in a team project to avoid a "cut and paste" appearance. To share accountability, however, ensure that all team members read the document and agree on its content and organization, before submission.

This chapter overviews major elements of teamwork, especially *team dynamics,* the *allocation of team tasks, project management* and *conflict management.* The chapter ends with some real-life testimonials of members of team projects, evaluating their strengths and weakness of their teamwork.

Team dynamics

At their best, teams can produce excellent results by combining the specialized skills that individual team members bring. At their worst, teams produce delays, misunderstandings and conflicts. For this reason, the ability to deal productively with other people, peers, juniors and superiors is a highly valued skill that contributes greatly to the smooth and successful management of an organization. The success of a team project is largely due to such skilled procedures as effective negotiation, duty allocation and conflict management.

In business, as in other contexts, teams can be effective problem-solvers for many reasons, including the following:

- Teams bring together experts from different specializations and skill sets.
- More extensive information is available in a team than an individual may have alone.
- Individuals bring different approaches to a problem within the team. This allows for a wide range of options to be considered.
- Improved understanding of the problem and possible solutions is possible, because team members are aware of the reasoning used in problem analysis.
- Risks can often be managed more effectively in teams. What can be a high-risk decision for an individual could actually be a moderate-risk decision for a team, because different team members bring new knowledge to the issue, and because risk is often a function of knowledge.
- Motivation and confidence are likely to increase in decisions made in team situations, because individual team members feel supported by others.

Major disadvantages of reaching important decisions as part of a team include the following:

- Decisions can be made too soon: teams that feel uncomfortable with conflict may decide on the first option which meets with some support from the team members, regardless of whether this would be the best option.
- On the other hand, decisions can take too long, if the team cannot agree on a topic.
- If the team structure has no hierarchy or leader, there may be a lack of initiative and responsibility.

- Teams may be influenced by one person, whose charismatic or persuasive strengths may induce members to overlook pertinent factors in the problem involved.
- If there is too much conflict in a team, the team may become inoperable or ineffective.
- Teams may displace responsibility so that it may be difficult to hold a team or an individual member accountable for a negative outcome.

Generally, good team dynamics are achieved in three main ways:

1 members are attracted to the team's purpose
2 members share similar values, needs and interests
3 members fulfil for each other important interpersonal needs, such as **recognition** (acknowledging each other's point of view), **inclusion** (allowing each member to play a role in activities) and **ownership** (allowing each member to determine certain actions pertinent to the member's role).

Task allocation

In order for teamwork to be productive more is needed than just faith in the goodwill and competence of individual members. What is more essential is a formally implemented system for duty allocation, negotiation, delegation of duties, monitoring of progress and feedback.

> **TIP**
>
> Divide the project into tasks and allocate the tasks to each team member. Also, ensure that everyone knows and agrees to his/her allocated tasks at the beginning of the project.

Three common and effective models for organizing team projects are *the sequential, the functional* and *the mix-and-match*. These are broad categories that can be adapted and modified for particular situations.

The sequential model

In this type, each department/section in a company, or person in a group for smaller projects, is assigned a specific, non-overlapping responsibility in the project. Each department must finish its job before passing the material to another department for the next stage.

The sequential type of collaboration can be effective at times, especially when the work of each segment is specialized and each stage is self-sufficient. However, projects completed sequentially take longer than when other methods are employed, and a project manager is often necessary to coordinate the project and to ensure that deadlines are kept, all parties understand requirements and transitions from one stage to the next are smooth.

The functional model

This type is organized according to the skills or job function of the members. All stages of a project are undertaken concurrently, and all parties can monitor procedures at each stage. For example, a four-person team carrying out a user documentation project for software might be organized as follows:

- A manager schedules and conducts meetings, assists team members, issues progress reports to management, solves problems by proposing alternatives and generally coordinates efforts to keep the project on schedule.
- A researcher collects data, conducts interviews, searches the literature, administers tests, gathers and classifies information, and then prepares notes on the work.
- A writer/editor receives the researcher's notes, prepares outlines and drafts, and circulates them for corrections and revisions.
- A graphics expert obtains and prepares all visuals, specifying why, how and where visuals should be placed and designing the document layout. S/he might even suggest that visuals replace certain sections of text.

All parties work on the project at the same time and interact regularly through meetings and other forms of communication.

The mix-and-match model

In this type of collaboration, team members agree on shared objectives, and then work independently on separate sections of the project by undertaking all tasks. The team members meet at specified times to compare their work and choose the best samples from each other's work. This approach is constructive in smaller-scale projects, when team members have similar skills but cannot meet regularly.

A different version of this approach occurs when all members share the same interactive software and can work on the same project concurrently, each contributing according to their own skills which may or may not overlap. This would most likely cut costs and reduce time, compared with the sequential model, but it would necessitate that all members work cooperatively, and that project milestones and outcomes are very clearly set out and agreed by all in advance (to reduce the risk of "You're treading on my toes" situations).

The leader

In any kind of collaboration model, the role of a leader is vital. Even in cases where, seemingly, the team works on egalitarian principles, and all team members know their duties, liberties and constraints, the presence of a leader can act as a unifying force that helps to maintain cohesion and stability. It is a good idea to select a team leader to avoid the situation where the most dominant personality takes over unofficially. Regardless of whether their focus is to maintain cohesion or to initiate tasks, effective team leaders share certain characteristics. According to Qubein (2008), these common characteristics are that:

- They value people: they acknowledge the importance and contribution of others
- They listen actively: they make an effort to understand the needs and desires of others
- They are tactful: they criticize sparingly, constructively and diplomatically
- They give credit: they praise others and their contributions publicly
- They are consistent: they control their personal moods and are fair in their exchanges with others
- They admit mistakes: they take the blame for errors they committed
- They have a sense of humour: they maintain a pleasant disposition and pleasant manner
- They set a good example: they follow their own regulations.

Effective leaders are not only personally ambitious and well-organized, but should also be people-oriented, willing to assist and direct subordinates, and able to improvise and innovate in their field within ethical parameters.

Project management

A project in business and industry consists of a series of activities leading to one major goal or purpose. *Project management* refers to the planning necessary to complete a major project on time, within budget, according to specifications, and with the consultation and consent of all relevant parties. Projects tend to be undertaken by a *project team*, a group of people responsible for managing a project. Projects usually begin with a proposal and end with a completed outcome, and a final report showing how the initial goals were reached or not. During the progress of a project, the team is generally required to submit progress reports at specified times in order to keep management informed of what has been achieved and what still remains to be done.

The components of effective project management are *definition, planning* and *direction*. Briefly, *project definition* involves describing the envisioned final product and its place in the market; *planning* involves identifying and prioritizing the tasks necessary for the completion of the product; and *direction* involves allocating roles to team members and setting a timeline for the execution of tasks. Consider each component more carefully.

Definition: As the first step, a project is carefully defined. Aspects of project definition include:

- Project overview: is the project attempting to solve a problem? If so, for whom is this a problem? How is the problem defined? Is the project creating a new product? What are the characteristics of this product? What types of markets will it target?
- Scope: what issues, topics or features will the project cover? How much detail will it provide? What are the parameters that project team members must work within?
- Outcome: what will the result of the project be? For example, if a computer system is being developed, what functions should it perform and to what standard?

Planning: Each step in the process is planned before further action is taken. Tasks undertaken in the planning stage include:

1 Identifying the steps required to complete the project
2 Listing the priorities: what should be done first, second, third?
3 Identifying dependent and independent tasks: which tasks need to be put aside while other tasks are being completed? Which tasks are urgent, and which may be delayed without damaging the project?
4 Creating a timeline for task completion and allocating roles to project team members.

Project Managers usually divide tasks into three categories:

1 **A critical task** must be completed on time for the entire project to be completed on time.
2 **A milestone** is an event that signifies the accomplishment of a series of tasks during a project. A milestone often signals the ending of a stage or section in the development of the project.
3 **A deliverable** is a concrete object produced at specific stages in the project (and usually delivered to a manager or client). Deliverables are used in some types of project management, like, for instance, software design and engineering. For example, the systems requirements report, produced near

the beginning of the project and describing what the projected software will achieve, is a deliverable.

Direction: Each project is directed according to a line of responsibility. Project managers are responsible for monitoring and controlling progress and activities. Members of the project team report to managers, who in turn report to upper level management and clients. Team members who are able to meet all the requirements of the project at a minimum cost and on time are highly valued.

The direction of a project also involves issues of resources, constraints and risks, which may propel the project forward or inhibit its development:

- Resources: what advantages do the team have in undertaking the project? Are they highly skilled? Do they have a large budget? Do they have adequate time to complete all the tasks? Is up-to-date technology available to them?
- Constraints: is the budget modest? Is the staff limited, in numbers or in knowledge? Are there tight deadlines? Is there a lack of appropriate technology?
- Risks: what are the possible dangers of the project and what can be done to minimize them?

Two particular dangers that often arise in project management are known as *scope creep* and *feature creep*. Both of these can lead to delays, incomplete projects and conflicts within the project team.

Scope creep is exemplified by the tendency of stakeholders and project participants to expect increasingly more from the outcome of the project as it progresses. For example, businesses and users might expect increasing functionality and performance from a computer system as the process of developing the system unfolds.

Feature creep refers to the tendency to add more features and details to the expected product of the project without bearing in mind that the incorporation of these features will take extra time and money. The type of project determines what kind of feature creep may exist. In software design, for example, feature creep leads to the uncontrolled addition of technical features to the software under development.

One way to keep the project under control and monitor progress is to have a clear plan at the beginning, agreed upon by all members, to implement a feedback process where any conflicts or miscommunication can be aired and resolved, and to discuss progress at regularly organized meetings.

Team roles

Understanding the roles that are required for projects to progress smoothly can help to allocate duties to individual team members and to select members who are most likely to contribute positively to the successful completion of the project. These are the concerns that led organizational psychologist Meredith Belbin to formulate his inventory of team roles. Belbin distinguished nine roles that team members tend to play in high-performing teams. These roles refer to behaviours that team members exhibit, and they relate to individual personalities but also to contextual factors such as the interactional exchanges that take place during team projects. Belbin's roles are:

Action-oriented roles

Shaper

Shapers urge the team to improve. They are dynamic and enthusiastic and challenge others to find solutions to problems. They keep the team moving and challenge the other members, keeping them from becoming too complacent. Their potential weaknesses are that they can be aggressive and are not very tactful.

Implementer

Implementers have good organizational skills and get things done. They can turn ideas into actions and are product- and results-oriented. Their potential weakness is that they can be stubborn and adverse to change.

Completer–finisher

Completer–finishers finish projects. They are good at checking for errors and delivering high-quality final results. They are detail-oriented and disciplined. Their potential weaknesses are that they worry too much and can be control freaks.

People-oriented roles

Coordinator

Coordinators have good leadership skills and they know how to organize others and delegate duties. They can identify objectives and select appropriate people to meet them. Their potential weaknesses are that they can delegate too much and, although they are excellent listeners, they can be manipulative.

Team worker

Team workers bring people together and cheer people up. They are supportive and make good negotiators. They can be diplomatic and flexible. Their potential weakness is that they can be indecisive.

Resource investigator

Resource investigators are inquisitive and resourceful. They know how to find information and bring together resources. Their potential weaknesses are that they can be over-optimistic and may lose their enthusiasm if discouraged.

Thought-oriented roles

Plant

Plants are the eccentrics in the team. They can be creative geniuses, who keep the ideas coming. They are good at innovating. Their potential weaknesses are that they can be hard to work with and may be impractical and uncommunicative.

Monitor–evaluator

Monitor–evaluators are good at analyzing and evaluating ideas. They can be shrewd and they have good judgement. They have a balanced approach and are good critical thinkers, able to evaluate possibilities objectively. Their potential weaknesses are that they can be detached and too critical.

Specialist

Specialists provide expert knowledge in the team and are skilled and competent. They have a professional attitude and can focus on technical details easily. Their potential weaknesses are that they might lose sight of the big picture in favour of details and might overload people with information (www. belbin.com).

Conflict

Conflict is embedded in human relations. It arises when there is incompatibility of orientation between individuals or groups, and it can form in such situations as when people have incompatible goals and behaviours, when resources need to be allocated, and when decisions need to be made. Conflict is associated with:

- Value: underlying values are different. This is arguably the most important and serious type of conflict because values are entrenched in social interaction and behaviour and are very difficult to change.
- Interests: what promotes one's self-interest opposes another's. For example, when two colleagues compete for the same promotion, inevitably some degree of conflict will arise.

- Policy: existing regulations do not reflect current needs. This often manifests in cases where conflict leads to employees' strikes or group protests. This is what happens, for example, when prices increase but salaries remain static, leading to a strike, or when women have achieved breakthroughs in social equality, but legislation regulating gender issues remains at a primitive level, leading to demonstrations or legal proceedings. Policy is very closely aligned with value.
- Goals: there is controversy or disagreement about where a project is heading. In a project, for example, some members may think the goal is to produce routine results, whereas others may want to produce a radical breakthrough.
- Method: there is controversy or disagreement about how to arrive at the desired outcome. Such conflict may arise when one side is more optimistic about the future, while the other side wants more control over a situation, leading them to choose high-risk methods (such as war over negotiation, for instance).

Similarly, conflict can be *structural* or *substantive*. In structural conflict, it is the actual structure of the organization that creates the conflict. In substantive conflict, the conflict exists in the issues associated with particular problems or situations.

Managed properly, conflict can be constructive and result in growth because it allows for different points of view to be aired and considered. Managed badly, it can be destructive and costly – in resources and relationships. Groups can suffer from two opposite evils: too little conflict, and too much conflict. A little conflict can be a good thing for change and rejuvenation of outmoded structures and beliefs. A lot of conflict, however, can destroy a project and in serious cases even lead to costly lawsuits and official investigations.

When teams are not working well, it can be a very serious matter, costing the organization money and time. While the reasons that make a team unproductive are not fixed or universal, there are some guidelines regarding what could not be working right that can be used to clarify the situation:

- The team may lack a leader, or be burdened by an incompetent leader, making it disorganized and dysfunctional as a result
- The team may be lacking the required specialist skills to tackle a project expertly and confidently
- Members may feel their personal skills are not appreciated and they may lose motivation (often the result of weak leadership or bad management)

- The team may feel their efforts will not be supported by authorities and funding agencies, especially if they are working under budget constraints and/or on obscure or unpopular projects
- A conflict of values or expectations may exist where some team members may expect different results from the project or the team may be expecting different results from the management
- The objectives and scope of a project may be unclear, leading to confusion
- Personal conflicts may hinder the achievement of goals. This is especially true of competitive environments where people are not accustomed to working cooperatively.

Managing conflict

As it probably has become clear from the preceding discussion, managing conflict is no easy matter. In most aspects of interpersonal communication, contextual factors, such as the setting of the interaction, the background of the participants and the nature of the interaction, are important in pointing to the most appropriate reactions, and conflict management is no exception to this. However, as regards teamwork, a general process for managing conflict could take this form:

1 **Define the problem:** The definition of the problem is the most important step in finding a solution. In many cases there is low morale and a lack of commitment by team members because there is a problem that has not been voiced or made conscious within the group dynamics. An effective method of discussing the problem that caused this conflict is to describe it in writing. Each conflicting side should describe their perspective on the matter as clearly and as objectively as possible, avoiding "I said/he said" type criticism. It is also important to avoid generalizations, such as "they", "always", "never", etc., and to determine if the reaction is proportional to the situation. In describing the issue, consider if it had objective grounds to escalate into conflict, or if it is likely to have been caused by misunderstanding.

2 **Analyse the problem:** Once the group agrees on the nature of the problem, the next step is to analyse it in terms of size, causes and criteria of evaluation. At this stage, it is important not to succumb to the temptation of listing possible solutions before having analysed the problem thoroughly. Before answering the question "What can be done to solve the conflict?", team members should answer "Why is this a conflict?" and "For whom is it a conflict?"

3 **Generate possible solutions:** Brainstorming is usually an effective way to generate ideas that could lead to the resolution of the conflict. At this stage, evaluation or nitpicking criticism of ideas should be avoided, and team members should produce as many possible solutions as they can.

4 **Evaluate and test the various solutions:** After the brainstorming stage, each possible resolution should be examined to ascertain its merits and drawbacks. Factors to consider carefully include if the solutions are likely to work, if they are fair to all and if they can be implemented easily. This should eliminate the solutions that are not worthwhile and leave a reduced number of options.

5 **Choose a mutually acceptable solution:** From the reduced number of possible solutions the one that seems to be the most effective can be chosen for a trial period. The best way to articulate this would be, once again, in writing. At times choosing an option is a risky act, with no guarantees that the selected solution will work. However, if the decision was reached by (relative) consensus, all the parties involved will be responsible for testing it and providing feedback.

One way to maximize the chances for keeping conflict under control is to institute a feedback process, through which all team members air complaints, express satisfaction and propose changes to the team structure at specified intervals. During such feedback sessions, consider evaluating your own and others' contributions and participation with the criteria in Table 9.1:

Table 9.1   Criteria for Evaluating Team Member Contributions

1 Team members are available when needed and are punctual and reliable
2 Team members communicate clearly and constructively – they provide feedback
3 Team members contribute equally to the project and carry out their tasks as assigned
4 Team members help each other to manage conflict and act as intermediaries in negotiations with other team members
5 Team members are serious about deadlines, protocols and constraints of the project.

Effective listening

Effective listening contributes enormously to group dynamics and conflict resolution. In interpersonal communication, poor listening skills are at fault in many cases of misunderstanding. Being a good listener makes one not only an effective communicator but also a strong leader.

Listening involves the whole physical presence. When working with others, much of the communication that takes place when suggesting, instructing, requesting, criticizing, praising and negotiating is non-verbal. Listening actively by making a physical and mental effort to understand what someone else is saying engages the whole body, not just ears. It is a way of communicating that signifies that you understand the feelings of the speaker and are interested in their position, and that you are available and willing to consider the situation impartially without judging or laying blame.

Here are six tips for active listening:

1 **Stop talking:** Many people talk too much because they feel uncomfortable with silence. However, you cannot listen if you are talking.

2 **Remove noise as much possible.** "Noise" is used in the communication sense of distractions to the unhindered transmission of the message. Therefore, it refers not only to external factors such as street noise, but also other factors, such as excessive heat or cold, and distracting mannerisms. Common distracting mannerisms include clicking pens, shuffling papers, checking clothing or fingernails and gazing around the room. If you need to talk to a team member or colleague about something serious, it is advisable to arrange a meeting in pleasant and relaxed surroundings.

3 **Ask open questions** which begin with the 5Ws and 1H: what, when, why, where, who and how. This helps to keep the conversation on the topic and to obtain as much information as possible on it. When people answer W and H questions, they must reply in full sentences, and so their replies are more factual than they would be if the questions were of the "Do you..." type, which elicits, simpler "yes-no" answers.

4 **Be supportive.** Let the other person know that you *want* to know what they are talking about. It is well attested that most people will talk if they get attention and interest from the listener. Sensing indifference or impatience discourages a constructive response.

5 **Respond to feelings.** If the situation at hand has an emotional investment by one or all the participants, it is best to acknowledge this. Hidden or "bottled" feelings may cloud or sabotage the information you require.

6 **Summarize to check mutual understanding.** A summary ensures that both parties have the same understanding of what has been said and helps to create closure to an issue or topic of discussion. In business, for example,

a summary is formalized in a Statement (or Memorandum) of Understanding, which lists the points that have been agreed upon in a previous discussion.

Avoiding Groupthink

The absence of conflict, although at first sight a good thing, can be problematic if it indicates a phenomenon known as *Groupthink*. Groupthink was explored by Yale sociologist Irving Janis, who was interested in understanding historical cases where teams reached disastrous decisions because of Groupthink. Janis found that in many of these cases the free voicing of concerns and dissent was not encouraged, leading to parochialism and reluctance to express disagreement, even when team members knew problems existed. This uniformity of thought leads to stagnation and should be avoided in team projects. Janis's study identified some factors which can lead to Groupthink (Table 9.2).

Table 9.2   Groupthink

- Belief in being invincible: excessive optimism and unnecessary risk-taking.
- Attempts to rationalize all issues: explaining away warnings or threats.
- Belief in inherent morality: the belief that the team can do nothing wrong.
- Stereotyping: the belief that others are too evil, stupid or weak to take seriously.
- Direct pressure: forcing everyone in the team to conform.
- Self-censorship: preventing oneself from voicing concern so as to maintain consensus.
- Belief in unanimity: the belief that everyone in the team agrees because no one raises objections.
- Imposing mind-guards: setting some team members as gatekeepers to keep external influences at bay.

Adapted from Janis, 1982: 174–175.

Testimonials on teamwork

Below are extracts from evaluations of engineering team projects. These extracts describe problems in unclear task allocation, inadequate structure of meetings, lack of leadership and inadequate planning.

Skills, tasks and roles

> One good rule in forming a team is to pick members who have a nice distribution of skills. A group whose members all specialize in the same field may be very strong in that one area but lacking in many others.

> Considering the allocation of roles, it took us some time to organize ourselves. Our roles were overlapping and after some time we decided to attribute ourselves some more precise functions. We realize that a better way to do this would have been to have a clear definition of our roles from the start, which would have optimized the time spent during meetings by preventing significant overlap. For future teams, we would recommend that the attribution of roles be done with common accord and discussion between team members as early as possible.

> Defining roles and responsibilities at the beginning of the project would have led to better distribution of work. More clear responsibilities would also have been a good motivation for team members to contribute to the project.

Agendas and structure of meetings

> Agendas and schedules are helpful. Project groups cover many issues in a meeting, and it is difficult to keep track of them all. Making a list ensures that all points will be addressed and not forgotten. Schedules help in time management. The large task of tackling a big design project is much more manageable when broken down into smaller tasks that can be knocked off one by one.

> Our meetings were first planned electronically through email and initiated by any member. During this preliminary organization stage, an agenda could have been delivered, which would have added structure and routine to our meetings.

> Another way to enhance team efficiency is better routine. If we always had the same meeting time on the same day, it would prevent confusion and wasted time. The meetings would have more value since people would always be conveniently prepared.

The lack of agendas and minutes also led to inefficiencies during team meetings. This problem combined with the lack of clearly defined roles, led to uncertainties during meetings as to what work needs to be done. Without the project brief, which set milestones and deliverable dates, little progress would have been made during meetings.

Intra-group communication

A group should be flexible. It should be able to account for mistakes and accidents and be able to change plans in case of emergencies or failures. A team should not be so set on one solution that the whole group dissolves when something goes wrong.

Problems that one member encounters should be brought to the entire team, to make everyone aware of the issues that need resolution and possibly to allow the team to resolve the problem during a meeting.

Leadership

We recommend having a leader. Leaders help organize a group which could otherwise be chaotic from miscommunication or personal conflict. It is good to have someone who can mediate when there is a problem or make executive decisions when the group cannot decide together. The leader can also impose schedules to continue pushing the project towards its goal in a timely manner.

Planning

Planning ahead and not procrastinating is key. Although teams can complete a divided workload more quickly than an individual, gathering and organizing the completed work takes extra time. Procrastination is always bad, but with a group it can be even worse. It is more difficult to gather a group, and not everyone may be available at the same time.

Planning ahead allows more flexibility in schedules and allows for unexpected conflicts. It also prevents the whole burden of the project from being dumped on one responsible individual at the last minute.

Team charter

Here is a team charter template that you can use or adapt to plan and monitor team projects.

Project title	Objectives		
Deliverables	**Milestones**		

Team Member Roles and Responsibilities			
Name	**Role**	**Tasks**	**Deadline**

Communication Protocol		
Team rules	**Meeting dates**	**Mode of communication**

1 Assume you are the Founder and CEO of a new business. You have an executive team of five people and are now preparing to write a business plan to gain investments and funding. Organize the tasks leading to the business plan in project management fashion, and allocate roles and responsibilities to all team members. Set your project out using the templates and guidelines proposed in this chapter.

2 What would you say are the organizational problems that the following statements signify? Some statements may indicate more than one communication problem.

- "Our team could tell you how to achieve this in half the time and cost, but if this became public, they'd probably dismantle the team."
- "I could have told management this would happen, but I didn't think they would listen, and I wasn't asked anyway."
- "There's a better way to do this, but I doubt the project manager would want to learn about it."
- "The design team originally made this suggestion, and it eventually made millions for the company. But the design team got nothing out of it."
- "I didn't know this was the correct procedure."

References and further reading

Belbin, M. (2012) *Team roles at work*, 2nd edition. London: Routledge.

Cobb, A. (2013) *Leading project teams: The basics of project management and team leadership*, 2nd edition. London: Sage.

Csikszentmihalyi, M. (2003) *Good business: Leadership, flow and the making of meaning*. London: Hodder & Stoughton.

Dowling, G., & Moran, P. (2012) Corporate reputations. *California Management Review*, 54(2), pp. 25–42.

Janis, I. L. (1982) *Groupthink: Psychological studies of policy decisions and fiascoes*, 2nd edition. Boston: Houghton Mifflin.

Joshi, A., Lazarova, M. B., & Liao, H. (2009) Getting everyone on board: The role of inspirational leadership in geographically dispersed teams. *Organization Science*, 20(1), pp. 240–252.

Northouse, P. G. (2012) *Leadership: Theory and practice*, 6th edition. New York: Sage.

Qubein, N. R. (2008) *How to be a great communicator*. Oxford: Wiley.

Walker, R., & Aritz, J. (2014) *Leadership talk: A discourse approach to leader emergence*. New York: Business Expert Press.

CHAPTER 10

Revising and Editing

Focus:

- Revising a document
- Editing a document
- Sentence structure
- Grammar

This chapter provides guidelines on revising, editing and sentence structure. It aims to give an awareness of the communicative effects of grammatical structures and enable you to gain control over the "mechanics" of writing. The chapter begins with an overview of sentence structure, and proceeds by explaining some common language troublespots – *active and passive voice, participial phrases, subject–verb–pronoun agreement, punctuation* and *relative clauses.* The chapter ends with a discussion of revising and editing considerations.

The guidelines presented here should help you to produce grammatically correct prose, whatever the context and purpose of the document. Knowing rules and conventions of writing confers confidence and credibility, even in cases where a writer decides to deliberately ignore these rules and conventions. In the famous words of T.S. Eliot, "it is not wise to violate the rules until you know how to observe them" (cited in Ivers, 2010, p. 46).

Sentence structure

A. Sentences and phrases

The minimal definition of a sentence is a word group that contains a *subject* (someone or something that carries out an action – the agent of an action) and a *verb* (the action carried out). This minimal word group is called a *clause.* Many sentences also contain an *object* (the recipient of the action, or the thing or person acted upon).

The report	recommended	changes
Subject	Verb	Object

If the word group has no subject or no verb, but still makes some basic sense by evoking an image, it is a *phrase*. This is not a complete sentence; it is a fragment. Fragments do have their place in writing: they create colourful and imagistic effects. However, although their use is justified and often even expected in creative writing and many kinds of journalism, fragments are basically ungrammatical and should be avoided in formal or specialist style.

Phrase: Trying to come to a decision.
Sentence: Trying to come to a decision, the project members considered all options.

To write complete sentences, make sure you have these elements:

1 **A verb that shows time:** something happens or is described in the past, present or future. If the word group has no verb at all, it is a fragment, because nothing happens. Also, make sure your verb has a *tense* (time element). Even if a word group contains a verb, it fails as a complete sentence if the verb has no tense.

Fragment: The committee considering the proposal.
Sentence: The committee considered the proposal (past tense).
Sentence: The committee considers the proposal (present tense).
Sentence: The committee will consider the proposal (future tense).

Some verbs have no tenses, for example, infinitives (to do words) and gerunds (-ing words).
-ing words can function in different ways in a sentence:

1 **A participial form of a verb:** *Having agreed to collaborate on the project, the engineers formed their teams.* This is actually a reduced subordinate clause: *After they had agreed to collaborate on the project, the engineers formed their teams.*
2 **A verb in a continuous tense:** *The excavation continued while it was raining.* In this case, the -ing word is preceded by the verb *be* (was, were, am, will be, etc.).
3 **A gerund:** *Walking is good exercise.* A gerund can be the subject of a sentence, and functions as a noun.

4 **An adjective:** *It is tedious to attend boring meetings.* In this case, the -ing word qualifies a noun by describing its attributes (interesting, exciting, frustrating, amusing, etc.).

2 **The absence of a subordinating conjunction:** a word group ceases to be a complete sentence if a subordinating conjunction is placed in front of it. Subordinating conjunctions include:

after	if	until
although	in case	when
as	provided that	whenever
as if	since	whereas
as though	so that	whether
because	that	which
before	unless	while

Consider, for example, this:

While common law has long implied that there is a requirement for mutual respect and fair dealings in the employment relationship.

The word "while" at the beginning of the sentence implies that there is a second part to this sentence, which contrasts the information given in the first. Without this second part, the sentence is not complete. To correct this problem, either put a comma after "relationship" and add another clause or remove "while".

B. Types of sentences

Sentences are classified into four categories:

Simple sentences contain one main clause.

The report recommended changes.

Compound sentences contain two or more main clauses connected with conjunctions.

The report recommended changes and established deadlines.

Complex sentences contain one main clause and one or more subordinate clauses (clauses that would be fragments if disconnected from the main clause).

(a) The report, which will form the basis of our decision, recommended changes.

(b) The report recommended changes because these are the only way to solve the problem.

Compound-complex sentences contain two or more main clauses and one or more subordinate clauses.

> The report recommended changes and established deadlines, because that is the only way to solve the problem.

Note that sentence types are more about the prioritization of information than about length. In fact, a simple sentence can be much longer than a complex one, as seen in these examples:

Complex sentence: The applicants who were rejected were permitted to apply for the other position.

Simple sentence: After much deliberation and a lot of debate over several meetings, the project members decided reluctantly to accept the committee's proposal to re-design the bridge.

The first stage where you begin your crafting of style is the sentence. Therefore, the more practice you give yourself in constructing different types of sentences and observing their effects, the more aware you become of writing style.

C. Coordinating, subordinating and adverbial conjunctions

These words are important because they show if the information you write can be put in one sentence or two. Using different conjunctions brings variety to your writing and also allows you to distribute information in different ways, with a different rhythm and effect. To use these correctly, you must be aware of some grammatical rules.

Coordinating conjunctions can connect two clauses in one sentence, which becomes a compound sentence, giving equal value to both clauses. Coordinating conjunctions are known by the mnemonic FANBOYS – *for, and, nor, but, or, yet, so.*

The weather was treacherous but the project team did not postpone the expedition.

Subordinating conjunctions connect a subordinate clause to a main one and create a complex sentence. The information placed in the subordinate clause is of secondary importance, even if it comes first in the sentence. Subordinating conjunctions include *although, because, whereas.*

> Although the weather was treacherous, the project team did not postpone the expedition.

Adverbial conjunctions are actually adverbs that qualify the relationship between two sentences. They always link two sentences and require appropriate punctuation (see section on punctuation below). Use these conjunctions when you want to elaborate on two points and develop them into two separate sentences. Adverbial conjunctions include *however, nevertheless, furthermore, therefore, consequently.*

The weather was treacherous. However, the project team did not postpone the expedition.

Relative clauses: *which* and *that*

Subordinate clauses can be *adverbial*, showing contrast, cause or result (although, because), or they can be *relative*, showing detail about a person, event or thing (who, which). Grammatically, both *which* and *that* are subordinating conjunctions, signalling a subordinate clause. However, they are not used interchangeably and some thought is needed on their use.

The clause that begins with *which* gives information about the noun that directly precedes it. If the *which* clause in a sentence is necessary to define the identity of the noun that precedes it, do not separate the noun from the *which* clause with a comma. In such cases, the *which* clause is called a *defining* or *restrictive* clause. The sentences below illustrate this.

1 The committee accepted the proposal which the project team had been working on for months.
2 The committee accepted the proposal, which the project team had been working on for months.

In the first sentence, the word *proposal* is relative. That is, the sentence literally means that the project team submitted several proposals and the committee accepted the one that the team had been working on for months. In this case, the *which* clause is *defining* and does not require a comma preceding it. It defines which of the proposals was accepted. In a defining clause, *which* could be replaced with *that.*

In the second sentence, on the other hand, the word *proposal* is absolute. That is, the sentence literally means that there is just one proposal in question here. In this case, the *which* clause is *non-defining*, meaning that it is not necessary in order to determine the identity of the noun that precedes it. In a non-defining clause, it could not be replaced with *that,* and always requires a comma to set it off from the main clause.

> **TIP**
>
> Because of this double use of *which*, it has become common practice in professional contexts to avoid it in defining clauses. Use *that* in defining clauses, and *which* in non-defining clauses.

1 Entrepreneurs, who have an adventurous spirit, need to be resilient and adaptable.

   – All entrepreneurs have an adventurous spirit.

2 Entrepreneurs who have an adventurous spirit need to be resilient and adaptable.

   – Only the entrepreneurs who have an adventurous spirit need to be resilient and adaptable, not the rest.

Global *which*

You can also use a *which* clause to refer to the whole statement that precedes it. In such cases, do not use *that*. In these cases, always put a comma before the clause that begins with *which*.

1 The troops surrendered their weapons, which surprised the army command.
2 The candidate did not get the position, which was a mistake.

However, because a global *which* is often ambiguous, it is best to avoid it where possible in formal writing. For example, the above sentences would be more precise as below.

1 The army command was surprised that the troops surrendered their weapons.
2 Not giving the candidate the position was a mistake.

Relative clauses activity

Rewrite these sentences to avoid ambiguity.

1 The interest rates fell by 5%, that is interesting.
2 The equipment which we ordered arrived on time which was a great relief.
3 There is only one solution to the problem, which is the course of action, which we must take.
4 Here is a program which eliminates many of the problems which the team has had with previous models.
5 Methodologies which are a formalized approach to implementing the system vary in their approach which involves both analysis and design.

6 One major problem in science is that no matter how extensively a subject is researched, there will still remain the unknown variable of "time", which often reveals something which was not considered.

Active and passive voice

The active and passive voices are a major concern for writers, as they can colour a text profoundly by disclosing or revealing information and by highlighting different elements of the sentence. The active voice emphasizes the agent and the action of a sentence. The passive voice, on the other hand, emphasizes the object, person or thing acted upon. Therefore, using one or the other should be a strategic choice. For example:

> **Active**: The manager signed the contract.
> **Passive**: The contract was signed by the manager.
> **Word order of active voice**: subject + verb + object.
> **Word order of passive voice**: object + be + past participle [optionally + by + subject].

Using active or passive voice is not just a matter of variety. As happens also with other forms of sentence manipulation, it orders and prioritizes information and, therefore, has an evaluative function. Some people (and grammar checkers) harbour deep suspicions about the passive voice. They will tell you to use the active where possible. There are three reasons for this:

1 The passive voice emphasizes the object, which does not carry out any action (it is acted upon). Therefore, the verb of the sentence becomes weaker. The information content of the sentence appears to be static rather than dynamic. This may be required in some cases (as discussed below). However, if it is not a deliberate choice, the passive may better be avoided to prevent weakening the sentence.
2 Often, the passive voice conceals the agent of the action, or at least subordinates it. This may be unacceptable in certain cases where stated responsibility for an action is required for clarity or ethics.
3 Conciseness is valued in many contexts, especially in business and public writing, and the passive voice adds words to sentences.

However, the passive voice has a definite role for these purposes:

1 The agent is unimportant and, in fact, mentioning the agent may make the sentence awkward:

> **Awkward active**: I/we use the passive voice to move components around in a sentence.

Preferred passive: The passive voice is used to move components around in a sentence.
Awkward active: Trucks take the logs to the factory for processing.
Preferred passive: The logs are taken to the factory for processing.

This purpose of the passive is most evident in scientific writing, where processes and procedures are important because of the results and observations they lead to, rather than because of the personal role of the scientists themselves in carrying out the process. Notice also that, in this case, the agent is not mentioned at all in the sentence.

2   The agent is unknown:

Awkward active: Someone stole the computer from the lab.
Preferred passive: The computer was stolen from the lab.

In this case, the agent is unknown and emphasis falls on the event. In fact, in some cases, such as in police reports, it would be misleading to include an agent as perpetrator of a deed, if the identity of this agent is unknown or uncertain.

3   The agent is collective:

Awkward active: People/Farmers grow tea in India.
Preferred passive: Tea is grown in India.

In this case, the subject is not an individual, and the result or process is more important.

There are occasions where using the active voice is a far more advisable choice. As noted above, one occasion is when you want to produce a sharp, energetic and concise style. Another occasion is when your writing involves assuming or attributing responsibility for decisions and making these decisions more personal. In many occasions, the passive voice is used to conceal the agents responsible for certain actions, and this can give a harsh and impersonal impression. For example, the impersonal nature of the following sentence gives it bad audience dynamics:

Awkward passive: Your proposal has been considered and it has been decided to reject it.
Preferred active: The Housing Board considered your proposal and the executive committee decided to reject it.

In important writing, such as proposals, formal business reports and official documents, the readers want to know who they are dealing with in order to ascertain who is responsible for different actions. In such cases, use the passive voice with the utmost care to avoid misunderstandings and conflict. The same situation occurs when you write about plans, decisions and reactions to events. Using the passive in such cases mystifies the topic, since the agents remain unknown, and produces a generalized and vague effect unsuited to professional writing.

Consider this extract. The first sentence is acceptable because it sets the scene and focuses on a process. Notice, however, how the use of the passive voice in the other two sentences puts the writer in a distant and detached position that leaves the reader with a general impression of the situation but with no specific, factual information. Who raised questions? Who questioned the ethical viability of GMF procedures?

> Genetically Modified Foods (GMF) have been used commercially in food products available to the general public since 1996. This was met with general outcry, and many questions were raised about the safety of the products. The ethical viability of such procedures and the impact that GMF would have on the environment were also questioned.

Passive sentences in the active voice

Sometimes a sentence is considered passive because its content is not dynamic even though the sentence might be written in the active voice. A passive sentence is not necessarily a passive voice sentence.

Passive voice sentence with dynamic content: One third of the country's population was killed by the hurricane.

Active voice sentence with passive content: There is tranquillity and peace in the tropical island lifestyle.

Active and passive voice activities

1 Convert these sentences into the passive, if possible, and discuss their effects.

   1 The experts that the CEO invited confirmed the gravity of the situation.
   2 The terrorist squad disarmed the bomb that threatened to destroy the building.
   3 The project team leader could not organize the meeting because he broke his leg.
   4 The manager decided to extend the deadline by a week to allow the team to finish the first part of the project.
   5 Astronomers have discovered a bizarre planet, which is said to orbit our sun in the opposite direction, far beyond Pluto.

Now convert these sentences into the active and discuss their effects.

1   The chemicals are sealed in containers and taken to the laboratory for tests.
2   The analyst felt sure that the files had been tampered with.
3   The plan was approved and permission has been granted to begin implementing it.
4   Your report should be revised carefully before it is submitted for consideration.
5   The discovery of the double helix of DNA was announced by James Watson and Francis Crick in 1953.

2   This extract is written mostly in the passive. Rewrite it using active structures and making any other necessary changes. Then observe and discuss the effect of the two versions.

> The Employment Contracts Act 1991 has been controversial since it came into force. Generally, it has been opposed by trade unions and supported by employers' organizations, although different views might have been held by individual unions and employers. In this Act, the machinery of Industrial Conciliation as the primary means of wage fixing was abolished. Also, state sponsorship of the trade union was ended, and protected status taken away from employees. Trade Unionism has been affected substantially by the 1991 Act, and the power in industrial relations was tilted towards employers.
>
> In contrast, in the Employment Relations Act 2000 unions are given the right to represent their members in bargaining for collective employment agreement with employers. This is particularly significant because only union members can be covered by collective agreement. Collective bargaining may be undertaken by non-union members, but any agreement that is reached will be individual.

Participial phrases

Participial phrases contain the past participle of a verb (generally, verbs ending in -ing, -en and -ed) and no subject. Participials reduce clauses that show a temporal (before, after), or a causal (because, so) relationship. They add variety and, often, formality to your writing, and are useful stylistic choices. Study these sentences and their participial alternatives, and notice how using this construction can introduce variety in your writing:

Compound sentence: The CEO agreed to support the proposal, so she attended this month's meeting.

Sentence beginning with participial phrase: Having agreed to support the proposal, the CEO attended this month's meeting.

Sentence with subordinate clause: Many investors are turning to mutual funds this year, because they think that interest rates will fall even further.

Sentence beginning with a participial phrase: Thinking interest rates will fall even further, many investors are turning to mutual funds this year.

Participial phrases generally serve the following functions:

(a) they help keep your writing concise by reducing words
(b) they provide you with a tool to give your writing more variety
(c) they can make your writing more formal.

Frequent error with participial phrases

Using participial phrases incorrectly may lead to the common error known as **dangling modifier**. This occurs when the verb of the participial phrase does not agree with the noun immediately following the participial phrase:

Dangling modifier: While inspecting the nuclear reactor, a loud crash alarmed the supervision team.

– was the loud crash inspecting the nuclear reactor?

Corrected: While inspecting the nuclear reactor, the supervision team was alarmed by a loud crash.

– note that to correct the relation while keeping the participial phrase, the sentence has to change from active to passive voice.

Corrected: The loud crash alarmed the supervision team, while they were inspecting the nuclear reactor.

– this removes the participial phrase and adds a full subordinate clause

Dangling modifier: Having solved the problem, it was easy for him to get any job he wanted.

Corrected: Having solved the problem, he could get any job he wanted.

Participial phrases activity

Combine the following sentences by turning one of them into a participial phrase.

1 The Managing Director allocated an extra $2 million to our department. He was pleasantly disposed towards our supervisor's project.
2 The General Manager was faced with numerous accusations of misconduct. He was forced to resign in June.

3 Small business owners can give too little attention to choosing a good location for their business. This results in lower profits or even bankruptcy.

4 She attained a good reputation and the admiration of her colleagues in the corporation. Because of this status, she had no problem finding a new job.

5 The Employment Relations Act is based largely on the presumption that the employment relationship is a human relationship. With this attitude, it has been possible to solve successfully many disputes.

6 The unexpected settlement money that the company won in the court case gave them the opportunity to expand their business internationally. This resulted in a surge in confidence and increased optimism among all company members.

Subject–verb–pronoun agreement

A common troublespot in writing is misusing a singular verb with a plural subject and vice versa, or a plural verb with a singular pronoun and vice versa. This sentence, for example, comes from a professional document:

Incorrect: The facts in the case and all the evidence provided has been considered in the final decision.

Correct: The facts in the case and all the evidence provided have been considered in the final decision.

In the incorrect version of the sentence, the verb "has been" does not agree with the subject, which is "the facts in the case and all the evidence provided". The writer wrongly assumed that the word closest to the verb, "evidence", is the subject.

Some general guidelines for correct subject–verb–pronoun agreement are:

1 Collective nouns (such as *police, family, government, team, audience,* etc.) can take a singular or a plural verb. Your choice depends on whether you want to emphasize their collective nature or the fact that they are composed of individuals. However, ensure that if you use a pronoun to refer to a collective noun, it has the same number as the verb:

Incorrect: The audience showed its appreciation. They gave the speaker a standing ovation.

Correct: The audience showed their appreciation. They gave the speaker a standing ovation.

2 Correlative conjunctions (*either-or, neither-nor, not only-but also*) have two subjects. In this case, the verb must agree with the subject closest to it:

Incorrect: Not only the workers but also the supervisor were affected by the fumes.

Correct: Not only the workers but also the supervisor was affected by the fumes.

Incorrect: Not only the supervisor but also the workers was affected by the fumes.

Correct: Not only the supervisor but also the workers were affected by the fumes.

3 Phrases separating the subject and the verb do not affect the number of the verb or pronoun:

Incorrect: The scientist, together with his troupe of devoted followers and supporters, have occupied the second floor of the building.

Correct: The scientist, together with his troupe of devoted followers and supporters, has occupied the second floor of the building.

However, subjects joined by "and" or "both-and" are plural and take a plural verb:

Incorrect: The scientist and his troupe of devoted followers has occupied the second floor of the building.

Correct: The scientist and his troupe of devoted followers have occupied the second floor of the building.

4 The pronouns "each", "every", "anyone", "everyone" "no one" are singular and should take singular verbs and pronouns.

Incorrect: He stated that anybody is welcome to apply for membership; as for applications, each is to be assessed according to their own merit.

Correct: He stated that anybody is welcome to apply for membership; as for applications, each is to be assessed according to its own merit.

In informal writing, as in speaking, this rule is often bypassed to avoid cumbersome sentences.

Informal: Everyone brought their books.

Formal: Everyone brought his/her books.

Subject–verb–pronoun agreement activity

Select the correct verbs in the following sentences:

1 The mob (was, were) mindless of the consequences of their actions.
2 Neither the general nor his men (was, were) prepared for the sudden attack; not only the men but also their leader (were, was) ready to retreat.
3 Assessments of essays and the exam (is, are) expected to be completed tomorrow.

4 An estimation of profits and losses (are, is) advisable before deciding.
5 The lecturer, together with her tutors (are, is) going to attend the meeting.
6 Confidence and initiative and courage to take risks (lead, leads) to promotion in that field.
7 The issue most on his mind (are, is) efforts to negotiate a settlement.
8 The audience (were, was) conscious of its power to influence the course of the performance.
9 The decision to install the new computers and to update the software programs (has been, have been) finalized by the executive committee.
10 Sharks, because of their secretive nature, and potentially aggressive behaviour, (has been, have been) a difficult topic of study.

Punctuation

Punctuation marks introduce rhythm and pace to the written text. Although they do serve to reflect in written form the dynamic aspects of speech, it would be misleading to equate them with the breathing patterns of speaking because punctuation follows syntactic (that is, grammatical), and not phonetic or physical aspects of language. Therefore, reading a text aloud is not an accurate means of deciding where to insert a punctuation mark nor what this mark should be. In this respect, punctuation is one of the most misunderstood aspects of writing. There are some grammatical rules that writers should know. This section overviews these rules.

A comma is the weakest pause mark. Others, in order of increasing duration or suddenness of the pause, include:

    semicolon – ;
    colon – :
    ellipsis – …
    en dash – –
    quotation marks – "…"
    full stop (period) – .
    exclamation mark – !
    question mark – ?

Correct use of punctuation has changed over the years. Older texts often use punctuation quite differently from modern texts. The following guide gives you an overview of punctuation usage that is the current international standard.

Comma

Three main categories cover most of the cases when a comma is required:

1 Inserting words, phrases or clauses into a sentence

We often add extra information to the basic core of sentences by adding phrases that give more detail, help to keep the reader on track or just generally add more variety to sentence structure. When adding phrases to a sentence, or moving phrases out of place to add variety, set off these additions and interjections with commas. These changes are made in three places:

a) Sentence openers

> **Adverbial conjunctions:** However, I ...
> **Interjections:** Well, I ...
> **Adverbs:** Often, I ...
> **Prepositional phrases:** In board meetings, I ...
> **Participial phrases:** Having completed the project, I ...
> **Adverbial clauses:** Whenever I try to think, I ...
> **Appositives:** A successful entrepreneur, Steve Jobs ...

A frequent question is if a comma is always needed after a prepositional phrase that begins the sentence. The ideal answer is yes: you cannot go wrong by including a comma after a phrase, to set it off from the sentence that it modifies. However, if the sentence is easily read and understood without the comma, and there are typographical space limitations, omit it.

> **Easily understood sentence:** At present (,) the company does not have a financial manager.
> **Confusing sentence:** After moving the tenants, who inherited one million dollars, bought their own mansion.
> **Corrected:** After moving, the tenants, who inherited one million dollars, bought their own mansion.

b) Sentence insertions

These have the same function as the openers but produce a less emphatic effect. For example:

> **Inserted participial phrase:** The executive, having completed the project, decided to take a break.

TIP

If you use insertions, remember to use commas at both ends.

c) Sentence enders

Inserting a phrase or clause at the end of a sentence gives the least emphasis to the information contained in that phrase or clause. For example:

> **Participial phrase ending the sentence:** Give this to the President, the woman sitting next to the door.

2 Joining two clauses with *for, and, nor, but, or, yet, so* (coordinating conjunctions).

Two sentences can be joined with a coordinating conjunction:

> **Simple sentences:** I took part in the competition. I came first.
> **Compound sentence:** I took part in the competition and I came first.

A frequent question is if a comma is needed before a coordinating conjunction. Grammatically, the conjunction is enough to combine two clauses and no comma is needed. The comma before a coordinating conjunction, also known as *Oxford comma* or, more disturbingly, as *serial comma*, is attributed to Horace Hart, printer of the Oxford University Press from 1893 to 1915, who recommended using it for clarity. Some style guides, such as the American Psychological Association (APA), endorse its use, while others, including, paradoxically, the University of Oxford style guide, propose using it only in cases of ambiguity. The best advice is to be guided by context and clarity in this.

3 Listing items in a series

A comma is used to list items in the same category in one sentence.

> **Listing items:** The position requires writing annual reports, internal memoranda, newsletters and online documentation.

Frequent errors with the comma

A. Comma Splice

Comma Splice occurs when you join two full sentences with a comma. This is corrected by inserting a period (or full stop in UK), a semicolon or a coordinating conjunction in the place of the comma.

> **Comma Splice:** The committee contributed to the project by sending delegates to the meeting, however, these delegates were not adequately informed of recent developments in software design.
> **Corrected using full stop:** The committee contributed to the project by sending delegates to the meeting. However, these delegates were not adequately informed of recent developments in software design.
> **Corrected using semicolon:** The committee contributed to the project by sending delegates to the meeting; however, these delegates were not adequately informed of recent developments in software design.

Corrected using coordinating conjunction: The committee contributed to the project by sending delegates to the meeting but these delegates were not adequately informed of recent developments in software design.

B. Subject–Verb Disjunction

Subject–verb disjunction occurs when the subject is separated from its verb with a comma. Subjects may be separated from verbs only with phrases and subordinate clauses. In these cases, commas are inserted at either end of the phrase or clause. This way, the phrase or clause is set off from the rest of the sentence.

Incorrect: Authorized to seal the agreement, the company representatives, will meet with each board member individually during their visit.

Correct: The company representatives, who are authorized to seal the agreement, will meet with each board member individually during their visit.

Incorrect: Designers, play a pivotal role in the success of marketing products, through their skills in attractive presentation.

Correct: Designers play a pivotal role in the success of marketing products, through their skills in attractive presentation.

Correct: Designers, through their skills in attractive presentation, play a pivotal role in the success of marketing products.

Semicolon

The semicolon is used in the following cases:

1 It joins together two independent sentences. It indicates a stronger pause than a comma, but a shorter one than the full stop, and shows that there is a close relationship between the two joined sentences. For instance, the first example below consists of two sentences that distribute information equally. The second example below consists of one sentence with two clauses joined with a semicolon. This suggests that the second clause is directly related to the first as an explanation or result.

Two sentences: Branding is a major stage in the marketing process. It determines how consumers will visualise and relate to the product through its name.

Two clauses joined with semicolon: Branding is a major stage in the marketing process; it determines how consumers will visualize and relate to the product through its name.

2 It separates items in a list, when one item or more in the list already contain a comma. The sentence below illustrates this.

Listing with semicolons: Attendees from overseas should submit a copy of their passport, showing the photo page; a certified cheque or money order, payable in local currency; and a completed application form.

Frequent errors with the semicolon

A. Connecting a phrase to a sentence

This error occurs when a semicolon is used to connect a phrase to a clause. The correct punctuation mark for this case is the comma.

> **Incorrect:** The project team could not continue with the intended plan; having encountered unexpected opposition from major stockholders.

> **Correct:** Having encountered unexpected opposition from major stockholders, the project team could not continue with the intended plan.

> **Correct:** The project team could not continue with the intended plan, having encountered unexpected opposition from major stockholders.

> **Correct:** The project team, having encountered unexpected opposition from major stockholders, could not continue with the intended plan.

B. Introducing a list

This error occurs when a semicolon is used to introduce a list of items or bullet points. The correct punctuation mark for this case is the colon.

> **Incorrect:** With your application include the following;

- A complete CV with contact details of three referees
- Transcripts of academic qualifications
- A completed application cover form.

> **Correct:** With your application, include the following:

- A complete CV with contact details of three referees
- Transcripts of academic qualifications
- A completed application cover form.

Colon

The colon has the following uses:

1 It introduces quotations a sentence or longer in length. If the quotation consists of a few words, a comma will suffice.

> **No use of colon before quotation:** The CEO made it clear that "only under exceptional circumstances" will the plan change.

> **Use of colon before quotation:** The CEO made it clear that "only under exceptional circumstances" will the plan change. He said: "The situation is pretty clear-cut. The majority of stockholders have voted for the new system to be implemented on an experimental basis for three months. Until this trial period passes, there is nothing more to be done."

2   It introduces a list of things, whether the list is written in-line or vertically. Three groups may attend the meeting:

- Members of the executive committee
- Press representatives
- Stockholders

3   It shows the outcome or effect of an action. In this case, the colon plays a similar role to a semicolon. However, it has a more visual, and, therefore, more dramatic effect than a semicolon.

He looked at an amazing sight: the house had totally collapsed.

Ellipsis

Ellipsis marks are much rarer in business writing than in creative or informal writing, because they reflect an incompleteness that is inconsistent with the purposes of professional documents. Ellipsis marks are mainly used for the following purposes:

1   To show hesitation or interruption. This is the most conversational use of the ellipsis, very rare in business writing. The extract below, from one of Ian Rankin's Inspector Rebus novels, exemplifies this in the representation of Rebus' meandering train of thought:

Rebus commiserated for a couple of minutes, thinking of his own doctor's appointment, the one he was missing yet again by making this call. When he put the phone down, he scribbled the name Marr on to his pad and circled it. Ranald Marr, with his Maserati and toy soldiers. You'd almost have thought he'd lost a daughter... Rebus was beginning to revise that opinion. He wondered if Marr knew how precarious his job was, knew that the mere thought of their savings catching a cold might spur the small investors on, demanding a sacrifice ... (Rankin, 2001, p. 352).

2   In quotations, to show that a part of the speaker's statement has been omitted, usually because it was irrelevant to the writer's main concern. This is the most common use of ellipsis in business and academic writing. To show that the ellipsis is not part of the quotation, enclose it in square brackets. For example, in the quotation below I have included the introductory sentence to a section, then omitted the remainder of that paragraph going straight on to the next paragraph, from where I have also omitted a few words that refer to a diagram that is irrelevant to my discussion:

"All researchers must support contestable claims with evidence, but they must then explain that evidence, treating each major bit of evidence as a claim in a secondary argument that needs its own evidence. [...] If you like doing things visually, put this on a wall-sized chart. Pin up index cards [...], then try different combinations of secondary arguments."

Dash

Dashes have the following uses:

1 They enclose information that is secondary to the main point of the sentence and that can be omitted or skipped – similar to brackets (parentheses). In this case, a dash goes at each end of the additional information. Avoid this in sentences that contain important information or when you want the readers' undivided attention, because, like brackets, dashes show a divergence from the main issue and can be distracting. Also, keep in mind that they can make a sentence unnecessarily long, so, where conciseness or directness are your aim, avoid them.

> 1 She would have liked to see those letters. Chances were, they couldn't be recovered, either because they'd perished – been disposed of with Lovell's effects when he'd died – or had gone overseas. An awful lot of historical documentation had found its way into collections overseas – mostly Canada and the US – and many of these collections were private, which meant few details of their contents were available (Rankin, 2001, p. 228).
>
> 2 Both developers were away from the meeting – one at home sick, the other attending a trade fair – so no major decisions were made that would affect the outcome of the project.

2 They have a similar function to the colon in introducing a set of items, and to the comma in setting off a comment on the information presented in the main clause. As opposed to the colon or comma, however, the dash makes the information it sets off more emphatic. In this case, the dash can actually make the sentence more concise by enabling the omission of introductory phrases or subordinate clauses. Place the dash before the additional information at the end of the sentence.

> 1 The CEO's decision to support the proposal was welcomed by stockholders – an unusual reception given the controversial nature of the proposal.
>
> 2 An unprecedented number of professionals attended the meeting – most of them engineers.

Apostrophe

Apostrophes are used for two purposes:

1 They show possession or ownership. In this case, they come before the possessive *s*. If the word already ends with an *s*, such as in plurals (pen-pens), in some names (Mars, Ross) or in some nouns (boss, albatross), the apostrophe comes after the *s*.

– the dog's tail (one dog)
– the dogs' tails (more than one dog)
– the student's grade (one student)
– the students' grades (more than one student)
– the boss' plan (one boss)
– the bosses' plans (more than one boss)

2 They make contractions (combine two words into one). In this case, the apostrophe shows that there is a word, like *is, has* or *not*, missing. This is not a frequent use of apostrophes in professional writing, because contractions are avoided in formal documents.

isn't it a nice day!
don't say it!
it's important
they've arrived

Frequent errors with the apostrophe

A. Incorrect apostrophe in plurals

This error occurs when an apostrophe is inserted before a plural *s*, as it would be before a possessive *s*. Distinguish between the possessive *s* (which requires an apostrophe) and the plural *s* (which does not).

Incorrect: The information is in two video's.
Correct: The information is in two videos.
Incorrect: The presidents move was foreseen by many.
Correct: The president's move was foreseen by many.

B. Omission of apostrophe in contractions or incorrect inclusion in a pronoun. This error occurs when two words are contracted into one without an apostrophe to indicate the contraction.

> **Incorrect:** In all, its an interesting idea.
> **Correct:** In all, it's an interesting idea.
> **Incorrect:** The deadline has arrived for students to submit they're assignments (this is a contraction of "they are").
> **Correct:** The deadline has arrived for students to submit their assignments (this is the pronoun "their").

Quotation marks

Quotation marks are used when reporting the exact words of a speaker or writer. Like the Oxford comma and spelling, they are another confusing part of punctuation. The confusion is compounded by the fact that British, Commonwealth and American texts use quotation marks differently. The best advice is to select a method and be consistent, and, if your organization has a style guide, to adhere to it.

Here are some general guidelines:

1 If the quotation takes up more than three lines, indent it in a block paragraph and set it off the rest of the text. In this case, do not use quotation marks – the indentation signals that the text is a quotation.
2 Use double quotation marks for the beginning and ending of quotations, and single quotation marks for words or phrases that are quoted within a quotation.
3 Use double quotation marks when you want to show that a word or phrase should be taken figuratively or is out of context.
4 Place full stops, commas, semicolons, colons, exclamation marks and question marks outside quotation marks, unless the quotation itself contains them. In American publications, periods and commas are placed inside quotation marks, whereas colons and semicolons are placed outside. Question marks and exclamation marks are placed inside quotation marks unless they apply to the whole sentence.

ACTIVITIES

Punctuation activities

1 Insert suitable punctuation marks in the following sentences, if necessary:

　　1 Proposals a common business document are a major problem for writers.
　　2 The hotel chain provides its customers with affordable reliable and comfortable service.

    3 Travel is educational it broadens your horizons.

    4 The operator ran the program the disk drive was faulty.

2 Discuss and correct the punctuation errors in these sentences.

    1 In addition to cleaning the assistant janitor must safeguard building keys.

    2 In some cases students have doubled their reading speed; effectively halving their time spent in researching for assignments.

    3 Everything seemed so different, the buildings were all made of red brick and were all very new.

    4 The government "red tape" has hindered business operations therefore it is important to assist these businesses in such issues.

    5 The majority of young shareholders voiced opposition to the proposed plan, this shows that what older generations took for granted is unacceptable for the younger generations who are better informed on alternative options.

    6 If you are tired of three-dimensional reality of the laws of physics and of cause, and effect; then virtual reality games will be congenial for you. As here you can: continually defy the odds, encounter firsts, and lasts, and perform miracles.

    7 Martial arts training brings many benefits to stressed professionals; it is good for self-rehabilitation in the health of body mind and spirit. An excellent method for the ailing to energize themselves in the search for well-being, vitality is enhanced and can lead to the confidence required for professional success; in any field.

Spelling

Unfortunately, English has no specific rules that you can learn to improve your spelling. The best way to improve your spelling is to read, read, read. A more systematic method is to focus on words that you repeatedly misspell, memorize their spelling and practise writing sentences with these words. For example, set yourself a weekly limit of about 30 words and give yourself 15 minutes a day every day for a specific period (from three to six months, or even a year depending on how bad your spelling is). Every couple of weeks or so test your learning to see if your programme is working. There are no quick-fix schemes for spelling.

As a writer, it is important not to underestimate spelling. Bad spelling is not a minor problem for writers. It shows that you are, at best, sloppy, at worst, illiterate. Also, relying on spellcheckers is not a good idea, as they do not always identify the context a word is used in. For example, they do not distinguish between *homophones* (words that sound the same but are spelled differently and have a different meaning). *Sun* and *son*, *I* and *eye*, *there* and *their*, *so* and *sew*, *weather* and *whether* are all pairs containing homophones with radically different meanings.

Table 10.1 contains a list of commonly confused words to practise.

Table 10.1 Commonly Confused Words	
accept	receive (verb)
except	with the exclusion of (preposition)
advice	recommendation (noun)
advise	to recommend (verb)
affect	to produce an influence on (verb)
effect	consequence of an action (noun)
already	by this time
all ready	fully prepared
altogether	thoroughly
all together	everyone or everything in one place
brake	device for stopping
break	destroy, make into pieces
canvas	material (noun)
canvass	solicit, ascertain, survey (verb)
choose	to pick
chose	past tense of choose
complement	round out, add to, complete
compliment	praise, flatter
council	administrative body (noun)
counsel	advise, consult (verb)
device	a plan, an implement
devise	to create

eminent	distinguished, notable
imminent	impending, about to happen
ensure	make certain of
insure	take out an insurance policy
envelop	to surround (verb)
envelope	container for a letter (noun)
formally	conventionally, with ceremony
formerly	previously
lead	heavy metal; to guide
led	past tense of lead
loose	unbound, not tightly fastened (adjective)
lose	to misplace (verb)
personal	intimate
personnel	employees
precede	to come before
proceed	to continue
principal	foremost; chief, leader
principle	moral conviction, basic truth
quiet	silent, calm
quite	very
stationary	standing still
stationery	writing paper
wave	surf
waive	to relinquish, give up
weather	climatic condition
whether	if
which	one of a group
witch	female sorcerer

General proofreading activity

These sentences contain errors in grammar, style, accuracy, clarity, spelling or punctuation.

1 Having approved the project, the necessary staff was recruited.

2 The basic principal of good writing is clarity.

3 Today pneumatic tyres are fitted to almost all road vehicles, originally they were developed for use on bicycles.

4 One has to be aware of all the facts before you reach an opinion.

5 The decision to introduce computers have already been made.

6 It is estimated that more than a thousand people were effected by the radiation leak.

7 In advertising the brand information includes not only information about the product but also the image related to the product.

8 Although the situation required expert advice, however they attempted to solve it on their own.

9 The refinement process has already started when the minerals will be sealed in the special containers.

10 The report was logical, short, and reading it was easy.

11 In the last couple of years, a pattern has emerged on campus that shows an increase in student enrolments.

12 Everybody must agree for the recommendations to be implemented. This being the standard course of action for implementing recommendations.

13 Through public education, controlling manipulation techniques by making all testing of Genetically Modified Food (GMF) products compulsory, and increasing government funding, safety and acceptance of GMF can be established.

14 The objectives of this report are to establish and strengthen the relationship between small business and government organizations.

15 Judging from the growth rate in small business at 1.4 %, it shows that the country's economy is in good shape.

16 The government "red tape" has hindered business operations therefore it is important to assist these businesses in such issues.

17 With the change in government policy there represents many potential problems that translate to higher costs for employers and a less flexible work force.

18 Having an information system that is not integrated and cohesive could result in X company's inability to effectively capture business information about its operations and customer base, which will in turn affect its competitiveness in the market and have a negative effect on its reputation as a company that produces cutting edge products valued by international business world-wide.

19 The Museum offers people a general range of activities, whether as members of the audience, attending events, being part of a guided tour group, retail therapy, enjoying the restaurants and bars or simply taking a stroll.

20 The using of function keys by a user allows the user to carry out some specific functions within the program.

Revising and editing

For many writers, revising is the most important stage of the writing process. Although some creative writers, for example science fiction novelist Isaac Asimov (1993), claim that they spend minimal to no time revising, most others emphasize the value of revision in taking a draft to its final stage. In fact many of the problems associated with written communication are due to a lack of revision: inexperienced writers often jump straight from writing to proofreading without going through the revising process – with unfortunate results.

Revision is the process of seeing the text anew (which is, in fact, the literal meaning of "revise"), so that you gain some distance from it and are able to make extensive changes, if necessary. Revision is not correcting errors in spelling and grammar – the task of proofreading – but rather, a reconsideration of the whole text, its meaning, flow and significance, from the readers' perspective. When revising you must decide, honestly, whether the writing is really effective in relation to audience and purpose. If it is not, it takes creativity and vision to figure out what needs to be changed and how. Revising can also be brutal; sometimes the best way forward is to delete material that may have taken hours or days to draft.

An important part of revision is making sure you have a sustained focus and purpose throughout the document. Focusing encourages you to establish what the main point of your document will be. Every document, from the shortest memo to the most intricate report, must contain one overriding point – the main message of the text. Make sure this point stands out, by stating it in a complete sentence at several different stages of the writing process.

Editing is the process of ensuring that a text complies with company house styles, and that it follows the conventions of its genre. Editing can be *substantive* and *mechanical*.

Substantive editing involves deleting and reorganizing sections, and adding or rewriting content. During substantive editing, you may need to do some more research and to rewrite sections of the document.

Mechanical editing involves checking for style consistency, genre formatting and grammar. During mechanical editing, you proofread for sentence structure and punctuation problems and you check for compliance with house styles.

Editing can be done by the writer or by another person. In collaborative writing in business contexts, for example, one team member acts as an editor to the team's reports, compiling and synthesizing material from different members' work. Also, the publishing industry has professional editors, who ensure consistency and appropriate formatting of all texts published by a particular publishing company.

The following guidelines are relevant for both revising and editing:

When you have a complete document, start revising from the big picture or conceptual content to the details: have you included all necessary information? Did you respond to the brief appropriately and effectively? Don't begin with mechanical editing because this would draw your attention away from logic, meaning and clarity.

After checking for overall meaning, look at the organization of the document: is this the most appropriate ordering of information, or should you reorganize paragraphs? Remember that, in addition to a "logical" sequencing of information, there is also a "conventional" sequencing that depends on the genre of your document. Some journalist genres, for example, would begin with the most important information first, Inverted Pyramid style, and would have a catchy lead instead of a formal introduction.

Then rethink the audience: is the style appropriate? Do you need to define terms or give more information? Have you given too many details on a subject your audience is expected to be fluent in? Look at examples and explanations: are they specific, clear and interesting, and not exaggerated, vague, repetitive or contradictory?

Afterwards move to paragraphs and check for unity and cohesion: is each paragraph about one main point? Is all information included in the paragraph relevant to this main point? Does each paragraph flow from the previous one, so that the reader can understand the transition between one point and another?

Finally, proofread the text for grammar, word-choice, punctuation and spelling: do your sentences and words provide the appropriate "rhythm" for the type of document and audience? Are all sentences grammatically correct, clear and concise? Have you avoided unnecessary repetition or wordiness?

Table 10.2 is a chart to guide you in asking the right questions, which will lead to the delivery of a polished and professional final copy.

Table 10.2   Revision Chart

Context
- Am I writing to the right person?
- Have I learnt as much as I can about my readers?
- Will there be an immediate and secondary audience and have I catered to them?

Content
- Is all the information I intended to convey there?
- Do I need to reformulate my argument or main message?
- Do I need to deepen or extend my analysis?
- Do I have irrelevant information? Should I narrow the scope?
- Do I need to reorganize information?
- Do I need to add information to strengthen a point?

Organization
- Do I need to reproportion the amount of space given to particular topics to reflect their importance or complexity?
- Have I used informative headings that reflect the content of the sections?
- Have I used sectioning and point-listing so as to highlight important points?

Style
- Do I need to simplify anything or make it more complex?
- Is my degree of formality appropriate?
- Is my tone acceptable for the purpose and content?
- Are my sentences active and concise?
- Have I used enough sentence variety to make the writing less monotonous and more compelling?
- Have I used enough flow and transitions to make the writing coherent?
- Have I ensured that my expression is gender-neutral?

Layout
- Have I formatted paragraphs correctly and consistently?
- Do I need to add, delete or adjust graphics (tables, graphs, charts, drawings, photos)?
- Do I need to adjust the visual aspects (font size, style and consistency, white space, formatting)?
- Is my referencing appropriate and correct? Have I cited sources for all information?

Style guides

Many corporations, large organizations and government agencies have style guides or manuals that describe the stylistic and formatting conventions followed. This is a very useful item, since it directs writers on how to structure their documents. If your company does not follow the conventions set out in a style manual, consider creating such a manual, proposing that one be created or suggesting that an available manual be adopted. Existing manuals include the APA (American Psychological Association), MLA (Modern Languages Association), and Chicago Style manuals.

Even in cases where you only need to produce one document, it is useful to create a style sheet documenting the spelling, formatting and other choices that you made. This not only helps you when revising the document, it also helps others who may take over writing the document, or who may wish to write a similar document.

Style guides and style sheets help to maintain consistency within a document and in a set of documents produced by the same source. They also answer writers' questions about how they should present their writing. Table 10.3 lists some sections to include when designing a style guide.

Table 10.3   Style Guide Sections

Spelling: do you use American or British spelling? Or are both acceptable as long as consistency is maintained?

Fonts: what are the rules about size and type of font?

Formatting: how much space will you allow between lines? How much margin? How will you section and how will you number sections? How will you organize sections in a report?

Numbers: when do you use figures and when words? The standard convention is to use words up to ten and figures after that, returning to words when you reach thousands, millions and billions. Will you keep this standard or use another?

Abbreviations: what will you abbreviate and how? For example, will you write Mr or Mister? Dr or Doctor? How will you punctuate abbreviations?

Punctuation: how will you punctuate? Will you use any punctuation at the end of bullet points? Will you include punctuation marks inside quotation marks or outside?

Visuals: what rules will you have for visuals? Will you have any restrictions on size of visuals in a document? How will you title visuals?

A final note...

The book ends with an overview of some major reasons for difficulties or failures in communication in professional contexts. These are taken from specific cases where miscommunication led to disasters or serious damage. Having worked your way through this book, you are now equipped to handle such situations expertly.

Major reasons for faulty communication, on both conceptual (thinking and planning) and writing (drafting and revising) levels, are:

Ignoring the company or project's role distribution: in many cases, time is wasted, with documents being exchanged between parties that will not be the final decision makers. When dealing with important projects, involve the right people in the chain of communication, and speak (or write) to them in ways they can understand. For example, in engineering projects, administrators, and possibly even marketing managers, are most often involved in the lifecycle of a product. They may not be engineers themselves, so they would require technical concepts to be interpreted.

Not following the rule of "one document – one message": if you have many pieces of information to communicate, write different documents. Do not attempt to cut corners by cramming as much data as possible in one document. Documents that lack a main message, or "bottom line", fade in significance, and the important issues they may contain are lost if they are buried in a maze of facts presented indiscriminately. For example, when delivering PowerPoint presentations, do not clutter slides with all the information that you want the audience to know. Use the slides to complement, not contain, your oral explanations, and supplement the talk with written documents, such as technical and progress reports.

Adopting an unsuitable style: readers are offended if their "attitude" (the frame of mind in which they receive the document) is not respected. Do not be overly friendly and casual with readers who may expect more respect and formality and do not adopt a lighthearted approach with topics that the reader treats with gravity. Remember that your sentence structures emphasize different elements, and construct them deliberately and with a clear intent. Remember that after having lost a client or alienated a manager, it will be very difficult to regain their trust.

Not being clear, accurate and concise: if you are vague, confusing and inaccurate you come across as unprofessional and untrustworthy. Plan your writing carefully so that you can collect appropriate and adequate data to make it informative for your readers. Revise well to avoid repetitions and what may come across as self-indulgent verbosity. Remember that time is precious for business readers.

Not having enough signposting, highlighting and closure: readers are not in your mind, so direct their reading by signalling changes in direction (such as contrast, exemplification, additional point, etc.), distinguishing data according to its order of importance, and indicating where one chunk of information ends and another begins. Readers in professional contexts do not have the disposition to work laboriously through stream of consciousness-type writing, trying to trace the important points. Preview the structure and purpose of your documents in a clear executive summary and introduction, sum up points in appropriate places in the text and make sure you make clear what action you require the reader to take.

Being unconvincing or irrelevant: people respond more positively to those who communicate on their "wavelength". Also, they pay more attention to information that is relevant to their needs, desires and expectations. If you want your advice or warning to be heeded, make sure it is pertinent to the values and goals of your audience. To achieve this, do your "homework" by learning as much as you can about your readers, and relate your descriptions and explanations to situations that are familiar to them.

Not acknowledging the "big picture": documents concerning projects with a public relevance may become public at any time. Even if you are an engineer working on technical equipment, your correspondence and notes could come under public scrutiny, if, say, the users of your equipment are harmed because of malfunctions. Therefore, always write documents about professional projects with the idea that more than just your intended readers may end up reading them. An example is email. If a message you send to a particular person includes information that is pertinent to others, your recipient may distribute the email. Be careful how you phrase emails that may be distributed. Have you insulted someone who may receive it? Have you written something that may be misunderstood by some readers? Use foresight when writing.

Not paying enough attention to deadlines: this is a very common problem in all types of writing tasks. The best advice is to not be over-optimistic about how much time you have to complete a task. Plan your time carefully and at different times during the task. Have contingency plans: if you get stuck during a task move to something else that you can do more easily. Train yourself to multitask. And always remember to leave some time for revision and for unexpected delays.

References and further reading

Asimov, I. (1993) Revisions. Dozois, G. et al (Eds.) *Writing science fiction and fantasy.* New York: St. Martin's Press, pp. 221–225.

Biber, D., Johansson, S., Leech, G., Conrad, S., & Finegan, E. (1999) *Longman grammar of spoken and written English.* London: Longman.

Dwyer, J. (1997) *The business communication handbook*, 4th edition. Sydney: Prentice-Hall.

Faigley, L. (2012) *The little Penguin handbook*, 2nd edition. Boston: Pearson.

Greenbaum, S., & Quirk, R. (1990) *A student's grammar of the English language*. Harlow: Longman.

Hacker, D. (2007) *The Bedford handbook*, 7th edition. New York: Bedford St. Martins.

Ivers, M. (2010) *Random House guide to good writing*. New York: Ballantine Books.

Jones, D. (1999) *The technical communicator's handbook*. New York: Allyn and Bacon.

Kennedy, G. (2014) *Structure and meaning in English*. London: Routledge.

Rankin, I. (2001) *The falls*. London: Orion.

Rude, C. (1998) *Technical editing*, 2nd edition. New York: Allyn and Bacon.

Stott, R., & Chapman P. (2001) *Grammar and writing*. London: Longman.

Sword, H. (2016) *The writer's diet*, 2nd edition. Chicago: University of Chicago Press.

Appendix

Job applications

Focus:

- Career values
- Curriculum vitae formats
- Covering letters

The shape of the workforce and the idea of a "career" have changed dramatically over the last few decades worldwide. Since the 1990s, rapid changes in technology, the globalization of the workforce, competitive international markets and the growth of short-term contract work have made the contemporary workplace anxious and fast-paced.

In some instances, people setting out in the workforce today are likely to change careers several times over the span of their working life. Accordingly, employers now look for graduates who can demonstrate transferable skills, particularly in communication, leadership and teamwork. Such skills are transferred from one job to another, indicating a willingness and ability to adapt to new business procedures and new technology.

To survive in this quickly-changing environment, you must be flexible and ready. This chapter will prepare you to "market yourself" in the workforce by illustrating successful methods of compiling a job application consisting of a CV and a covering letter. Although many of the tips given here will interest all jobseekers, the main target readers are those starting out in the workplace.

Knowing your values

Your chances of being good at what you do increase if you actually enjoy what you do. If your job is just a set of gruelling tasks, it is highly unlikely you will excel or stand out in any way. And you can only really be successful in what you value. In fact, successful professionals are unanimous on this. Advice given to new generation professionals by both corporate CEOs and adventurous entrepreneurs emphasizes the importance of enjoyment at work for success. For such reasons, before setting out on a new career, or before changing your current career, you should assess your values. Table App1 lists some questions to guide you on your career quest:

Table App1   Career Values
What do you want to achieve in your life?   Determine your goals and ambitious. Do you value wealth? Fame? Spirituality? Independence? Do you want a centre stage position in life or would you prefer to work behind the scenes?
What are your skills and talents, and can you make best use of them in your career?   Think of all your talents, interests and abilities. How can you adapt them so that they will be functional in your work? Break down all the work you have done into constituent skills and reshuffle them. For example, if you have been successful in sports, this could indicate endurance, high energy, collaborative skill, fast thinking, etc. There are plenty of other contexts where these skills would be useful.
How good a communicator are you?   Are you good at writing? Speaking in public? Explaining? Have you ever taught? Do you prefer one-to-one communication or would you rather address a large number of people?
Are you project- or process-oriented?   Do you like doing short-term projects that you can finalize quickly and move on to something else, or do you prefer being part of a chain, contributing to an ongoing process?
Do you prefer to lead or to follow?   Do you prefer following others' instructions, or would you rather instruct others? Do you work best in a corporate, hierarchical environment, or does self-employment appeal to you more?
What sort of culture would you prefer to work in?   Do you like strict guidelines or a more liberal way of achieving goals? Do you want to be given specific goals or would you rather work with broad parameters? How closely do you want to be managed? Would you rather be left alone to find solutions your own way? Do you want strict hours of work or more autonomy to choose your timetable?

What drives you?
Do you want status? Recognition? Money? Independence? A combination?

What location suits you?
Are you happy in a high-rise building in the centre of town, or would you prefer a suburb, or a specialized location like Silicon Valley? Do you want to have the option of working at home? Travelling? Working in two or more different places?

Adapted from Morgan and Banks, 1999, pp. 28–30.

CVs, résumés and cover letters

A **curriculum vitae** (CV) lists your education, work skills and work experience. A CV is often glanced at or skimmed rather than carefully read. In many cases, potential employers spend about 30 seconds on a first viewing of a CV, before deciding whether the candidate is worthy of further consideration. Thus, you should structure your CV in such a way that the potential employer can tell at a glance if you are suitable for a job.

A **résumé** is similar to a CV but shorter. Résumé is the French word for "summary", so a résumé summarizes the items included in a CV, which includes full life details (vita=life).

A **cover letter** addressed to the prospective employer accompanies the CV. In the letter, introduce yourself and draw attention to your achievements relevant to the position. The cover letter gives you the opportunity to "showcase" your talents, including your ability to write convincingly and correctly. A covering letter is also called a "letter of application".

Job searching

When looking for a job, make an action plan using this four-step framework to guide you.

1 Assess yourself
Examine your goals, and make sure you understand what motivates you, what your values are, what your strengths and what your priorities. Ask yourself the questions listed earlier in the *Knowing your values* section. Think about where you would like to be in five years, and what you would like to have achieved. What are your lifestyle preferences, and what role do work and professionalism play in these preferences?

2 Research your career goals
After the first, introspective stage, open up to the world and see what is available to assist you in reaching your goals and achieving your desired lifestyle. The obvious

way to look for a job is to peruse the classifieds in major newspapers and visit employment websites. In addition, major recruitment consultants have their own databases where you can access information on professional job vacancies.

Another major way to find out what your options are and what opportunities are available is through **networking**. Tips for networking are:

- Get to know people at courses and through business, trade and professional associations
- Subscribe to a business, trade or professional magazine or newsletter; or join online discussion groups and forums
- Join online social networking sites devoted to professionals, such as www. LinkedIn.com and participate in the blogs and activities posted
- Establish mentors. A mentor is a senior colleague whose work and personal character you respect. A mentor takes an interest in your career and is willing to advise you. If you leave a company or a programme, keep in touch with your mentor. For example, if you know your mentor is working on a particular project or has a special interest, send clippings or other relevant information
- Contact career professionals, such as recruitment consultants and "headhunters", and discuss your options with them
- Do voluntary work in a related field. This can help you to meet people in the field and achievements performed as a volunteer can go in your CV.

When networking, take care to:

- Send a thank-you note to people who give you helpful leads and stay in touch
- Never ask directly for a job! Asking directly puts people on the spot and can make you seem desperate or pushy.

3 Develop a self-marketing strategy
Market yourself as if you were a product (which, in fact, you are, in relation to the employment market). Use the five Ps of marketing:

- **Product:** what do you have to offer? What key skills and qualities can you offer to potential employers?
- **Price:** what is your value in the marketplace? What value do your educational background, experience and professional strengths give you?
- **Promotion:** what themes, signs, phrases or messages can you use to communicate what you have to offer?
- **Place** (distribution): how will you "circulate" yourself? For example, will you focus on advertised positions, rely on your networking, send your CV to a

senior member of a targeted company (known as **cold contact** or **speculative job searching**) or post your CV online? Start a blog?

- **Positioning**: what distinguishes you from other candidates? Do you have a Unique Selling Point (USP)?

4   Prepare some versions of your CV for different purposes
Have two or three versions of your CV ready. Each version should highlight different qualities, but they should also be relevant to the job profile that you will have created using the previous three steps.

Finding information about a company

Before applying to a company – and particularly before attending an interview – find out details such as share price, company structure, annual turnover and product lines. Take advantage of the following resources:

- Visit the company website. Most companies recruit through their websites
- Browse through magazines relevant to the industry in which you hope to work and to which the company belongs
- Browse through company literature, such as brochures, newsletters and annual reports
- If possible, visit the company itself and get a feel for its culture and atmosphere.

Find out as much as possible about the industry of a company, by asking these questions:

- What products or services does this industry offer?
- Who are the major players and up-and-comers?
- What are the critical success factors for a company in this industry?
- What is the outlook and hiring potential for this industry?
- What type of talent does this industry attract, hire and need?

Find out as much as possible about the particular company you are interested in applying to, by asking these questions:

- What distinguishes this company from others in the industry?
- What are the company's culture, values and priorities?
- Who are its leaders and what do they stand for?
- How does this company treat its employees?
- What is the company's reputation?
- What would it be like to work there?

CV formats

CVs tend to be classified into three main categories: **chronological, functional** and **targeted**. All types of CVs should satisfy certain general standards. They should:

- Provide information that is relevant, clear and concise
- Highlight and provide evidence for your strengths and achievements
- Inspire confidence
- Form an agenda for the interview.

Chronological CVs

The chronological format lists education and work experience in reverse chronological order (most recent items listed first). Chronological CVs are useful if you have a steady work history, and/or all or most of your recent work experience is relevant to the position.

Do not use a chronological CV if only one or two jobs in your work history are relevant to the position sought, or you have a complicated or diverse work history that may raise doubts as to your reliability, or you have many gaps in your work history that are difficult to explain, or you are pursuing a career change and wish to highlight transferable knowledge and skills.

Functional CVs

Functional CVs focus on knowledge and skills, rather than on dates or places of employment. They are useful if you are changing careers and some of your previous experience is not relevant to your target job or want to highlight specific skills rather than list your employment history.

In a functional CV, the most marketable information is presented at the front of the document. The functional format allows for selective organization of information and enhances your ability to customize the CV for the particular position.

To become aware of all the knowledge you have gained in your experience, list all the responsibilities you had for each job. Think of everything that you did each day at work, including all the small tasks or the tasks that were so routine that you hardly noticed them. If your list gets too long, edit it by deleting activities that may not be directly relevant to the job you are applying for. Table App2 contains some action words to help you compile your list:

Table App2 Action Words to Describe Skills

Accomplish	Define	Inform	Provide
Act	Delegate	Initiate	Publicize
Adapt	Demonstrate	Innovate	Publish
Adjust	Design	Inspect	Recommend
Administer	Detail	Install	Record
Advertise	Determine	Institute	Rectify
Advise	Develop	Integrate	Relate
Affect	Devise	Interview	Review
Analyse	Direct	Investigate	Report
Anticipate	Distribute	Invent	Represent
Approach	Draft	Lead	Research
Approve	Edit	Maintain	Resolve
Arrange	Educate	Manipulate	Revise
Assemble	Enlarge	Market	Scan
Assess	Establish	Mediate	Schedule
Assist	Evaluate	Modify	Select
Assign	Examine	Moderate	Serve
Budget	Exchange	Monitor	Speak
Build	Execute	Motivate	Standardize
Calculate	Expand	Negotiate	Staff
Catalogue	Facilitate	Obtain	Stimulate
Chair	Formulate	Operate	Summarize
Clarify	Fundraise	Order	Supervise
Collaborate	Generate	Organize	Survey
Communicate	Govern	Originate	Synthesize
Conceive	Guide	Participate	Systemize
Conceptualize	Handle	Perform	Teach
Conciliate	Hire	Persuade	Team-build
Consult	Identify	Plan	Train
Contract	Implement	Present	Transmit
Control	Improve	Preside	Utilize
Cooperate	Increase	Produce	Write
Coordinate	Index	Promote	
Counsel	Influence	Propose	

Always use verbs in the active voice to describe the activities you perform or performed in your work experience. Use the present tense for positions currently held, and the past tense for positions previously held. Omit "I".

Where possible, use the *STAR (Situation, Task, Achievement, Result)* method to highlight your successes, either in the CV itself, or in the cover letter. First, state the situation where you had to perform a task; second, describe the task; third, go to the outcome of your effort; and fourth, state how your employer, or profession as a whole, benefited from the way you carried out the task.

Targeted CVs

Targeted CVs follow the specifications or templates given in an application package or job advertisement. They are often similar to functional CVs but concentrate on skills that are directly relevant to the requirements listed in the position description. When writing a targeted CV, answer the question or follow the formatting directions given by the recruiting company.

Optional features

These features are not necessary. Analyse your audience, context and professional culture, and decide whether or not you wish to include them. If in doubt, leave them out.

- **Personal information.** In most Western societies, gender, religious beliefs, age, ethnicity and marital status are irrelevant to many kinds of employment, and, in fact, are considered confidential by law. You are not obliged to state any of these in your CV. Find out about cultural practice in the particular job contexts that interest you for a decision on this point.
- **Photograph.** Employers in certain countries and in certain sectors of the economy, such as public relations, may favour photographs on CVs. Others find them irrelevant or even misleading, because they de-focus objective skills and capabilities. For example, in the information technology sector or in education, a photograph is generally not necessary.
- **Hobbies/Interests.** Include a brief list of hobbies and interests if they indicate knowledge or skills relevant to the job, such as leadership, teamwork, resilience or determination. You can also set your CV apart from others if you specify unusual hobbies, or if you demonstrate excellence in a particular pursuit. If your hobbies are humdrum or irrelevant, leave this section out altogether.
- **Career objective.** A career objective states the applicant's goals and ambition within a specific industry. If you are unsure or undecided about your long-term goals, or if you want to project versatility and resilience, leave this section out (unless, of course, it is specifically requested in a targeted

CV). If you do decide to include an objective, make it short but focused. It should inform the employer that you are moving in a certain direction, specify your work preferences and serve as a focal point from which to review your CV.

- **Referees.** You do not need to include names of referees or references unless they are specifically requested. However, since referees will play a role if you are shortlisted, it is wise to include a statement such as "Referees are available on request", either at the end of the CV or in the cover letter.
- **Nationality or residential status.** This is only relevant if it affects your availability for employment – for example, if you are on a working visa. Include this if you have an international background, and the potential employer may wonder if you are eligible to work in the particular country.

Presentation of CV

How the CV is set out depends on the medium of communication. For example, if posting the CV on a website, where it might be read off a screen, use more highlighting, such as bullet points and headings, and minimize the information on each page. If sending out a hard copy, where you were specified to limit the CV to one page, obviously you need to set it out differently to maximize the limited space. Adapt the following guidelines in relation to the specific circumstances of each application:

- Ensure readability by leaving as much white space as specifications allow, and by using a clear font, size 11–12.
- Align points down the page and preferably indent them.
- Do not use more than two fonts, perhaps one type for the main text and another for headings. Consider using only one font unless creativity is required by the job and you have flair for design.
- Do not use more than one highlighting technique: Bold or Underline or Italics – not all three.
- As with other business documents, include a header or footer on each page, and page numbers, in case pages get mixed up when printed.

CV templates

It is not wise to copy a standard CV format from a book to which countless others also have access. Instead, by making your CV as individual as a signature, you increase your chances of attracting the attention of those that can further your career. So use these templates as a guide or inspiration, but tailor them to suit your individual aspirations and strengths.

Template for chronological CV

Name	Your full name
Address	Your current residential or business address
Phone numbers	Home and/or business numbers
Email address	Your business or personal email address
Education	List your educational qualifications with most recent first
Employment History	Name of employer, Position (job title), Period of employment, Duties, Achievements. Begin with current or most recent position and work backwards.
Professional Memberships	Briefly list them, if relevant
Computer skills	List your skills of operating systems and software packages
Languages	State the languages that you know and degree of fluency
Interests	List, only if relevant

Template for functional CV

Name	Your full name
Address	Your current residential or business address
Phone numbers	Home and/or business numbers
Email address	Your business or personal email address
Skills and abilities	List the major skills you have acquired from your experience. List only those skills that you can demonstrate but be creative in highlighting their relevance for the job you seek.
Education	List your educational qualifications with most relevant first. Include all professional development and short courses that you attended.
Computer skills	Depending on the kind of job you seek and the kinds of skills you have, you could list your computer skills separately to highlight them. Include operating systems and software packages.
Languages	State the languages you know and degree of fluency

Professional Memberships	Again, briefly list them, if relevant
Awards and Achievements	List, only if relevant to the new job
Employment History	Name of employer, Position (job title), Period of employment
Interests	List, only if relevant

Table App3 lists some commonly used phrases to summarize and highlight skills.

Table App3   Skill Phrases

General
Works well under pressure
Able to adapt to new situations
Ability to learn quickly
Capable of accepting responsibility
Works well without supervision

People Skills
Ability to work as a team member
Good sense of humour
Ability to deal effectively with clients
Handles people with patience and understanding
Works well with people from different cultures

Communication Skills
Ability to communicate effectively with clients
Capable of initiating and completing projects
Trained and supervised new staff
Able to communicate effectively with others
Excellent communicator

Organization Skills
Excellent organization skills
Ability to plan, organize and supervise projects
Capable of working on different projects
Completes projects accurately and on schedule
Punctual
Dependable in all situations

Leadership
Excellent leadership skills
Accepts responsibility
Dealt efficiently with emergencies
Comfortable with taking the initiative
Supervised activities of team members
Successful project manager
Successfully organized staff/team members to attain goals

Look at the following chronological CV and notice how the writer summarizes their skills at the beginning and then demonstrates how they used these skills in particular work situations.

Lee B. Wilson

Address, Phone number, Email address

Summary

Accounting Professional/Payroll Administrator combining cross-functional competencies in all phases of accounting, information systems, and staff supervision and management. Proficient in managing and developing financial reports and controls using staffing and technology efficiencies. Ability to contribute as a team player and interface with professionals on all levels. Expertise includes:

* Payroll administration
* Quarterly & Year-End Reporting
* Automated Accounting Information Systems
* Inventory Control & Purchasing
* Financial Reporting
* Corporate Tax Compliance
* Corporate Accounting
* Job Costing

EDUCATION

2017: Masters in Business Administration, Y University
2015: Bachelor in Business Management, X University

PROFESSIONAL EXPERIENCE

2015–present: **Controller**, Platinum Choice Corporation, City, Country

Plan, manage and provide leadership for accounting department including payroll, budgeting, cost accounting, managerial accounting, financial reporting, financial analysis and purchasing. Scope of responsibility spans both the corporate and divisional level. Provide financial expertise to outside firms, including banks, auditors, and government authorities.

• Managed $4 million in annual operating budgets allocated for personnel, facilities, and administrative expenses

- Established improved accounts receivable that reduced outstanding receivables by 25% during the first quarter
- Implemented automated cost accounting systems to analyse profit improvement opportunities
- Worked in cooperation with management teams to restructure corporate pricing on all major product lines, resulting in a 14% profit improvement
- Successfully guided the company through annual outside audits.

2010–15: **Accounting Consultant**, XYZ Consultants, City, Country

Recruited to provide diverse finance, accounting, payroll and tax preparation functions for one of the largest international consulting firms.

- Responsible for preparation of financial statements: payroll, sales and property tax returns, and income tax return.
- Streamlined accounting processes to reduce workpaper and document requirements
- Worked closely with clients in structuring general ledgers and evaluating their software needs.

COMPUTER SKILLS

- Experienced with the following software for payroll preparation: QuickBooks/ QuickBooks Pro, Peachtree, PenSoft Payroll
- Skilled in most accounting software programs including Impact Encore, Peachtree, Preform Plus, ProSystems and Quicken.
- Proficient in Excel, Word, Access SPSS and Lotus.

The cover letter

A cover letter must be professionally presented in format, grammar, and spelling. It generally is one to two pages long and should have a "bottom-line" organization – that is, it should go straight to the point. Remember, employers may be reviewing hundreds of applications and may spend as little as 30 seconds reviewing each one. You covering letter should have something that stands out.

There are three main kinds of cover letter:

- A letter written in response to a job advertisement.
- A 'cold contact' letter, written unsolicited (without being requested in advance) to a senior member of a targeted company. This should not be

more than one page, so as not to take the recipient's time. Always follow up a cold contact letter with a phone call after a week to ten days.

- A referral letter, mentioning a contact within the company or a previous conversation held with a staff member. A referral letter may open with a line such as, "I am attaching my CV, as you requested during our recent conversation regarding the Human Resources counselling position opening up at your firm."

The cover letter generally has four paragraphs, covering the following material:

Opening paragraph indicate the purpose of writing

Second paragraph state relevant skills and experience

Third paragraph demonstrate your knowledge of the company or organization

Fourth paragraph close with confidence and request an interview

When sending a "cold contact" letter, it is best to address it to the manager of the section you want to work in (rather than to the HR Department). The advantages of this are that, even if you are not employed, the manager will at least know your name and may remember you if you apply for an advertised position within the company later. People who are eager and take initiative make a good impression professionally. Also, if the manager is dedicated to his/her area of specialty, chances are that he/she would be willing to help newcomers to join the industry. Therefore, he/she may refer you to someone or give you some very useful advice, if you approach him/her directly. It is unlikely that the HR Officer would have the same commitment.

Cover letter tips

Here are some general tips for writing an effective cover letter:

- Keep paragraphs short (2–4 sentences)
- Adapt the content to the particular organization and job position for which you are applying. That is, show that you are an insider to the industry
- Include contact details (name, address, phone number, fax, email), either in a letterhead or in the concluding paragraph
- Do not point to any of your weaknesses. Instead, match your skills and experience to the requirements of the position
- Do not refer to personal interests or hobbies unless they are directly relevant to the position, or you share an interest with the recipient of the letter
- Do not use sarcasm or irony
- Do not criticize a former employer.

Watch out for...

How bad can your writing get on your CV? We end the chapter with some real-life examples of CV "howlers" (Table App4):

Table App4 Bad writing in CVs
Education: Curses in liberal arts, curses in computer science, curses in accounting.
I am a rabid thinker.
Proven ability to hunt down and correct erors.
My intensity is at supremely high levels, and my ability to meet deadlines is unspeakable.
Personal details: Married, 1992 Chevrolet.
Personal interests: Donating blood. 15 gallons so far.
Covering letter: Thank you for your consideration. Hope to hear from you shorty!

Sources: Gordon, B. (2008) The Apprentice: When your CV contains no information to misconstrue. *Monday Morning Funnies*, http://www.families.com/blog/monday-morning-funnies-mistakes-to-avoid-on-your-résumé

References and further reading

Carter, C., & Izumo, G. (2013) *The career tool kit: Skills for success.* New York: Pearson.

Littleford, D., Halstead, J., & Mulraine, C. (2004) *Career skills: Opening doors into the job market.* London: Red Globe Press.

Morgan, G., & Banks, A. (1999) *Getting that job: How to establish and manage your career into the new millennium.* Sydney: HarperCollins.

Index

Printed in the USA
CPSIA information can be obtained
at www.ICGtesting.com
LVHW020611190124
769389LV00012B/673